This book explores the alluring landscape of erotic and sexual love, its passion, intrigue and ecstasy, and the com\ldots patterns of human relationships. From the rich mater\ldots the great love stories of the world the authors draw uni\ldots meaning and significance and take the reader on a fascin\ldots journey of discovery.

With extraordinary insight they retell the famous love stories of three major cultures: the Indian – Hindu, Perso – Islamic and Western which range across the broad spectrum of innocent first love, as in the Persian tale of Layla and Majnun, to the darker and more ambivalent tales of adulterous and incestuous love as in Tristan and Isolde, and finally the erotic obsessions of Nabokov's novels.

SUDHIR KAKAR, a psychoanalyst, is currently a Nehru Fellow at the Centre for the Study of Developing Societies, Delhi. He has been Homi Bhabha Fellow, Fellow at the Institute of Advanced Study, Princeton, and Professor of Behavioural Sciences at some of the major universities of India, Europe and the USA. He is also the author of several books; two of these – *The Inner World* and *Shamans, Mystics and Doctors* – have been translated into French, Spanish, German and several other languages.

JOHN MUNDER ROSS, a psychoanalyst in New York City, was educated at Harvard and is currently Associate Professor of Psychology in Psychiatry at the Cornell Medical College. He is the chief editor of *International Journal of Psychoanalytic Psychotherapy* and co-editor of the book *Father and Child: Developmental and Clinical Perspectives*.

TO LOVERS

ACKNOWLEDGEMENTS

S. K. is deeply grateful to the Institute of Advanced Study, Princeton, where he spent the year 1983–4 working on the book as a Visiting Fellow at the School of Social Sciences. He also thanks Apeksha Kakar for her help in the preparation of the manuscript.

J. M. R. wishes to thank Katherine and Matthew Ross for their unwavering support and affection and acknowledges the help given by Keith W. Bradley.

TALES OF
LOVE, SEX
& DANGER

Sudhir Kakar and
John Munder Ross

UNWIN PAPERBACKS
London   Sydney

First published in Great Britain by Oxford University Press 1986
First published by Unwin Paperbacks ®Paperbacks, an imprint of Unwin
Hyman Ltd in 1987

UNWIN HYMAN LIMITED
Denmark House, 37–39 Queen Elizabeth Street
London SE1 2QB
and
40 Museum Street, London WC1A 1LU

Allen & Unwin Australia Pty Ltd
8 Napier Street, North Sydney, NSW 2060, Australia

Unwin Paperbacks with the Port Nicholson Press
60 Cambridge Terrace, Wellington, New Zealand

British Library Cataloguing in Publication Data

Kakar, Sudhir
    Tales of love, sex and danger.
1. Love in literature
I. Title   II. Ross, John Munder
809'.93354   PN56.L6
ISBN 0-04-440042-X

Printed in Great Britain by Cox & Wyman Ltd, Reading

CONTENTS

Contents

CHAPTER ONE

INTRODUCTION

It was nearly twenty years ago that the two authors of this book on sexual love first met. We were brought together under the aegis of Erik Erikson and his well-known course for Harvard seniors on 'The human life cycle'. Erikson was in his prime then, a sort of folk hero for young intellectuals, a psychoanalytic guru from the Rhine, Vienna and Stockbridge. He stirred the faculty with his conjunction of intellectual playfulness and artistic sensuousness, and he moved the undergraduates with his white-haired sagacity and love of youth.

John Munder Ross, one of Erikson's tutees, and Sudhir Kakar, an assistant in the course whom Erikson had met in Gandhi's Ahmedabad, were among the few in this heterogeneous assemblage of twenty- to thirty-year olds who were later to pursue psychoanalysis in earnest. Admiring Erikson and awed by Freud, we loved analysis with its promise of momentous revelations and, above all, its implicit passion. Psychoanalysis to us was reason as well as reason's mysticism, to which we felt greatly drawn, pushed towards it by forces from our personal pasts. Our scrupulously irreverent and atheistic fathers had stood for the primacy of rationality and fought against all who would seek to dim the clarity of intellect. They provide us with a common ground, an intellectual heritage that found expression in psychoanalysis.

About our love lives, different at the time as they are now, when the passage of time has levelled the disparity between our ages, we shall say little. We are analysts after all, with at least a pretense to discretion. But this much we can reveal: as much as art (and sometimes metaphysics), women and our love of them—with love's tender discoveries, sudden torments, and consuming desires—occupied those long nights of mildly inebriated talk in the niches of Harvard Square. We would discourse on our fumbling overreaching quests, trying to make sense of them by putting into words what we had suffered or were suffering (the one after all was older than the other). Or else, without knowing, we groped to realize in our lives the passions of the poets. Love and sex seemed to reverberate with the great ideas enveloping us in the university lecture halls and libraries and resonated with the innermost reaches of our selves. They pointed as beacons illuminating our future work identities.

We are older now, fathers with families, teaching, writing and with workaday practices from which we glean a living. Life, we have learned, should live itself for the most part or at least remain unfettered and unworried by obsessive and excessive scrutiny. Yet our pasts and our commitment to the sublimity of love have remained with us. As soulmates separated by cultural as well as literal gulfs, continental and oceanic, when we turned at last to the collaboration we had so long planned it was natural that we should alight upon the brilliant and ephemeral yet universal matter of erotic love.

Initially, given our deference to the poet and the musician as the supreme interpreters of romantic feeling, we were hesitant about our enterprise. Are not analysts, we wondered, reputedly the theologians or, if you will, ideologists of Eros, barred like Moses from themselves entering passion's portals? But then, we said to ourselves, not all analysts are equally inclined towards the virtue of abstinence in everyday life, of stoic self-possession, or find philosophizing and chilly intro-spection more congenial than hedonistic entrancement. Personal predilections aside, there is a fundamental feature of passionate love that makes it singularly accessible to psychoanalytic exploration and discourse. Denis de Rougemont has proclaimed that either the description of unalloyed sexuality, on the one hand, or the agape of brotherly love, on the other, soon become tedious, the one degenerating into pornography, the other into parable.[1] In contrast, the forces of passion transcend action and reality, permit of a poetic and dramatic tension, and lend themselves best to the enduring life of the narrative. 'The passion of Eros', as de Rougemont observes, 'is true first in dreams, and perhaps never exists better than in the lyric impulse of its narrations'.[2] The analyst, along with the bard, can take heart. His efforts are not in vain. The narrative of individual dreams of passionate love, and their resonance with those great and compelling cultural dreams we call myths or tales of love, is familiar turf for the psychoanalyst. Treading as he does the 'royal road to the unconscious', the analyst has been privileged, in fact, to analyse the mysteries of what Kierkegaard, in characterizing love, called 'the psycho-sensual synthesis'. So the philosophers have granted us a place, a vantage on love. Solaced by them, we were heartened in our pursuit—the retelling of some of the best-known, most compelling and terrifying stories of love, and through these the passionate individual's history of longing and desire.

There were problems, of course, unavoidable with two different men, analysts or no, exploring a subject whose enormity discovers itself not in easy generalization but in serendipity and idiosyncracy—to borrow from Milan Kundera, in the 'unimaginables'. Speaking of the objects of passion, Kundera has described his philandering hero's erotic impulse as follows:

'What did he look for in them? What attracted him to them? Isn't making love merely an eternal repetition of the same?' Not at all.

There is always the small part that is unimaginable. When he saw a woman in her clothes, he could naturally imagine more or less what she would look like naked (his experience as a doctor supplementing his experience as a lover), but between the approximation of the idea and the precision of reality there was a small gap of the unimaginable, and it was this hiatus that gave him no rest. And then, the pursuit of the unimaginable does not stop with the revelations of nudity: it goes much farther: How would she behave while undressing? What would she say when he made love to her? How would her sighs sound? How would her face distort at the moment of orgasm?

What is unique about the 'I' hides itself exactly in what is unimaginable about a person. All we are able to imagine is what makes everyone like everyone else, what people have in common. The individual 'I' is what differs from common stock, that is, what cannot be guessed at or calculated, what must be unveiled, uncovered, conquered . . [3]

Kundera's is a literary impulse—poetic, fictional. His stress is on the manifestation of the universal in countless particulars. Each erotic act and actor is unique. How, then, could two men, however deep and tested their spiritual and intellectual friendship, find concordance in their understanding of the multitude of love's irreducible forms of expression? After all, the novelist takes such pains to trace love's vagaries in narratives of lovers—limiting himself to a portrayal of one or two or three characters at most. How dare we speak of worlds of love, when all love and are loved so differently? What can we hope to add?

It is here that our discipline serves us, an enterprise whose stock and trade is the 'unimaginable' and its peculiar lawfulness. Analysis aims to adumbrate those corners of the mind—the locus of what Kundera calls 'poetic memory'—where the poetry of the erotic and exalted abide. Our theory 'thinks' about them and makes imaginary maps to help us find each individual's hidden treasure. In clinical practice, where people unfold the details and minutiae of their real and fantastical love lives, these conceptual generalities serve early on as transient expectations about uniquely personal truths. In due course they are to be discarded lest they make of the analytic couch a procrustean bed, maiming and disfiguring the patient and his heartfelt desires. Yet they offer a paradigmatic plot for life, into which each of us inserts his or her psychic personae and the variations to which our individuality gives rise. What, then, are some of the themes or motives which seem to characterize passionate, consuming love for another—represented time and again in the arts which have celebrated them with clarion calls so unusual in life as it is lived? Many meanings converge on passionate love, one rising to the fore in one moment of the erotic encounter, another next. Our book title tells it all—the inevitable triad: love, sex and danger.

Spiritualists and ascetics to the contrary, there can be no love without sex, that is, without its real or imagined or sometimes unconscious enactment in the sexual embrace of two persons. Inevitably there arise with this physical commingling of body and soul, seemingly so simple, a host of psychic dangers. That is, when love is brought to bear on pleasure. In the artist's narrative, as in the patient's associations, these risks find palpability and, perhaps, consequence. Sensual intimacy can evoke terror at one's helplessness. Love's insatiability, with its waves of violent, consuming hunger, threatens the loss of those we hold dear. Naked in our desire we are vulnerable to disapprobation, mortification, rejection. Challenging the keepers of the social order and guardians of its taboos, we tremble at the punishment fitting the crime, emasculation, or more generally a pervasive unsexing. Worse still for many is the spectre of relentless self punishment; searing, burdensome guilt.

Ironically, the dreads are also the 'meanings' of love seen from the vantage point of the clinician, the historian of psychic life. In what is feared we may find what is desired. If we follow another precept inherited from Freud: the fear *is* the wish, especially so in matters of love. Proponents of 'free love' and authors of those handbooks greedily devoured by teenagers miss the mark; there is no such thing as 'love without fear', certainly no heights of pleasure, communion, exaltation. Tales of love are therefore inevitably also tales of terror and torment which the reader can vicariously savour, secure in the protection of a safety-net woven by the narrator's art. Herein the veracity of the love story, almost inevitably tragedy, averted by most of us in our lives even as we dull our sensibilities and obscure our insight with one or another facetious lament.

It used to be that Freud's 'Oedipus Complex' was the shibboleth of psychoanalytic explanation. Little boys of three to five years, and in more convoluted ways little girls too, harboured wishes, in Freud's nineteenth-century diction, 'repugnant to morality' yet 'forced upon us all by nature'. Sexually they coveted their parents, especially but not exclusively those of the opposite sex, while more violently they would depose the reigning overlords and matriarchs who tended and protected them but who claimed their conjugal rights. Stricken by guilt or more primitively dreading retaliation in the form of castration, they fled their incestuous initiative, subsiding first of all into a sexual latency and then as adolescents and adults looking for lovers other than mother or father. At the same time, finding them, they played out with these persons their childhoods and indeed (Freud asserted) ancient and predestined dramas filled with awesome and alluring beings. Or perhaps they succumbed to symptoms in which the personages of the mind found an even eerier presence in symbolic phobias and compulsions. In this, the so-called 'classical analytic point of view', the incestuous and rivalrous oedipal constellation shapes all ensuing erotic and romantic strivings as well as the terrors and moral quandaries to which it gives rise.

After Freud, baby watchers of the 1940s and '50s learned more about what he had dubbed the 'prehistory' of the Oedipus Complex—the equally arduous journey of Everyman (or woman) towards the goal of self-identity. Jung and Rank had already intuited as life's core task the individuation of the single person out of some primordial mass of non-self, non-other being. In their and Freud's wake, Rene Spitz and Margaret Mahler, perhaps the foremost of psychoanalytic infant observers, chronicled in detail this process in the real life of the developing baby. Mahler has shown that it is our mothers, both their prenatal bodies and their felt animas after birth, from whom we must extricate ourselves in a process of self-definition which can never be completed. Prompted by a preordained destiny to disengage and thereby seek separateness (such is our Kierkegaardian fate, solitude), bawling babies and scrambling toddlers are none the less drawn back by their own longings into a 'dual unity' with their mothers. In this union the self is suffused with an everlasting sustaining warmth but one which compromises a hard-won individuality and the striving for self sufficiency. Herein the most elemental of love's paradoxes; here, too, the core of love's exhilaration and terror.

Adult passion reaches into the extant past where yearning and danger coincide. In the spirit of his disciple Ferenczi, Freud once wrote that a man's penis is precious indeed, for it alone ensure a re-entry and access to the great womb of our individual and collective origins when mother seas covered the world. True, yet there is more irony and tension here. In regaining the paradise lost through interpenetration of the genitals, our image of our body, the bedrock of our felt identity, is swept away, its contours and contents dissolved by the tides of merger and engulfment. Conquering a woman, a man simultaneously surrenders as he cedes to her his self and his sex. For that matter, in being possessed the lover too loses outline and representation. Intermingling with the beloved, one at least momentarily loses consciousness and awareness of a being who no longer has the shape of a separate life seen from a distance. In this elemental sense desire and dread meet as one.

The secret of erotic love, its synthesizing illusion, probably lies at the junction of these two primal developmental dilemmas—the impossibility of oedipal possession and the half-wanted birth of the self. The genital freedom and orgasmic capacity of the adult further charge this synthesis with a special and electrifying potential. They allow it embodiment, permitting man and woman to meet physically, to conjoin. They wed physiology of the body with the illusions of the soul—granting neither a supremacy over the other. Conceptually, psychoanalysis is a dialectical cosmology and trades in paradoxes such as these: wish as fear, illusion in sensation, in the act of sexual masculinity the attainment of femininity, and more—conflicts that lend to passion and development a poised unity, a sense of striving towards unattainable resolutions of mystery and inquiry.

Moreover, in Freud's tradition, as we shall elaborate it, psychoanalysis, in theory and especially in practice, is very much a psychology of love. Indeed the analyst counts on love, on being the prime object of his patient's passion, to do his work. He exploits this binding force in the uses of the so-called 'transference', to subdue resistance to unwanted truths and to discern love's wellsprings in all manner of suffering and sublimity.

We are not literary critics or intellectual historians. But we have out of shared passion chosen to focus on shared texts to illuminate our subject matter, to draw our readers into the larger love story we have in mind. The tales range across three cultures with which we are familiar—the Indian-Hindu, Perso-Islamic and Western worlds—and span the millennia. Ours is, obviously, not an exhaustive collection but a sampling deeply personal, asymmetrical at times, and even arbitrary. We are confident, though, that the selection is an emotionally representative one in which members of the cultures will hear and recognize the whispering of their desires.

Apart from 'vignettes' and cases in point, we have deliberately eschewed the use of clinical case histories. Poems, tales, epics, plays have, to put it crudely, an intensely evocative appeal since their authors, who are artists, have voices more melodious or stirring than our own. To portray the love lives of our patients would require narratives of an equal poignancy and, certainly, comparable length. Moreover, to do so would entail the selfsame persistency of detail in which a character's or mythic figure's plight is given life. To provide such detail would be to violate trust, breaching the codes of our consulting rooms. We thus make only passing references to our ample clinical backdrop in the form of anecdote and commonality, leaving our patients in their optimal state, incognito. So, rather than confess for others, we have largely let the public poets speak for us.

As we have said, we are of two cultures, further steeped in the interdisciplinary view which would wed life-history with historical and cultural study. Does erotic passion as it is rendered or valued, sought and feared, reveal distinct differences across the cultures and their millennia? Just as each individual reveals his own personal hierarchy of dangers and desires yet suffers all the passions at one level of consciousness or another, so too do cultures stamp their imprint, their variations, on universal themes—emphasizing some of love's dangers and exaltations while obscuring others. Moreover, though our instinct is to try and make the love story fit the mystique of its culture, yet in every culture, it seems, the love story is the prime subverter of its official mores, especially those relating to authority and the relations between the sexes. Cultures, we found, use their myths of love in much the same way as do individuals their central sexual fantasy: to express their deeper wishes which are utterly at odds with the accepted ideologies of the man-woman relationship.

Finally there is the book's form, the sequence of our exposition. Each great love story contains all others in that it includes within its gambit all of love's paradoxical associations and radii—conquest, possession, surrender, the savouring of unbearable and raw transports, time held still in a poised nostalgia, sensuality and sensuousness, and the loss of visual, distal perceptions in another mode of knowing. Yet each story also uniquely highlights the wishes and fears related to love from one or other period of individual life-history, specifically from the early stages of childhood. Thus, as if spontaneously, our stories simply fell into their order, as intuitively we responded to *the* story at hand. We begin with young loves in our three literatures portraying the purest, if not the most 'innocent', or, better, benign, of passions. Manifestly, the lovers in these stories are adolescents, yet, as we shall see, their wishes and fears hearken back to the prehistory of the individual before guilt and guilt-inducing intruders happen upon the developmental scene. This is an era shrouded in forgetfulness and betrayed by a vanishing epistemology, a time before love becomes a surreptitious thief, avoiding the vigilance of watchful eyes, real and imaginary. We then turn to love adulterated, to the triangles of persons and the ambivalence of each, which gradually alloy guilt and passion, trespass and longing, fantasy and reality. Our scheme mirrors life-history, and in our conclusion we elaborate upon the phenomenology and what we have called the ontogeny of love, sex and danger.

PART I

PURE CULTURES OF LOVE

As myths, the great paradigmatic love stories speak directly to our psyches, which are after all, by definition, our amorous souls. They repeat in relief and in variation a finite number of elusive themes. The outcomes seem expected and inexorable. Like the audiences of the Greek tragedies or Christian passion plays, we have a sense of ritual, pleasing and reassuring in its reaffirmation of the cultural and personal myths we entertain to explain the course of our lives.

Yet these stories still stir us with the surprises they contain. Each hearing reveals a new perspective or a kind of truth in the prism of love. Because of the refractions in our hearts we learn something new about our own desires and longings. The experience is analogous perhaps to that of psychoanalysis, in which patients reiterate their same old inner stories, each time with new romantic twists and signposts towards the past, until at last they and we understand the better part of it all.

In this spirit of rediscovery we turn now to three prototypical *histoires d'amour* which are perhaps pre-eminent in their cultures' respective mythologies of passion. These are tales of young lovers who are believed to express the purest of romantic sentiments. As we shall see, however, theirs is anything but a simple innocent love. Unalloyed, their love is none the less ridden with paradoxes and wants which are but dimly perceived through the mists of their childhoods. Rushing pell-mell towards each other, the lovers embrace the very terrors most of us unconsciously avoid.

We begin in the Western world with Romeo and Juliet, whose names are almost synonymous with romantic lovers. We then explore the tales of those young lovers who served as similar models for the Islamic and Hindu worlds. The commonalities in these stories of 'true love' are striking all the more so because of the history and geography which separate them from one another. At the same time, each story sets in relief a particular theme from within universal clusters of primal longing. These themes seem alien, quite at odds with normal expectations and the accepted notions of the society in which the tales are embedded. Yet the cropping up of the unforeseen in the familiar may well reveal what a culture's members most want but which the community finds so upsetting to acknowledge.

CHAPTER TWO

THE AMOROUS DEATH OF ROMEO AND JULIET

If music be the food of love, play on;
Give me excess of it, that, surfeiting,
The appetite may sicken, and so die.
That strain again! It had a dying fall.
—Orsino, in *Twelfth Night*.[1]

Shakespeare told many love stories. Perhaps none has better transcended the context of the specific work than the tale of *Romeo and Juliet*. A classic verging on a latter-day myth, the story is no longer Shakespeare's alone but has become the common property of Western culture—a narrative available for all manner of personal and artistic reference. Romeo and Juliet offer themselves as *the* star-crossed young lovers, their purity of feeling and spirit betrayed by cruel fate and misguided relatives. Theirs is seen as an archetype of passion laid low by petty vanity masquerading as kinship honour, and as such has lent itself to the artistic forms of different centuries and to settings other than Shakespeare's Verona. The lovers have drifted across the stage, garbed in the costume and customs of successive eras, Romeo paraded now in the powdered wig and broad belly of the seventeenth-century thespian, now in the jeans, T-shirt and switchblade of *West Side Story*.

In our era Dame Margot Fonteyn performed the role of the fourteen-year-old Juliet in the MacMillan–Prokofiev ballet until she was well into her fifties, retaining in silent motion all the while the now virginal now expectant sense of imminent womanhood. Perhaps the most poignant moment in one of her final appearances in this part came when her Romeo, that legendary Tartar and sybarite Nureyev, his huge penis packed like a coiled snake against the pubic wall, finds what seems to him the corpse of his beloved in the Capulet mausoleum. Vainly he tries to bring her back to life, lifting her limbs in imitation of the balcony and bedroom scenes in which the two have first touched each other's souls and then their flesh. The parts of her body rise but fail to respond with a will of their own, as unclasped they arc and fall ethereally in an aesthetic rendering of dissembled death. Juliet, whether dead or alive, is no longer young.

Perhaps a decade following her swan song, Dame Margot appeared once again in the ballet, restaged this time by a Nureyev, bulging still, dancing his heart out on the brink of middle age. This time, however, she was Juliet's still young-enough mother, the severely beautiful and narcissistic Lady Capulet, the sort of character role given to the aging prima donna, a lithe body tucked beneath folds of brocade.

Such is the normal course of human events. After all, we hold onto our youth and vigour for as long as we can until we must acquiesce to, and with luck embrace, what the life cycle has in store for us next. In contrast, to borrow from Shakespeare's *A Midsummer Night's Dream*, 'quick bright things', like the dramatized love of Romeo and Juliet, 'come to confusion', devoured 'by the jaws of darkness' before they are eroded from within. Hence its nostalgic appeal for most of us and its memorability as a tale of love, sex and danger.

We see in it, as in our screen memories, the long-lost fire of impassioned youth. A married woman in her thirties complains that she and her husband carp at each other on the eve of what should have been their love-making, which is postponed by their bickering. Her life is tedious compared to the flame of her teenaged heart, and she recalls the delicious tension of touching but not quite meeting in intercourse for many months. Perhaps sex has become too easy, too commonplace, she muses, and her fighting serves to jazz it up somehow. Maybe she's bored and that's why she interrupts herself on the verge of orgasm, even when her husband succeeds in exciting her. Many dreams and nocturnal narratives later, the analysis will reveal her still fierce love, her urge even now to wrench with the muscles of her vagina her husband's penis, to envelope and ensconce his whole vitality within herself. Like so many people, she had idealized her first love in order to obsure its essence and the desires still alive within her, yearnings deadened by the difficulties of an ongoing marriage.

Our sentimentality, our need to idealize our own pasts and to disclaim responsibility for the subsequent course of our lives, leads us to ignore any human agency in Shakespeare's young lovers' plight, and therefore to see it as a simple tragedy of fate. In so doing, however, we overlook the secret, universal appeal of the story. We treat it not as a tragedy, metaphorically capturing our own universal struggles to transform and so sustain passion in the lover's inevitable inward ambivalence, but rather as pathos brought on by extrinsic cruelty and caprice. We defend against the drama even while extolling its beauty.

A psychoanalytic exegesis of the play can, we believe, help adumbrate its tragic quality and this without treating the work on anything but its own terms, without 'psychologizing' or reading people into dramatic characters.

Here, with the text, its diction and metaphors as our reference points, we shall argue that *Romeo and Juliet*, which at first glance seems a story of love endangered from without, is in fact very much a drama of tragic flaws wherein the threats to the unfortunate lovers are to be discerned in the paradoxical intentions of the drama's protagonists. Whatever else may have been made of it, *Romeo and Juliet* is neither about innocence (betrayed), nor about the romantic absorption and tenderness of young love, so idealized in the Western cultural tradition. Rather it has as its theme a singular aspect of erotic union—its *savagery* when denied. It tells us also of the violence inherent in the frustrated femininity of men and of their carnivorousness once they taste a woman's beauty and then are kept from it. Normally, night envelops and obscures these mysteries. Lifting the comfort of darkness, exposing them to the light of day, risks catastrophe.

The play's setting is an Elizabethan England's imaginary Verona—Italy, a locale for the workings of passion and intrigue. Two noble families, the Capulets and Montagues, feud with each other because of slights long obscured by the passage of time. Their ancient quarrel terrorizes the citizenry and rankles the overseeing Duke.

The Capulets have a young and only daughter, Juliet, who at fourteen has become marriageable. Young Romeo, scion of the Montagues, lies outside her kinship lines and indeed her purview. Romeo's cherished companions are steadfast Benvolio and witty Mercutio, the latter a relative of the Duke's.

When the play begins Romeo has become a courtly lover, enamoured of love itself. We are introduced to the drama by a Prologue. The notion that Romeo's and Juliet's is a tragedy of misfortune probably derives rather literally from the words of the Prologue:

> From forth the fatal loins of these two foes
> A pair of star-crossed lovers take their life.[2]

Theirs is a 'misadventure . . . of death-marked love', we are told.

Were this all to the story, however, we would need no play. The Prologue, rather than necessarily expressing the viewpoint of the creator and the narrative, seems a theatrical conceit akin to the pomp of the Chorus which introduces us to Henry V, formerly Prince Hal. As with the rhetoric of courtly love, Shakespeare plays upon the accepted form, using it to reach the psychic pulse of his audience. He seduces us with seeming convention, only to surprise our easy expectations. Like a psychoanalyst, Shakespeare begins with the surface but takes us ever deeper into human nature. The Prologue's perspective is, in fact, that of an audience which at the outset superficially sentimentalizes the passion of the young lovers and which only gradually, as in any great drama, beginning with *Oedipus Rex*, learns the truth. Somewhat later, after they have met and spoken to each other, he and we will change our 'tune'.

As we shall show, the language of their love will reveal that this eerie and unsettling 'death mark' is not only to be discovered in the social and ideological forces which obviously victimize them but lies as well within the darker forces of their own nature. It is the lover's own, their doom; Eros is infused and contaminated by Thanatos, in the manner suggested by Denis de Rougemont.[3] The sadism plaguing the city of Verona also resides within the lovers' hearts.

The play begins with yet another brawl. When one of the families' retainers is killed, the Duke pronounces his sentence: future killers in the name of kinship honour will be executed. In the wake of the fighting Romeo's father describes his pining son's 'artificial night' and wonders at the mysterious origin of the young courtier's sorrows. Entombed within his room, a claustrum of his own devising, Romeo is infatuated with his rejecting Rosaline and is in love with love—the burning, unrequited love for the cruel mistress whose virtue makes her cool. Rosaline shuns him, and he loves her all the more. Describing the boy, the elder Montague introduces another sort of metaphor, one which will find its way into Romeo's language later on, once the tragic events of the dra-

ma have become inexorable, and he is torn from Juliet: he is a
'bud bit with an envious worm'—sick, dying, cut down before maturity, cut off from life. Romeo is reminiscent of the
modern teenager 'on the make'—romantic yet itching, aching in
his loins and desperate in his almost metaphysical sense of pre-
destination for realms of the flesh and spirit still to be known.

Without knowing true love Romeo is already enamoured
of frustration and suffering; his is a self-consuming passion,
desire turned on itself. When he enters he tells his comrade
Benvolio that 'Love is a smoke made with the fume of
sighs . . . a sea *nourished* with a *choking gall*' in the face of
'beauty starved with [its own] severity'. The images are desperate, at times hostile and, specifically, altogether 'oral'.
Romeo would eat what he cannot have, in the absence of
which he feeds greedily and, as we later learn, even suicidally
upon himself.

We may chuckle at his proverbial foolishness but we are
offered presentiments of more fateful consequence, the horrific denouement of the tragedy. To the Elizabethans such
courtly love was a cliché, a conceit inherited from the troubadours, the court of Elinor of Aquitaine and the Silver Poets
in the half century before Shakespeare.[4] It is a legacy which,
as we show in the next chapter, reaches back into the deserts
of Arabia and the forlorn cries of nomadic worshippers of
women. Behind admirable chivalry or the foolery of unrequited love—love's tragic and comic masks of the time—there
lurks some primal, irrational and oddly sensual violence—a
self-devouring cannibalism. Shakespeare finds in these and
other conceits personal meaning, gradually but inexorably revealing his and our own culture's self-deceptions about the
nature of our cravings.

Romeo's callow histrionics reveal the ominous counter-
points to and dangerous possibilities inherent in youthful
naivete and sexual self-discovery. Romeo the adolescent, beside himself because he is beset by the erotic within himself, is
not free of the destruction and guilt which conspire to render

him, like most teenaged lovers, the abject 'masochist' *par excellence*. To love means to yield to the all-powerful woman, to cede the hard-won independence, braggadocio, humour, and 'phallic' masculine camaraderie epitomized in his banter with Mercutio and Benvolio. To love means to yearn, to offer oneself up to the receding breast as a sacrificial victim in the hope of a moment's beneficence. All passionate young men have probably loved in this way, though none have been so heartfelt as their prototype, or ideal, Romeo.

Romeo's proclivities and his idiosyncracies are, at all events, matters to be reckoned with and are prime movers in the action of his tragedy. In the first scenes of the play, stung with what is for him unremitting repudiation, Romeo is ripe for love. He remains 'bound . . . shut up in prison, kept without my love, whipped and tormented.' Will this predilection for such pain, *his* tragic flaw, simply abate once his yearnings are actually consummated, if incompletely reciprocated? We know in advance that Romeo and Juliet are fated to fall wholeheartedly in love with each other. We do not know how Romeo's predisposition will greet this reality of adolescence when desire becomes palpable. The collision of circumstance and inner nature remains to be seen, the love story to be told. Prompted by Benvolio he agrees to go to the masqued ball of the Capulets, a 'supper' he supposes, where his friend hopes he will, as the psychiatrist says, 'test the reality' of what has become a ridiculous obsession with Rosaline's beauty.

In the interim the audience meets Juliet, not yet fourteen. Her earthy Nurse's reminiscences focus again on a series of telling anecdotes wich might easily be dismissed as an old crone's senescent babbling did they not have to do once more with the themes of bitterness, rebuff, injury, and death. Lamenting her own dead child, the old woman recalls Juliet's weaning at three years, the 'wormwood' on her *dug* and the little girl's 'broken brow'. Wailing, the fallen toddler is said to have been swept up by the old woman's late husband, who prophecies:

> . . . dost thou fall upon thy face?
> Thou wilt fall backward when thou has more wit;
> Wilt thou not, Jule? and, by my holy dame,
> 'The pretty wretch left crying and said,
> 'Ay'.[5]

The man, half facetiously, is referring of course to Juliet's heterosexual destiny. But the bawdy witticism implies something further about the nature of this fate and of woman's sexuality in its more servile aspect. Juliet (and the point is driven home as the nurse perseveres, repeating herself three times) is also *by nature* a victim. She is dutiful, modest and fair, yet headed for another fall. She seems to have embraced life more wholeheartedly than her morbid Romeo; indeed she rushes pell-mell into it. Her self-destruction is more headlong than languorous: hence her virtue, her beauty, yet also her own potential for disaster, as she too is impelled to seek it out in the seeming expectation of exhilaration.

The next scene introduces us to the witty Mercutio, and with him a third adolescent's window on love. Mercutio disparages and parodies Romeo's lovesick reveries. His author's spokesman at this point, Mercutio likens his friend's unanchored obsessions and specifically his dreams to all manner of vanity—to the courtesies craved by courtiers, to lawyers' fees, to the blistered lips of haglike ladies, to a soldier's vainglory, and the like, all more fanciful than real, dream images that are 'children of an idle brain, given life by a fairy midwife'. But Mercutio himself, despite his protestations, is not immune to such sentiments, which are indeed betrayed in his banter. He is in love with Romeo, Romeo the gay blade, and he would have him dance. Mercutio represents, we believe, the last gasps of the androgynous, vaguely homosexual, Peter-Pannish world of male adolescents, where wit and honour guard against and override heterosexual love. His allegiance is to friendship above all else, most certainly above any commitment to a woman. As with Romeo's and Juliet's love, the bonds of friendship beyond reason will exercise claim on his judgement and contribute to Romeo's downfall.

Future nemeses lurk among the revellers at the Capulet ball—
Tybalt, the fencer on the prowl, Lord Capulet, and the vain
and vindictive Lady who is Juliet's mother. Amidst the thick
darkness Romeo happens upon the snowy, brilliant, bejewel-
led 'true beauty' of Juliet. Their encounter is magical, love at
first sight epitomized. His love 'burning bright', he fore-
swears his earlier semblance of passion and discovers in Juliet
a willing recipient of his ardour. They dance towards and into
each other's arms, masqued yet open-faced, driven by a
magnetism that makes Romeo, at least, foolhardy. As quickly
as they find each other with a kiss, the young lovers discover
the kinship ties that divide them from each other. Destruction
and desire immediately converge as Juliet, having discerned
Romeo's identity, concludes the drama's first act:

> My only love sprung from my only hate
> . . . Prodigious birth of love it is to me
> That I must love a loathed enemy.[6]

Her words are reminiscent of Romeo's response to the crude
brawl with which the story opens and are portents of her
more warranted dismay at the dilemma she will face when, later, Romeo has personally acted to earn her family's enmity.
Meanwhile Tybalt has espied all and is only restrained by
Lord Capulet from attacking Romeo and disrupting the festivities.

The Chorus which introduces the second act now reverber-
ates, as we have indicated, with the more sinister undercur-
rents of the lover's poetry. Manifestly, the Prologue now
compares Romeo's base lust for Rosaline with his transcendent love of Juliet. Yet, more significant, the verse is charged
with metaphors that centre on death and greed.

> Now old Desire doth in his *deathbed* lie,
> And young affection *gapes* to be his heir;
> That fair for which love *groaned* for and would *die*,
> With tender Juliet match'd is now not fair.
> . . .
> And she steals love's *sweet bait* from fearful hooks.[7]

Outside the Capulet mansion Mercutio and Benvolio wonder where Romeo is to be found. Mercutio again ridicules Romeo, calling him an 'ape', a beast, and 'dead' to boot. But he now mistakes a complex longing for simple lust. Hearing his friend's cry Romeo privately rejoinders by once again equating love's imprint with injury—'scars' and 'a wound'— and this on the brink of anticipation, not in the aftermath of any experienced hurt. Mercutio, he further implies, cannot love a woman, has not been so seared. He is a man ensheathed by his wit, derision and misogyny.

Romeo vaults the wall to the Capulet's garden, the barrier—symbolic and real—separating him from his Juliet. The famous balcony scene which follows is indeed a rhapsody on true 'love's light wings', a lyric duet which elevates Romeo and Juliet above the stony impediments imposed by the petty prejudices of their families which render their houses fortresses and prisons. Yet even here the themes of envy, competition, murder and the savouring of suffering provide a sinister counterpoint to exalted feeling. In Romeo's monologues, as he observes her from below her window, Juliet, the 'fair sun', is seen to 'kill the envious moon', 'sick', 'pale and green', with narcissistic 'grief'. Her brilliance and Romeo's now tender submission submerge the uglier imagery—he would be a 'glove upon that hand', a part of her yet enveloping her, to touch her cheek.

On the balcony above, Juliet's musings on Romeo follow a parallel course. Juliet rails at the genealogical trappings that divide them. She would doff her and his names and be 'new baptized' in order to unite with him. Names are hateful enemies to be torn away. It is ironic, then, that their utterance—'Romeo!', 'Juliet!'—makes for their discovery of each other.

Romeo makes his presence known and Juliet recoils in fear for his life. Kinsmen are the murderers, Romeo acknowledges; yet in his sweet beloved's 'eye' he finds greater 'peril'. Juliet's person is not in the least forbidding; it is simply that she is a woman able to withdraw her love or her presence, severing her admirer from what has become, all too quickly, his better half. Juliet, too, is frightened of something inherent in their love, of Romeo the man's potential promiscuity, 'love's perjury'. There is nothing to fear, of course, as far as constancy and fidelity—their love's true passion—are concerned. Honour and vengeance will be the only other 'loves' to which Romeo will bow. In this sense their mistrust is unjustified.

The love is most dangerous in its mercurial intensity—'too rash, too unadvised, too sudden / Too like the lightning which doth cease to be / Ere one can say it lightens'. Paradoxically perhaps, Juliet's 'Bounty is boundless as sea / My love as deep; the more I give to thee / The more I have, for both are infinite'.[8] In loving she finds the reservoirs of her womanhood. Replenished by her own lavish devotion, she is immortal in her mind's eye in so far as she gives herself to another. Still, such boundlessness can be engulfing and mutually devouring. And once again, because desire is rapacious, 'oral' and predatory images intrude. Juliet yearns 'for a falconer's voice' to lure her male hawk back again; despite herself she is a siren. Notwithstanding 'how sweet lovers' tongues sound by night', Juliet likens her new betrothed to a 'wanton's bird', 'a poor prisoner', and she is 'loving-jealous of his liberty'. When Romeo assents to play this role Juliet warns him, 'Yet I should kill thee with too much cherishing', and, leaving for the time being, likens the bitter-sweet 'parting . . . [to] sweet sorrow'.

For the clinician these images resonate with the fears expressed by women in describing the heights of orgasm when making love with a cherished, adored man. Their vaginal muscles contract about the penis, as if they might wrench it and its possessor off, enveloping them within their innermost selves forever. Such is the erotic aggression of womanly inceptivity. Even tender Juliet becomes, like the chaste Layla of the next tale, La Belle Dame Sans Merci, luring her beloved into an erotic embrace, a snare which is his willing death.

Their leave-taking, with its aftertaste of sweet sorrow, is

not only regrettable but welcome, for it relieves the lovers of the urgency of their hunger for each other. Unending intimacy of this order must eventually exhaust itself. Where it is not attenuated or curtailed by artificial or external constraints, most lovers as they age and mellow erect their own walls, most often keeping their erstwhile beloveds at bay by fighting or fleeing them. In this way even romantic marriages grow stale and corrosive.

Romeo proceeds to his 'ghostly father', to Friar Laurence, the ascetic, scientific priest whose help, again in hungry imagery, he 'crave(s)'. Friar Laurence is reminiscent, in fact, of the modern analyst, who is his heir, the workmanly naturalist thinking and acting before the fact in the rational spirit of Freud and of the psychoanalytic dictum 'where id is there shall ego be', rationality growing out of blind impulses and thereafter reining them. Reason will preside over madness and irrational instinctuality, and conquer all. An onlooker and commentator on the world of love and hate, such a figure stands *hors de combat*, himself unmoved by and impervious to blinding passion and the twists of fortune that give it room to do its work.

Friar Laurence's opening soliloquy pays homage to the divine virtue he would draw out of all things, things insignificant or even poisonous until transfigured by his sage hands and natural lore. In his conjuring, much like ours of the unconscious, he makes a leap of faith. His informed yet spiritual truth would prevail over the forces of evil which, he tells himself, he knows so well, though impersonally. Hence the cleric's tragic liability when confronted by the inexorable, ineffable cravings of the flesh. In his herbs, as in an analysis, 'poison hath resonance and medicine power'; it is his conviction, rather than his inference, that the latter shall win out in the end. But how does one know? The turnings of powerful passions in concert with chance are more easily understood after the fact than predicted—and this is the great dilemma of all social or psychological sciences.

Romeo enters Friar Laurence's cell, tells him how 'on a

sudden one hath wounded me / That's by me wounded'. Can we doubt the 'sadomasochism' at the heart of his hunger? As if to purge himself of paradox, the young man seeks as a cure 'holy physic', and specifically marriage. Chiding his fickleness in discarding Rosaline from his affection, and the weakness of men in general, the old sage none the less accedes to Romeo's request in the hope that the lovers' alliance will serve as counterpoint to the hates which suffuse the Montagues' and Capulets' blood feud. He decides so rather quickly, perhaps drawn by the lovers' mutual magnetism. The wise man might have heeded the caveat with which, echoing Juliet's nurse's reminiscence, he himself admonishes Romeo—'they stumble that run fast.'

Does Laurence understand what Mercutio does in the next scene, when again he tells Benvolio that Romeo is 'already dead . . . run through the ear with a love song, cleft with the blind bowboy's butt shaft?' Such images call up a woman's more servile sexual stance, suggesting a reversal of roles and an abdication of masculinity. They are also prophetic of Romeo's progressive surrender to feminine feelings as the play progresses. Mercutio seems repeatedly both to dismiss and to fear any love of women, much as Friar Laurence tolerates and then exploits it. Yet he discerns the more problematic forces in the innocent rapture of his friend and would woo him back into the world of wit and swordplay. When Romeo engages him in this manner he concludes, 'Now art thou Romeo'. Phallic display and the ethic of bravery for bravery's sake, Mercutio implies, will reclaim his friend, helping him gird his loins.

In the mean time, unbeknown to Mercutio, Romeo has sent his proposal to Juliet. The nurse brings Juliet's answer and the wedding ceremony is set. Bawdily—her version of love is lust—the old woman teases Juliet. Romeo and Friar Laurence await Juliet, Romeo protesting, with some justice, that 'one minute's exchange of joy' more than makes up for 'hours of sorrow'. Like Romeo, Friar Laurence seems to have omens of disaster; he says:

> These violent delights have violent ends
> And in their triumphs die, like fire and powder
> Which as they kiss consume: the sweet honey
> Is loathsome in his own deliciousness.[9]

At some level he seems to know his charges' hearts, yet would magically impose order on their feeding on each other when he exhorts the groom to 'love moderately'. Or does his foreboding emanate from his own unknown and uncontrollable content? Again the images centre on orality and, specifically, insatiability, as if the lovers had stirred the old man's own long-abjured hungers.

Images of bounty and lightness attend the lovers' meeting on the brink of marriage. As if to tame the erotic and to control their rash press towards sexual union, Friar Laurence invokes the authority of the Church to 'incorporate two in one'. This they have already done and will continue to do themselves, needing no external sanction. Friar Laurence's is an illusion of omnipotence, and one for which the newlyweds will pay dearly. Without his help, we ask, would they not have found their union, unstoppable as the momentum was towards it?

The fateful scene that follows finds Mercutio quarrelsome, quite probably rancorous because of the vaguely felt loss of *his* Romeo. Tybalt then enters and provokes Romeo. None know as yet that he has become Juliet's husband. When Romeo refuses to answer Tybalt's challenge the friend is appalled at the 'calm, dishonourable submission' and himself addresses the crass affront with his weapon. They fight. Violating the code, his allegiance now belonging to Juliet, Romeo comes between the duellists and foolishly permits cunning Tybalt an opening. He thereby unknowingly facilitates Mercutio's murder and becomes one of his executioners. Romeo, it seems, has transiently identified with his 'ghostly father' and would reason with instinct. Inadvertently, in so doing, he further sacrifices friendship to erotic love.

When Mercutio curses them all, crying out 'a plague on both your houses', he may be seen to offer commentary on that same meddlesome, arrogant pretension to power—Romeo's and ultimately Friar Laurence's—that grants no room of its own to impulse, nature or fate. Mercutio's curse is also just that, a pronouncement foreshadowing an unfortunate turn of events which will interfere with Friar Laurence's plans and do Romeo in. A chance plague, after all, will later quarantine Friar Laurence's emissary John, delaying him and thereby giving Romeo's ready self-destructiveness time to fulminate. We shall return to this as the play moves to its inescapable conclusion, reason's omnipotence crumbling before both human and physical nature.

In the mean time Romeo decries the 'love' that has made him, in his words, 'effeminate'. As if to right one breach of trust with another, he forgets his nuptial vow. Martial masculinity and guilt—deference to the world of men—overtake him as he avenges Mercutio; in all good conscience he could not have done otherwise. Romeo's betrayals devolve from excesses of devotion—first to Juliet, then to Mercutio. Like Tristan, Romeo is buffeted by the love of man and woman. Like Hamlet, he is torn between the pagan laws of revenge and the Christian ethic of forbearance and mercy. Unlike Shakespeare's other hero, Romeo's genuine misery ensues upon rather than anticipates the act. He flees the scene before the arrival of the Duke of Verona, who sentences him to exile.

Ignorant of what has happened, Juliet invokes the black mantle of night, one of the play's recurring images. Unwittingly, she would deny all, including the inkiness of their love. In a startling fantasy, the gentle girl would have her beloved, once he is dead, 'cut into little stars' in order to overwhelm the firmament with his brilliance, in the process implying that the dead outshine the living. Is the innocent young girl, bounteous and capacious—Romeo's own soul now—morbid, self-consuming and violent? She knows him all too well. Theirs has become a 'symbiosis' of sorts, a confusion of identities.

Distraught when her nurse enters, raving that 'he is dead', Juliet immediately assumes that Romeo has slain himself. The 'storm' of passion and half-disclosed events 'blow[s] contrary', and when she learns what has occurred she is stunned by the betraval. Juliet gives full vent to ambivalence in oxymorons of death and desire, eros and agression. Romeo becomes all too quickly 'a serpent heart, hid with flowering face ... beautiful tyrant ... angelical raven ... wolvish ravening lamb ... damned saint ... honourable villain', and more. Yet she loves him still, unwaveringly.

The word 'banished' murders her. She is to be denied her Romeo. The ferocity of their need for each other is but whetted by their separation. Lifeless without him, Juliet threatens to have 'death, not Romeo, take my maidenhead'.

Fleeing, Romeo has sought the asylum of Laurence's monastic cell. When Friar Laurence informs Romeo of his doom, Romeo also finds more terror in exile than death. He seeks death as a boon, for his sentence, the exile, is a 'golden axe' cutting off his head. Juliet is everyone's but his. Desired and longed for, savagely, she is nowhere and everywhere. Friar Laurence would reason with and so support him. Romeo retorts, quite rightly, that the priest 'canst not speak of that thou dost not feel'. In despair the bereft lover takes 'the measure of an unmade grave'. Inversions of absence and presence, death and life, make for a natural insanity, a whirlwind of feeling known to all, yet impossible to articulate.

The grief of the two is beyond language; all they can do, in the nurse's description of her aggrieved Juliet, is weep, rise, fall, weep again. Neither can live without the other for they are as the two halves of a whole in desperate need of completion, each without identity or vitality in the absence of the other. When Romeo tries to stab himself, his first effort at suicide, Friar Laurence questions his status as a man. 'A man in form only', he concludes, whose 'tears are womanish' and whose 'wild acts denote / The unreasonable fury of a beast; / Unseemly woman in a seeming man! / Or ill-seeming beast in seeming both!'[10] The violence of longing unfulfilled undoes both Romeo's integrity and his masculinity. Laurence chastises Romeo for his raging, 'wench-like' weakness, and therefore implies that women (or the feminine in men) are wild or demonic. The confluence of femininity and bestial violence strikes an odd chord, overturning the ready equation of manliness and aggressivity. But we have already learned of womanly powers in Juliet's response to her lover's entreaties. In addition, the psychoanalyst would say, Romeo has succumbed to a 'de-differentiation of self and love object' and , with this, a 'destructuralization of drive-defense relations'. That is, as Romeo's sense of self collapses into his image of the vanishing beloved, so too does his civilized sensibility collapse before the press of instinctuality in both its loving and its violent aspect. No longer a man, both masculine and discriminating, he becomes a creature of unthinking impulse.

So beyond reason is Romeo that Friar Laurence must remind him that his Juliet in fact lives and that he can rediscover and reunite with her. The nurse, too, exhorts Romeo to 'Stand up' and be a man for Juliet, to rise from the vaginal 'O' into which he has collapsed. Together with the nurse, Laurence revives Romeo's hopes, offering him a lifeline with which to reverse his regressive descent into a state of sexual and destructive amorphism. He arranges for the consummation of the marriage and Romeo's escape from Verona. In his effort to order and manipulate passion and circumstance, however, the priest does not consider the unpredictability and raw power of the nature he would conjure and control. It is a nature which pre-dates all reason and is ultimately inaccessible to entreaty, although Romeo's collapse, his regression, is still reversible and yields temporarily to logic. But not everyone is to be reasoned with. If love is blind, pure reason tends towards tunnel vision. In the interim the ambitious, self-centred Capulets, ignorant of Juliet's wedding, have arranged her marriage to Count Paris.

Romeo steals off to Juliet's bedroom where they consummate their marriage. Once again the blackness of night, enclosing their secret nuptials, has proved a comfort to the lovers. In their clandestine shared solitude the lovers have found calm. The stillness of the bed chambers is broken by the sounds of the lark, heralding the dawn and replacing the nightingale. Having relished each other's softness it is the waking world, 'the envious streaks' of daylight, which harbours destruction. 'Dry sorrow drinks [their] blood'. At this point, as Romeo tells Juliet, their presence together, when brought to light, can only invite death. If Romeo is to survive and somehow reunite with Juliet, their division now is necessary. But can they stay apart and live? Romeo leaves. Juliet suffers a foreboding, overcome by a haunting image of her lover gone from her, descending into the garden below, 'as one dead in the bottom of a tomb'.

Juliet's mother enters and tells her of the marriage arrangements, to her horror. Not only passion now but allegiance to Mother Church opposes the secular convenience of the family. Lord Capulet vindictively spurns his daughter when she protests, threatening her with utter abandonment. Finally her trusted nurse, suddenly timorous (as Friar Laurence will prove to be), betrays her 'Jule's' love as well as the sanctified marital vows to which she bears witness when she sides with her employers. Utterly alone, perhaps unlike the weaker Romeo, Juliet rises up, fortified by her rage, towards the self-centred caretakers who would exploit and abandon her. 'Ancient damnation! O most wicked fiend!' she cries out after the nurse whose betrayal has cleaved their two 'bosoms in twain'.

Granted the nurse's pragmatism—she is a retainer bound to those who ensure her survival—it is inevitable that a man should sever a girl's ties to her mother. Union with him disrupts the vestiges of the symbiosis of mother and daughter and brings with it promise of ecstasy, loss and mourning.

Whatever the sources of her strength and womanly virtue, Juliet retains her integrity and with it her constancy to Romeo. She is still capable of faith in remedy. If any character is to be exempted from tragic responsibility it is she in her surprising courage and steadfast refusal to surrender to despair until the very last.

Juliet's grief 'stains' Friar Laurence 'beyond the compass of

[his] wits', suggesting that he finds himself somehow to blame for her plight. Faced with her suicidal despair he calls on his more mystical medical powers, his holy physic, and resorts to the 'dangerous flower' to which he has alluded earlier. He exhorts her to do what she has in fact already done in loving Romeo, to 'undertake a thing like death to chide away this shame / That cop'st with Death himself to scape from it'. His empathic words now unleash the horrid image of Thanatos skulking in the corners of the innocent girl's imagination. She would leap from battlements, walk in thievish ways, 'lurk where serpents are', be 'chained with roaring bears', sink under the skeletons and shrouds of a 'charnel house'—all 'to live an unstain wife to my sweet love'.

Manifestly, Juliet seems to envision herself the victim in these ghastly scenarios. Yet the verse is ambiguous as to its subject and object, and it remains unclear whether she suffers or participates in them as her own agent. Once again, perhaps, the initiative in Juliet's rage, unfettered by the further threat of shame, rouses her to act rather than submit, to take arms against her troubles, and this in contrast to Romeo's self-indulgent violence. Romeo's love, having made him effeminate, quite possible may have made Juliet rather manly in her resolve. The conceits of stereotypical sex differences have been shattered. Thus, though naive, she will assume the 'borrowed likeness of shrunk death' offered her as a means of life by Friar Laurence, undeterred by any 'womanish fear'. Friar Laurence further promises her that his letters shall reach Romeo in Mantua and apprise him fully of Juliet's plight. In the mean time the lovers have quite overturned the audience's expectations as to what is masculine and what feminine. So much, then, for the cultural image of love between lordly knights and damsels in distress; the fictions of sex difference have been shattered. Passion, the implication is, is charged with altogether surprising contradictions. As man becomes 'womanish', woman becomes 'masculine' in her forcefulness. And as the order of gender collapses, what was seemingly tender and life-affirming in eros is driven out by the forces of destruction, balm turning to poison, beneficence to malevolence.

Preparing to drink Friar Laurence's potion, Juliet recognizes that 'My dismal scene I must needs act alone'. This Romeo does not do. He is a creature of his need for her and cannot act in her absence. In his passivity, his paralysis of will and aspiration, he is now more 'effeminate' according to the terms overturned by the action of the drama. Even the Friar is not immune in Juliet's monologue to her mistrust, for those closest to her have failed her. Chance, too, is an enemy, for should she wake too early in the 'foul mouth' of the vault she will suffocate or else have to brave 'the horrible conceit of death and night'. And this Friar Laurence, who will free her at the crucial moment of her awakening, cannot do either. Alternatively, her own madness and 'rage' await her. In the end, about to imbibe the potion, Juliet shrinks from the murderous Tybalt's avenging ghost and the spectre offered by his rapier's point. In retrospect, this imagery is a presentiment of the tomb in which she will find herself at the story's close, surrounded by corpses—Tybalt's, Paris's, her very own Romeo's. But the dagger might also be interpreted as Romeo's, which she will later plunge into herself. The male phallus is Juliet's weapon, and she will use it to immolate herself in hope of eternal wedding. Drinking, Juliet offers herself up to sleep, but moves further towards the jaws of death.

Discovering Juliet's pale, limp body on the morning of the arranged marriage, her parents and the Nurse at last lament their selfish ambition. Images of coldness abound. Self-interest and narcissism are often chilling, for they destroy the love of another, erotic and parental. 'Death lies on her like an untimely frost', claiming the 'sweetest flower of all the field', as his bride. Death, her father recognizes, is Lord Capulet's son-in-law, 'barren emptiness' his 'heir'. He dies with his only child. The Capulet's punishment is apt, the Friar tells them, for it was their 'heaven', wealth and well being she should have advanced.

The audience, aware of the impending denouement, further

understands that it is also Friar Laurence's Christian heaven, albeit more exalted and less self-invested, that Juliet's and Romeo's rather over-hasty union was to have served. Eerily, he continues, echoing *A Midsummer Night's Dream*:

> She's not well married that lives married long:
> But she's best married that dies married young.[11]

No doubt this is a commentary on the eroding impact of inevitable ambivalence in human love relations. Yet, more than this, Friar Laurence's lofty intent may itself bespeak a half-acknowledged, self-serving objective, wherein he would have Juliet a politic martyr and exploit this martyrdom to create a more merciful or Christian climate in Verona. He is, in his almost Jesuitical logic, playing upon and with all too powerful passions, romantic love as well as family allegiance and narcissistic advancement. He concludes that tragedy is indeed the stuff of feeling, comedy of wit, that 'Yet nature's tears are reason's merriment'. He would have no one violate the heavens, the stars, save himself. Hence *his* hubris.

The final act of the play begins with the exiled Romeo's report of another dream, more 'real' and heartfelt than those parodied by Mercutio. Romeo's is a strange dream indeed, of being dead and then having 'such life breathed in him with kisses on his lips', that he revives and becomes an emperor. Why the optimism and seeming false prophecy? Is his spirit in memory destined to be more heavenly and glorious, as Juliet has earlier suggested, than his live, driven person? Better martyred than married? That is one of many possible interpretations.

Keats, it seems, confronted with unrequited love and the inchoate spectre of his own imminent death, may have alluded to Romeo's reverie in the literary dream contained in the ballad *La Belle Dame Sans Merci*:

> And then she lulled me asleep
> And there I dreamed, ah woe betide!
> The latest dream I ever dreamt
> On the cold hill side

> I saw pale Kings, and Princes too
> Pale warriors, death pale were they all,
> They cried, la belle dame sans merci
> Thee hath in thrall.[12]

The implication seems to be a reverse in metaphorical direction. Where the love, a lady, was earlier represented in Romeo's images of suffocating and dying, the image of death is now incarnate in the form of a beautiful woman. Quite possibly, Romeo is simply envisioning his own suicide and its glorification.

His hopes dashed by news of Juliet's death, Romeo for the first time, curiously, defies the stars and prepares to kill himself—by poison, the only fitting conclusion of ill-fated craving. Friar John, Laurence's messenger, has been delayed by the plague and fails to reach Mantua; Mercutio's curse comes true. Because of this circumstance the truth of Juliet's true state eludes her lover's awareness. Even so, as Romeo himself confesses, 'mischief is swift / To enter in the thoughts of desperate men'. Impetuous self-surrender, as we have seen, is an abiding defect in Romeo, and of youth in general, a further fact of life to which the priest has proved resistant in his deliberations despite so many signs to the contrary.

Romeo's sadomasochism and greed find full rein now. Their first object is himself. Talking with the apothecary who is his euthenasiastic executioner she imagines the poison's work—'that the trunk may be discharged breath / As violently as hasty powder fired / doth hurry from the fatal cannon's womb'. This is another strikingly hermaphroditic image in which the violence of sexual union becomes a shattering merger and finds a hideous embodiment. Romeo then turns the weaponry of deprivation upon the apothecary who sells him his poison. Like the impoverished priest, Norman Holland has reminded us, the apothecary trades in lethal and miraculous herbs and may figure as the ascetic Laurence's proxy.[13] He and his damned holy physic are perhaps the objects of Romeo's rage—the cleric's insensitivity to the imperatives of the flesh and to the ways of the world when stripped of its civilized veneer. In any event, Romeo derisively enjoins the poor man to 'buy food and get thyself in flesh'. He himself will do otherwise, setting out for Verona, as he embraces the 'cordial to his breast'. The rapt lover has become a cynic.

Ruthlessness and cruelty overtake noble Romeo. Having returned to Verona and the Capulet necropolis, he approaches Juliet's tomb with mattock and wrenching iron, threatening to tear his servant 'joint by joint' should he disturb him. His intents, he tells him, are 'savage-wild / More fierce and inexorable far / Than empty tigers on the roaring sea'. Like the churchyard, into which he projects his yawning cannibalism, Romeo is himself 'hungry' in the most implacable sense, driven by a gnawing void. What was once the breath of life is now become the odour of fetid, ashen death. Deprived of Juliet, Romeo senses that the tomb is within as well as without. The mausoleum is a 'detestable maw', a 'womb of death', whose 'jaws' he forces to open, disgorging it with more 'food'—his dead self—perhaps in the secret hope of reunion and rebirth. Indeed Juliet's inner reaches have become his unmade grave—a genital, oral cavern subserving not life now but death. He would devour, be devoured and sleep forever. Yet these are not erotic promptings, but involuted and violent ones. Romeo must *have* Juliet, and when the innocent Paris bars his way he kills him, notwithstanding his own determination to die.

Mouths, food and wombs are everywhere. When Romeo sees Juliet her beauty makes the 'vault a feasting presence full of life'. The cannibalistic images continue. Death has 'sucked the honey of her breath' yet failed to destroy or drain her, especially the 'crimson' of her lips. He laments the loss of her innocence and his own part in cutting her youth, like his own, in two. Death, 'amorous' death, and love are now wedded; the 'lean abhorred monster' keeps her a paramour. Romeo is lean himself, now monstrous too, as once he was amorous. Death, engrossing death, obsesses him, as once the living Juliet did. He yields to it and 'with a kiss'—Juliet's lips and the dram of poison—he dies. In the process, ironically, he destroys her whom he would resurrect; for his corpse will suck the life from her.

It is some intuition into the dark heart of even such a noble youth that seizes Friar Laurence's soul as he now enters the tomb. The 'unkind hour', the 'lamentable chance', or rather the ghost of his guilt, returns to haunt him. He is terrified of the 'death, contagion' and 'unnatural sleep',—the latter his own artifice. He tells Juliet that her husband 'in thy bosom there lies dead', in yet another reference to themes of mutual merger and incorporation. A noise frightens him, and finally he too flees her in her moment of dire need.

Abandoned, Juliet is again alone. In solitude she seeks the 'restorative' of union, poison, and would dispatch herself before being once again divided from her love. Snatching Romeo's dagger, she proclaims her body 'its sheath' and stabs herself. Like the cannibalism and the merger, their hermaphroditism is final, terrible. Romeo has encompassed death, taking it into himself as a woman might a man, while Juliet does both, thrusting death into herself. Their togetherness in death is now beyond disquiet; they are inseparable and forever wed in a *Liebestod*, a love death of the sort permeating many Western narratives of love.

In the concluding moments of the scene, before the carnage of what the prince calls the 'mouth of outrage', we learn that 'grief of [her] son's exile hath stopped [the] trials' of Romeo's mother—apart from a brief appearance, the sole reference to her in the play. The Friar strives to purge himself of any complicity in the double suicide and is indeed exonerated by the secular authority of the prince as a most holy man. The warring families agree to memorialize their children's love in stony monuments to them. Their martyrdom is now secured, theirs having become a parable of the devastation wrought by barren feuding and of innocence betrayed. About their own passion we hear nothing more as the living lovers become merely moribund objects of fate, family and politics. Romeo and Juliet are now the stuff of which retrospective and stereotypical fantasies about youth are made. We are spared their torments and ecstasies; all is well with the world.

There have been attempts, some of them interesting, to psychologize psychoanalytically about the play. Romeo and Juliet's 'adolescent development' has been underscored along with their struggle to sever their so-called incestuous ties to Oedipal parents.[14] All such efforts, however, treat the central figures of the drama as if they were real people with a history behind and motives within them, rather than archetypes whose life is that of the imagination and of the play in itself. Perhaps the usage has its playful and illustrative uses, whatever the methodological pitfalls. A further problem, however, is that these applications most often impose the current psychoanalytic consciousness, and what Foucault has dubbed 'reason's monologue about madness' upon these nearly mythic figures. In so doing, analysts tend silently to moralize about rather than explain the characters and what they embody. We have not done this, we hope—have not, for example, tried to discern in Romeo's craving for Juliet his merely childish yearning for mother love. Indeed, we have sought to elaborate on the savage, deathly, heavy passion harboured in the bosom of these two light lovers, Romeo especially, and evident in their words. It is the rapacity, the urge to give up oneself to eternal sleep, the grip of union, the surrendering of a sexual bounded identity and self-immolation which savage their tender love for one another.

The stories from other cultures which follow also exemplify one or other of these elements from the prehistoric era of the individual's love life, the so-called pre-oedipal period. At the same time, in accenting these early aspects, the love story overturns the culture's particular platitudes on the nature of love. In our Western tale, for instance, voracious hungers, startlingly violent in their intensity, seem to lurk under the cultural idealization of love's tenderness and the lovers' mutual adoration. In our hearts, born in our infancy, we har-

bour 'death instincts' which are, as Freud put it, beyond not
only the reality but also the pleasure principle. Fitfully, we seek
the very cessation of life—Freud called it Nirvana—and as
Melanie Klein tried to tell us, we are moved to destroy her
whom we love. It is in the face of this horrifying violence
from within that we struggle to cherish and preserve the beloved, as we once did the mother who bore us and whose
psychic presence continues to affirm our very existence. For
the purposes of defence, moreover, we persistently confuse 'I'
and 'thou', even after the images of the baby and mother
have become distinct in each other's eyes. Especially when
denied, a lover like Romeo becomes the uroboros, the
mythical snake devouring itself in a never-ending mystery.

Romeo and Juliet's social milieu is at fault because it reflects and intensifies only one aspect of spontaneous passion,
the aggression. In denying passion its due, in deeming it illicit
and forcing it to seek out the dark night for its gratification, in
dividing what has become united, social mores and inflexible
moralisms re-infuse it with hatred and make sexual love life-
threatening and ultimately ugly. Even the more sympathetic
onlookers—the Nurse, Mercutio to some extent, and the low
life comics who punctuate the unfolding of the lovers' tragic
plight—confuse libidinal aspiration with self-serving lust. In
failing to understand or honour eroticism, in degrading it, the
characters who surround the lovers create a self-fulfilling
prophecy. Deeming pure passion evil or perhaps simply foolish and blind, they bring out the 'worst' in it. They separate
the lovers. Frustration and privation fuel the aggression inherent in Romeo's and Juliet's passion, and they begin to taste
blood, turning upon themselves, and therefore also upon each
other, with a ferocity which they are quite helpless to express
against an altogether entombing society. They become carni-
vorous and sarcophagous, eating greedily of their own flesh
and blood.

Standing apart from the common ambitions and prejudices
that rule families and nations, the priest, like the uninvolved
'neutral' psychoanalyst, has the wisdom to challenge any re-

flexive condemnation of the boy's and the girl's rebellious love. Manifestly, he sees and affirms their vitality and virtue, provides them with access to each other and serves their pleasure, though not in the name of hedonism or of the sensuality which he has himself abjured, but of a higher (or ulterior) purpose. Such ideals, however, in which people come to play a secondary role to the abstractions we make of them, are eminently risky and cruelly exploitative, deluding even the most savvy philosopher of human nature. In a series of careful orchestrations, Friar Laurence reveals that, like the altruistic Prometheus, he would steal the fire of the gods. But it is not he who suffers.

The most terrifying irony is that the sage and well-intentioned cleric, rooted in the Christian tradition of martyrdom in the service of Mother Church, achieves his aim. The Church, and what is there represented as well, reason and tolerance, succeeds in restoring secular peace at the expense of the souls of Romeo and Juliet, who ultimately are its pawns. No longer flesh, the hapless teenagers are prematurely sanitized as statuary, mere reminders to the ascendant generation of their own selfish ambition. They have been, as one critic has said, ripe fruit, awaiting sexual self-discovery in their love. But we pluck them, eat them, exploit them in the process, making of them object lessons for our own purpose and person. Once we do so, their passion, whose unruliness frightens us, is forgotten entirely. Dead, they will love forever, but in stone, no longer themselves.

Seventy years ago, in his first full work on human sexuality, his *Three Essays on Sexuality*, Freud cautioned the adult world not to succumb to consensual denial and whitewash the pre-emptory sensuality of the child.[15] Sexual passion and aggressive ambition were commonplaces of the nursery, he told us, frankly understood by every nursemaid, however denied they might be by the parents who were its objects. In similar vein, the poet and dramatist of the soul *nonpareil* and *sui generis*, Shakespeare has provided us with an urgent meditation on the adult world's misapprehensions about adolescent and, beneath this, infantile first love. This love is neither malleable nor innocent and tender, nor simply lustful. It is imperious and obsessive, suffused with the press to complete oneself sexually and with the deathly intent that arises when one's inevitable solitude and separateness are confronted. The violence inherent in these urges to merge lurks behind more obvious conflicts among filial duty, phallic conquest and sensual yielding. Teenagers are not merely virginal flowers, noble youths, gay young blades and devoted brides. They are at heart 'roaring tigers' and the 'loving-jealous' jailers of one another. Only when they grow older, if and when they do, do they quell their passions. As they age they make them conform to reason and reality and settle in the interest of survival, and of a capacity to serve as householders and caretakers of the next generation of youth.

Child of the Western nineteenth-century zeitgeist, increasingly oriented by virtue of time's passage towards the centre of society's cultural value system, middle class now, contemporary psychoanalysis cleaves to the notion of 'mature genitality'. This idea, first advanced by Sandor Ferenczi and then by Karl Abraham, both Freud's disciples, has it that as long as one is most interested in genital sex engaged in with a member of the opposite sex and aims finally to procreate, to reproduce the species, one can love both intensely and safely.[16] The erotic is thereby civilized into the social order as mankind is again enjoined to go forward, be fruitful and multiply. The spectre of Friar Laurence admonishes us, however, serving as a caution against a rationalism oblivious to the compelling and violent psychic forces which spin the wheel of fortune.

We psychoanalysts, the theoretical conjurers and ghostly confessors of our own era, must finally concede the real-life limits of our undeniable explanatory powers. We may understand something about passion but none the less we cannot temper it. The erotic requires the veil of darkness to do its unstoppable work. Marriage may allow for islands of the night, for the inky darkness behind closed doors, the inner sancta where lovers feed on each other for their revival before they face the familial and worldly duties of the day. Yet the institution of marriage and a couple's erotic secrets are essentially antipathetic to each other. Even Elinor of Aquitaine's court knew better, reminding us how hard it was for true love to survive marriage and, with it, the regulation of kinship relations. Social and sexual unions are not equivalent, however much they are propelled by the inherent urges of human beings to bind and bond with one another.

Love is a form of insanity, as Freud himself acknowledged. Madness constrained—whether by reason or by the social order—is madness contorted and madness indeed. All lovers must be fools, crazed in some transcendent, even mystical sense—as our next tale reveals. The most we clinicians can do is try to help such madmen find protection from themselves while they revel as best as they can in the feverish hedonism of their life-affirming 'illness'. We cannot, nor should we try, to tame them.

CHAPTER THREE

LOVE IN THE MIDDLE EASTERN WORLD: LAYLA AND MAJNUN

There is a peculiar phenomenon reported of certain patients on the analytic couch. Drifting into sleep, they have described a grainy screen before them, a gritty or sandy taste in their mouths. These visitations have been attributed by Freudian analysts as sense-memories of a personally distant past, one lying beyond the borders of verbal recollection. They are engrams of the advancing or receding breast on which as infants we have fallen into soporific repose, only then to lose its sustenance in the solitude of sleep. Were we of a Jungian bent, we might see in these tricks of consciousness legacies of our collective amorous origins in the deserts of Arabia. It is to the sands that we now turn, to a prototypical tale of love lost to Western remembrance but continuing to breathe life into its romantic traditions. It is a story which captures one of love's first developmental tensions—the predicament of separation.

With Romeo and Juliet we endeavoured to describe the

deathly nocturnal mysteries underlying their lilting romance. In the spirit of their creator, Shakespeare, we sought to challenge the clichés with which the lovers and their passion were subsequently reified and mystified. The story of Layla and Majnun tells us of passion's havoc, its cruelty towards the solitary breast which harbours it, and of the vistas granted the sufferer. Where Romeo and Juliet have united and lamented their division, Majnun or Madman pines in deep loneliness for a Layla who becomes a vision. But once more to the story itself.

> Two lovers lie awaiting in this tomb
> Their resurrection from the grave's dark womb,
> Faithful in separation, true in love
> One tent will hold them in the world above.

With these mournful lines the great Persian poet Nizami, the originator of the Persian romantic epic, concludes his version of the ancient tale of Layla and Majnun, the quintessential lovers of the Perso-Islamic world.[1] In poems and songs, in older tales and modern movies, Layla and Majnun live on and continue to enthral the romantic imagination of Islamic Asia and Africa. The essential elements of their legend recompose themselves again and again in the real lives of other lovers and in works of the artistic imagination. No Muslim man has ever been a Majnun, nor a woman Layla, just as in Europe none has been a Romeo or a Juliet. Yet without the compelling example of these great organizing myths of love we would not quite appreciate why and how men and women in a particular culture love as they do, nor could we truly fathom the individual depths of their passion. Born of dreams and not doctrines, wielding power through expressions of individual fantasy rather than through social codes, Layla and Majnun (as also the lovers of other similar legends), have set standards for the course of 'true' love and the aspirations of lovers.

Today the Islamic world tends to be perceived by many as a barbarous bastion of misogyny, of the *chador*—the veil

obscuring woman's beauty, curtailing her freedom and denying her humanity. In counterpoint it is salutary to remember that the Perso-Islamic world has produced some of the
larger human universe's finest love stories. These tales are
characterized by tenderness, by mutuality and by the adoration of the woman, who figures as no mere object of men's
wants nor slave to his needs, but rather as a subject herself in
the enterprise of love.

Indeed it is from this world that the modern theme of passionate love first reached Europe in the twelfth century. The
songs of the Provencal troubadours who raised love to an
ideal and woman to an idol, adapted and indeed often adopted
entire verses of the Perso-Islamic poetry cultivated in Muslim
Spain, as in other intellectual centres of the Islamic world.
Their derivatives are to be found in the literature of courtly
love, in Shakespeare, in the Romantics and on into the modern Western era, in its popular ballads of homage to womanly
enchantment.

Once upon a time among the Bedouin in Arabia, the legend
begins, there was a great chief who possessed everything except a son. The chief, aware that 'he only is truly alive who in
his son's memory survives his own death', gave alms and
prayed long for an end to his son-less state. His prayers were
finally answered and a gorgeous son was born, an event celebrated with much rejoicing. The child was committed to the
care of a nurse, so that under her watchful eye he should grow
big and strong. So he did, 'for every drop of milk he drank
was turned in his body into a token of faithfulness, every bite
he ate became in his heart a morsel of tenderness.'

After his tenth year the boy, named Qays by the doting
family, was sent to a school for the children of noble families
from various tribes. Handsome and intelligent, he excelled in
his studies and soon became everyone's favourite. One day a
beautiful young girl, Layla by name, joined the school. The
devastation her beauty caused was immediate and overwhelming. Nizami describes their falling in love thus:
'Whose heart would not have filled with longing at the sight

of this girl? But young Qays felt even more. He was drowned in the ocean of love before he knew that there was such a thing. He had already given his heart to Layla before he understood what he was giving away . . . '. And Layla? She fared no better. A fire had been lit in both—and each reflected the other.

What could have they done against it? A bearer had come and filled their cups to the brim. They drank what he poured out for them. They were children and did not realize what they were drinking; no wonder they became drunk. He who is drunk for the first time, becomes deeply drunk indeed. And heavily falls he who has never had a fall before. Together they had inhaled the scent of a flower, its name unknown, its magic great . . . As yet no one had noticed, so they went on drinking their wine and enjoying the sweet scent. They drank by day and dreamed by night, and the more they drank the deeper they became immersed in each other. Their eyes became blind and their ears deaf to the school and the world. They had found each other.[2]

It is now that Majnun's strange love story begins. The world, noticing their open flirtation and 'scandalous' conduct, reacts sharply with reproaches, derision and threats. Qays tries to be cautious and hide his love but is unable to do so. Away from Layla he finds no peace, yet searching her out is to imperil both. He becomes a *Majnun*, a mad man. Majnun's emotional story begins where Romeo's concludes. The impetuousness with which he accedes to bereavement and its insanity rivals that with which Romeo presses towards Juliet. Devastated at the outset by division, his frenzy is more awesome than Romeo's. His is a living death, his life therefore a mystery of mysteries. Walking about in the small alleys between the tents and in the bazaar, he sings songs in praise of Layla's beauty and their mutual love. This confession becomes too much for Layla's people. Preoccupied with the girl's honour and that of the tribe, they confine her to her home and guard her carefully, her parents ensuring that the lovers do not meet.

If Layla weeps secretly, Qays, now universally known as Majnun, displays his glorious unhappiness for everyone to see. More and more often and for lengthening spells, he leaves the dwelling places and pastures of his tribe, wandering aimlessly through the desert singing *ghazals*, those elegies of unhappy love where the lover bemoans the loss, the inaccessibility or the turning away of the beloved:

He was in rags and looked wilder each day. Overwhelmed by his melancholia, he did not listen to anyone or anything. Nothing that otherwise pleases or disturbs a man found an echo in his heart. His two or three companions had long since left him. From afar people pointed at him and said: 'There goes Majnun, the madman, the crazy one, who was once called Qays. He heaps shame and dishonour on himself and his people'.[3]

Deeply distressed at the growing deterioration in the mental faculties of his beloved son and with the threat to his tribe's reputation, his father decides to ask for Layla's hand in marriage for Majnun. Layla's family refuses him flatly, advancing the not unreasonable argument that they could not marry their daughter to a madman, albeit one by virtue of his love for her. Disappointed, Majnun's father tries to reason with his son, offering him other girls from the tribe, 'beauties who are perhaps even more attractive than she who has stolen your heart'. But Majnun, in the manner of all lovers whose choice is so rigorous that it retains only the unique (cf. Juliet when presented with Paris), is beyond such reasoning. For Majnun, as for the rest of us, the question as to why of all the thousands of persons one encounters in one's life and of the hundreds one may lust after, only one is loved, lastingly, longingly, remains intractable to rational explanation. Majnun now wanders the desert, a solitary, naked nomad imploring Layla's presence in his verses to save him from the unbearable anguish of the enforced separation while trying little to pursue her.

Having failed in the profane realm of arranged marriages,

the father tries to cure his darling son by taking him on a pilgrimage to Mecca. But now he is foiled by the mysterious inner workings of the young man's mind. Standing in front of the Kaba, the holiest of holies, Majnun does not ask God to save him from his madness, but, on the contrary, to increase it. 'If I am drunk with the wine of love', he prays, 'let me drink even more deeply. They tell me: "Crush the desire for Layla in your heart!" But I implore thee, oh my God, let it grow even stronger. Take what is left of my life and add it to Layla's. Let me never demand from her as much as a single hair, even if my plaint reduces me to the width of one!'[4] God answers Majnun's prayers. He becomes even more intoxicated with agony.

As Majnun's madness becomes a matter of common knowledge, there is no tent whose dwellers do not know of his love for Layla. The members of her tribe, ever more angry and bitter, send emissaries to the Caliph's prefect. They tell him how Majnun through his behaviour and his songs imperils not only the honour of their tribe but also the authority of the Caliph, since 'Whatever this impertinent fellow composes tears the veils of custom and decency a hundred-fold.' Sensing the greater social threat posed by the boy's insanity of love, the deputy advises them to kill Majnun. Once again his miserable father entreats his son to desist, to save his own life as well as assuage the grief it has caused the family and the shame it has brought upon the tribe. Majnun, however, declares his helplessness since his destiny seems not a matter of choice but rather comes from a power beyond his control. Moreover, it has assumed spiritual proportions. What began as infatuation is now a vision, the frustrated lover becoming a prophet of mysteries beyond the worldly logic of categorization or common sense.

Layla too burns in the fire of longing but her flames, as Nizami puts it, are hidden and no smoke arises from them. She cannot speak to anyone of her sorrow. Like Juliet, and women in general, whatever their gossip about more mundane peccadiloes, she is more discreet in matters of true love.

Yet her lover's voice reached her. Was he not a poet? No tent curtain was woven so closely as to keep out his poems. Every child from the bazaar was singing his verses; every passer-by was humming one of his love songs, bringing Layla a message from her beloved. Secretly she collected Majnun's songs as they came to her ears, committed them to memory and then composed her answers on scraps of paper wich she entrusted to the wind. Often someone who found one of the scraps would bring it to Majnun, wasting away in the desert, hoping as a reward to hear some of his poems that had become very popular. Thus many a melody passed to and fro between the two nightingales, drunk with their passion. Those who heard them listened in delight, and so similar were the two voices that they sounded like a single chant. Born of pain and longing, their song had the power to break the unhappiness of the world.[5]

The gorge in which the nomadic Majnun finally chooses to live is ruled by a Bedouin prince called Nawfal. One day, while hunting in that area, Nawfal comes across the wandering recluse and is struck by the sight of his wasted frame, wild, dishevelled hair and arms and legs scratched severely by thorns. Astonished at finding such a strange and pitiful apparition in the wilderness, Nawfal turns to one of his companions for enlightenment and is told the history of Majnun's ill-fated love. Greatly moved, Nawfal swears to Majnun that he will bring the lovers together and persuades him to accompany Nawfal's retinue. Like the fool in *King Lear*, Majnun is a poor, bare-forked creature, presenting to us an embodiment of our innermost mourning, a grief and deterioration beneath all palpable pleasure and success. His plight echoes an inaccessible ubiquitous truth: we have all loved and lost.

At the head of his fighting men Nawfal rides to the tents of Layla's tribe and demands that she be married to Majnun. When her tribe refuses to accede to this demand, two great battles take place in which Majnun does not take part. On being asked the reason for this desertion of his own cause by one of Nawfal's men, Majnun replies, 'The heart of my beloved beats for the enemy, and where her heart beats, there is my home. I want to die for my beloved, not kill other men. How then could I be on your side, when I have given up myself?' Such is a lover's love that he will betray the staunchest and most self-sacrificing of allies.

Though Nawfal is victorious, Layla's father still refuses to voluntarily surrender his daughter to Majnun, a position the chivalrous Nawfal quite understands: 'Even though I am the victor, I want you to give me your daughter only if you are willing. A woman taken by violence is like a slice of dry bread and a salty sweet'. Nawfal's men, too, incensed by Majnun's refusal to fight in his own cause, urge their lord to wash his hands off the whole affair. Majnun's love eludes the ken of men of the world, lying beyond fealty as well as reason.

Layla is now married off by her parents to one of her many noble suitors, Ibn Salaam. Secretly grieving, Layla submits to her fate but refuses to consummate the marriage, expressing her willingness to die rather than give in to force. Ibn Salaam, who was himself deeply in love with Layla, is also a man of lofty sentiments and says he will adore her from afar till she changes her mind. He is content if he is only allowed to look at her and would be a common thief if he asked for more. What riveting power is granted to the girl that she can hold so many men from afar and have her spirit, her abstraction, stir the listeners of her lover's lyrics!

Majnun in the mean while is back to his lonely desert existence. His ageing father, on the verge of death, once again comes to reclaim his son with the aid of a deep paternal love and sage counsel on the virtues of patience, prudence and the small joys of daily life. His life having run its more natural course, he laments his boy's premature morbidity:

Tempt yourself, be gay and happy, joke and dally; anything—be it as fleeting as a breath of wind. Why not? That is life; whether its promises are true or false, enjoy what the moment brings. What is of lasting value in this world? Enjoy what you have—today; and eat what you have harvested—now!

Having appealed to Majnun's sense of reality, the father invokes his filial sentiments:

> Oh my son! Be my companion for the few days which still remain: for me, night is falling. If today you turn away, tomorrow you will look for me in vain. I have to go and you must take over my task. Soon my sufferings will be ended, but you should be happy! Look, my sun is sinking, darkened by the haze of a long day. Dusk is waiting for me, my son—my soul is taking wing. Come then, come! Do not delay. Take my place, which belongs to you! Come![6]

Unable to lie even for the state of pity, regret or shame Majnun tells his father that he cannot follow his advice for—'you strike your coins with the die of wisdom, mine is the die of love; it cannot be changed! Can you see that I have forgotten my past? I am no longer the man I was, my father!' Nizami tells us that in this hour Majnun at last understood his fate in full. His final rejoinder to the ways of the world needs to be quoted at length:

> I have not only lost you; I no longer know myself. Who am I? I keep turning upon myself, asking 'What is your name?' Are you in love? With whom? Or are you loved? By whom? A flame burns in my heart, a flame beyond measure, which has turned my being to ashes. Do I still taste what I eat? I am lost in my own wilderness! I have become a savage with wild beasts as companions. Do not try to bring me back to the world of humans! Believe me, I am a stranger to them. I am drawn towards death—death is within me. If only you could forget that you ever had a son! Oh my father! You say that soon you will have to begin your last journey? You say, this was the reason why you came to fetch me? But it is late, too late for both of us. It is autumn, here and inside me, and I must depart—perhaps even before you. Let the dead not mourn the dead, my father.[7]

After his father's death Majnun grieves but he is also changed for the better in subtle ways. Nizami expresses the new inner peace in images of Majnun's increasing harmony with the wild beasts with whom he now stalks the desert. He talks to the animals who are mysteriously attracted to him. He rests in the shade of vultures' wings and is guarded by desert lions. He has found his and man's fierce yet balanced essence. Nature, his own and the world's, now fathers him.

The feeling of mystical unity extends to Layla too. Once, after picking up a scrap of paper bearing just their two names, Majnun tore it in two and threw away the piece with Layla's name. On being asked the reason for this by an astonished bystander Majnun replied that one name was enough for both: 'If you knew what it means to be a lover, realize that one only has to scratch him, and out falls the beloved'. Here Majnun echoes the Indian mystical poet Kabir who too claims that 'the lane of love is narrow / There is room only for one'.

Through the offices of a kind intermediary, Layla and Majnun exchange impassioned letters of longing. One night a secret meeting is arranged in a palm grove near Layla's abode. Fate is kind to the lovers, and the moment they had so longed for at last arrives. Yet, as the reader might suspect by now, the hindrances to their sexual union are more than a simple matter of external prohibitions. As Nizami describes the scene:

Wrapped in her veil and protected by the growing darkness, Layla rushed to the garden, her soul flying ahead of her feet. She saw Majnun, but stopped before reaching th palm tree against which he was leaning. Her knees trembled and her feet seemed rooted in the earth beneath them. Only ten paces separated her from her beloved, but he was enveloped by a magic circle which she must not break. Turning to the old man at her side, she said: 'Noble sir! So far I am allowed to go, but no farther. Even now I am like a burning candle. If I approach the fire, I shall be consumed. Nearness brings disaster, lovers must shun it. Better to be ill, than afterwards to be ashamed of the cure ... why ask for more? Go to him! Ask him to recite some verses to me. Let him speak, I shall be the ear; let him be the cup bearer, I shall drink the wine!' Majnun, who had fainted, revives and 'as his eyes found their way to Layla, the verses she had asked for began to flow from his lips ... Suddenly he fell silent, jumped up and fled from the garden into the desert like a shadow. Though drunk with the scent of wine, he still knew that we may taste it only in paradise'.[8]

It is he who eschews union, thereby perpetuating it.

Here Majnun exemplifies the Sufi mystic who contemplates the full perfection of the Beloved only in the Image. Without this 'imaginative union', the Sufi holds, physical union is a mere delusion, a cause or symptom of mental derangement. Pure imaginative contemplation is all that the mystic wants, a contemplation which can attain such intensity that any material presence of the beloved will only draw it down, contaminate it.

Ibn Salaam, who had lost all hope of ever winning Layla, dies from a fever brought on by his grief. Layla is now free, though, in accordance with the Arab custom, she must not see anyone for two years while she mourns her husband. Before the two years are over, however, Layla, who has become very weak from her own secret sorrow, also dies of an illness.

When Majnun in the wilderness learns about the death of his beloved, he sets out at once to find her resting place. Weeping at Layla's grave, he prays for a release from his own tormented existence. Embracing the gravestone with both arms and pressing his body against it with all the force he can muster, his lips move once more, then with the words, 'You, my love . . .' the soul leaves his body.

In the Perso-Islamic World the tale of Layla and Majnun is a central parable of the Sufi religious experience. Nizami's rendering of the story was written down in the twelfth century, when Sufism had become one of the dominant forms of Islam and when Sufi brotherhoods or *tariqas* had spread through the Islamic world. It is self-conscious in its uses of central Sufi ideas, imagery and metaphors, especially in Majnun's conversations with his father where Islam's mysticism and orthodoxy seem to be pitted against each other in a rather friendly confrontation. Nizami makes Majnun the spokesman of the Sufi view that 'save love, save love, we have no other work!' Love is 'the essential Desire' of God, earthly love but a preparation for its heavenly acme where all separations will be destroyed. There men will be 'united in the whirling, mystical dance and lost to themselves, living in a higher unity, no longer distinct as rose and thorn'.[9]

In interpreting the tale as a psychological account of passionate love in the Islamic culture, as a parable of the psyche rather than of the Sufi soul, our intention is not to reduce its avowed mystical content to psychological notions. Rather, we would seek to elucidate the plane of human love which, after all, is the experiential ground on which both the writer and the reader must first stand before embarking on mystical-religious flights. To do so, however, we must proceed from the surface, first locating the tale in its cultural context.

At least in the upper classes, sexual love in most Islamic societies has been marked by a cheerful sensuality.[10] Not for Islam are the Christian preoccupations with chastity or the Hindu fascination with asceticism. The tradition has preserved a certain number of *hadiths* which strongly favour the satisfaction of the sexual instinct. At least, that is, for the privileged male.

In spite of the early Islamic lore about women of the aristocracy living lives of the greatest freedom, pleasantly preoccupied with their pleasures, it is primarily the man who is the real beneficiary of Muslim sexual permissiveness. His are the benefits of polygamy and of the lawful indulgence of his sexual appetites. In contrast, women, in certain cases at least, are even deprived of the right to give their consent to his demands.

As in any other marked partriarchy, however, behind a manifest social consensus on male dominance and the ideal of a man's freedom to satisfy his lust when and wherever he will, there lurks the equally potent psychic reality of man's deeper seated fear of woman's fearful power. The terror is of women who extract their revenge for their typical denigration and exploitation. The vicious circle lies at the very core of masculine 'superiority', namely in a cycle of misogyny, female revenge and self-protective posturing.

The frame tale of *A Thousand and One Nights* is a good example of the ubiquitous male fantasy. This fabulous collection begins with the powerful king Shahriyar, who has ruled in justice and tranquillity for twenty years. The calm of his reign is shattered by the visit of his brother, who discovers that Shahriyar's wife is having an adulterous relationship with a slave. Shahriyar pretends to go away from his palace but, hidden, observes a great debauch in the garden involving the women of the harem and the slaves. The orgy is crowned by the queen's cuckolding of him with a black slave, the most inferior being that Islamic court society can provide as a counterpoint to the monarch's majesty.

This fantasy of the treacherous female—animated exclusively by her sexual passions ('Never trust in women, nor rely upon their vows / Since all their likes and dislikes are but the itch between their thighs')[11]—has certainly been an important theme in the established relationship between the sexes in Islam. For that matter, in most cultures, exaggerated male attempts at dominance have served to both defend against and provoked a vengeful female sexual rapacity.

Indeed, this, the 'other' view of women, is forcefully stated in *Layla and Majnun* by a stranger who attempts to persuade Majnun to give up his love. For a while the 'demonic' misanthrope even succeeds in making the lover waver in his steadfastness as he evokes the full power of the culture's baleful imagery of women:

She deceives you, don't you understand? The woman to whom you have entrusted your heart has handed it over to the enemy. Your seed has been scattered to the wind, and Layla has forgotten you. She has been given in marriage to another man, and, believe me, she did not refuse him. Oh no! Every night she sleeps in his arms: she thinks only of kissing and making love and swoons in sensual pleasure while you torture and exhaust yourself. . . Did you believe her to be the one and only among thousands, different from all others?

Ha! That is what women are like, fickle and faithless from beginning to end. One like all, and all like one. For a while she looks
upon you as a hero, and then, all at once, you are nobody. True,
they are full of passion, even more than we, but they pursue only
their own selfish interests. Women are cheats! Never trust a
woman! She will repay you with torture. And rightly so! A man
who believes in woman's fidelity, is even more stupid than she who
makes him suffer. What, after all, is a woman? A dustbin of falsity
and viciousness; peace, when you look at her from outside, and turmoil within . . . Happy when you suffer, she is eaten by grief when
you rejoice. That is woman's way, that and even worse.
Remember![12]

To speculate: the stranger's exhortation to Majnun to remember and beware the treacherous woman who, for a while,
'looks upon you as a hero, and then, all at once, you are a nobody', may possibly derive from some basic flaw in the early
mother-son relationship typical of the culture. The betrayal
by the woman which makes the man so angry and anxious has
already taken place; the loss he so fears has long ago occurred.
Majnun's shunning of Layla at the moment of potential consummation and his quickness to suffer in loving corresponds
not with Layla's person but instead with her womanly and
thus also her maternal archetype.

The representation of the woman in Layla and Majnun
stands in sharp contrast to her more conventional Islamic
portrait, wherein she is a cunning adversary in the war between the sexes, a war fought with the weapons of a legally
sanctioned violence on one side and deceit on the other.

In most Arab and Persian love tales, a woman is adulterous,
insatiable, deceitful. Her exquisite quickness of wit is considered on the whole cunning rather than intellect, insufficient
to make her a companion of the more 'soulful' male. Yet the
man will always 'fall' for her since she is the foretaste, however imperfect, of an afterlife.[13]

Layla, on the other hand, is not only faithful and chaste
but, caught in her society's definitions of 'right' female behaviour, she is willing to suffer acutely in daring to love

actively, as a subject, rather than acquiescing to her cultural fate as a mere object of a man's determination. 'My torments', she observes

are a thousand times greater [than Majnun's]! It is true, he also is a target for the arrows of pain, but he is a man, I am a woman! He is free and can escape. He need not be afraid, can go where he likes, talk and cry and express the deepest feelings in his poem. But I? I am a prisoner. I have no one to whom I can talk, no one to whom I can open my heart: shame and dishonour would be my fate: Sweetness turns to poison in my mouth. Who knows my secret sufferings? I cover the abyss of my hell with dry grass to keep it hidden. I am burning day and night between two fires. Now—love cries out in my heart: 'get up! Flee, like a partridge, from this raven father, this vulture husband.' Now—reason admonishes me: 'Beware of disgrace! Remember—a patridge is not a falcon! Submit and bear your burden'.[14]

Layla's subjecthood lies not in the rebellion against social norms but in the *choosing* of her fate. Many later Islamic romances also applaud the woman's choice of death rather than a betrayal of her love. Among them is the Pakistani legend of Sohni and Mahinwal.[15]

The Tale of Sohni and Mahinwal

Once upon a time on the river Chenab in the town of Gujrat there lived a potter who had a lovely young daughter called Sohni—the beautiful—who helped her father in his shop. One day a caravan from Turkestan, on its way back home from Delhi, arrived in the town and halted there for a few days of rest. One of the young merchants, Izzat Beg, while exploring the bazaars of the town, happened to come to the potter's shop where he saw Sohni, with whom he fell instantly and violently in love.

When the caravan left Izzat Beg stayed behind in order to be near his beloved. He opened a shop where he sold earthenware bought from Sohni's father at a price lower than what the goods had cost him. Such a business could not survive—not that Izzat Beg's mind was on business—and he was soon bankrupt. Destitute, he entered the potter's service where his duty was to daily take the family's buffaloes out into the fields to graze. Soon everybody started calling him Mahinwal—the herdsman.

Impressed by his determination to be near her and the sacrifices he had made for her, Sohni too began to return Mahinwal's love. Troubled by the thought of the long, dreary hours he had to toil in the sun for her sake. Sohni once drew Mahinwal aside and said to him: 'I cannot bear to see you suffer all these hardships on account of me. Why don't you go back to your own country where you can live a life of luxury in your rich father's home?' Mahinwal's eyes filled with tears. 'How can I leave you? Away from you I cannot live', he replied.

Sohni's mother, who had already noticed signs of the young couple's infatuation with each other, overheard this conversation and reported the state of affairs to her husband. The potter flew into a rage and turned Mahinwal out of the house. Mahinwal took refuge on the other bank of the river. Soon his clothes were in tatters and, like Majnun, he was reduced to begging for food. Sohni's parents hastily married off their daughter to another potter in the same town. Full of grief at being parted from her lover, Sohni went to live in her husband's home. She prayed to Allah to keep her true to her love, and it seems that her prayers were answered. Every time her husband approached her he was stricken by a mysterious sickness and could not consummate the marriage.

One day, Sohni and her mother-in-law were busy in the kitchen when they heard the voice of a beggar outside. Sohni went to the door with a cupful of flour as alms and saw that the beggar was none other than Mahinwal. 'Why have you come here?' she said in a low voice. 'If my husband's family sees you, they will kill you instantly. Go away and I'll come to you on the far bank of the river tonight'. That night, when everyone was asleep, Sohni slipped out of the house and, taking a large earthenware pot, she ran to the river. She plunged into the swirling waters of the Chenab, and, buoyed up by the air-filled pot, she managed to cross to the other bank and spend the night with her lover, returning the same way before dawn broke. The lovers' meetings continued till one night her sister-in-law, who had seen Sohni surreptitiously leave her bed and go out of the house, followed her to the river and discovered what was taking place. Full of rage at the dishonour Sohni was bringing to the family, she substituted an unbaked pot for the baked one Sohni used every night to cross the river, one that would crumble and sink in the rapids. The next night was stormy with thunder and lightning, the river rough and turbulent. Even though Sohni had noticed the substitution of the pots, she could not bear to disappoint the waiting Mahinwal. Clasping the earthen pot in her arms, she plunged into the river. Halfway across the pot began to crumble and dissolve in the water, and she was swept away by the current. In the lightning flashes that illuminated the scene, Mahinwal saw Sohni's struggle and jumped into the river to save her. Wasted by hunger, he was too weak to rescue her, and the surging current of the Chenab speedily carried the lovers away to their watery grave, where, we may presume, they were reunited.

Layla's suffering—as also Sohni's death—is an inescapable consequence of her assertion of an individual erotic freedom which clashes with the traditional Islamic morality, a code which decrees that loyalty to the norms of the family and the tribe are what really makes life worth living. The appointed guardians of this code—fathers or husbands—are relegated to a lesser spiritual status than the identified lovers simply by virtue of their allotted position in the debate between politics and eros. They are like parental figures in the 'representational world' of patients, their human complexities and yearning obscured by the stereotypical parts they must play. Psychoanalysts and poets know this, and know better.

There are no real villians in the tale who can be conveniently blamed for the erotic catastrophe that overtakes the lovers. From the depths of her grief Layla may call her father a raven and her husband a vulture, yet the story makes it abundantly clear that both are honourable men, with noble sentiments, men animated by genuine concern for Layla. Regardless of his legal mandate, Ibn Salaam does not force his attentions on Layla but forlornly awaits her change of heart, aspiring to receive a love free of all coercion. Nizami sympathetically portrays the protagonists caught in a web of conflict and misapprehension. The characters are forced into predestined roles that diminish their evident humanity in one another's eyes, making antagonists of would be idolators.

Layla, the enchantress, was a treasure to others, but a burden to herself. If to her husband she appeared to be a precious jewel, he was for her a serpent coiled around her. In his eyes, she was the moon; she saw him as a dragon holding her in his jaws. So each suffered from the other.

For Layla this existence was constant torment. Was she not like a ruby enclosed in the heart of a stone? She had no weapons but patience and deceit. She knew no other grief or happiness but her secret love which she hid from all eyes, especially from those of her husband, Ibn Salaam.

Was he in a better state? Was his fate easier than Majnun's? In the eyes of the world he possessed Layla, who was more precious to him than anything else; yet this possession was an illusion. He knew this and he too had to keep it secret. He guarded a treasure to which no path would lead him; he was not allowed to enjoy what was his. Such a wound smarts . . .[16]

The psychoanalyst is privy to this kind of quiet desperation as he or she hears the laments of patients whose poor spouses fail to measure up to some fanciful ideal or of those who realize the terrifying truth that they are not cherished by those whom they are wedded to. The analyst wonders whether such

failures of the heart can ever be 'analysed', entombed free-
doms liberated. Is the love of the unloved, he muses, any less
than that of one who is adored? How many unsung lovers are
there, their tales of love but complaints of countless rejections
and little abandonments.

If love is the word emblazoned on the flag of Eros, then
honour or *izzat* is the banner under which the forces of
morality march in traditional Islamic society. What, exactly,
is this honour which inevitably seeks the separation of young
lovers? In seeming contrast to Romeo and Juliet—where the
feud between the Montagues and Capulets is the ostensible
barrier in the lovers' path, the stony wall that isolates them—
the love of Layla and Majnun is simply termed 'scandalous'
from the very outset without further elaboration or explanation.

What is considered overtly scandalous in Islamic love
stories—it is more disguised in romances from other patriarchal societies—is the violation of the rights of older and
powerful men, especially fathers, to dispose of and control
female sexuality. The challenge to their rights of ownership,
of the use and exchange of young women, is the real affront to
the 'honour' of the family, tribe or caste. These rights over the
daughter's sexuality are a part of the same complex in which
older and powerful men, through systems of institutionalized
polygamy, mistresses, secondary wives and concubines, of
droit de siegneur, and so on, have always claimed sexual access to young women. Challenges to these prerogatives easily
turn into questions of honour and, by extension, threats to
the 'social order'. Tales of passionate love in patriarchal
societies are thus also tales of sexual and social revolution;
and the lovers—whether Tristan, Romeo, Majnun or
Krishna—are as much sexual revolutionaries as are Don Juan
and Casanova, who too in their different ways threaten the
established monopoly. In other stories, to which we turn later, this power struggle is rendered obvious.

There is no price that the group is unwilling to pay to protect its honour, even if this involves the death of a daughter,

sister or wife. In a male dominated social order it is the woman who is the embodiment of the group's honour, as she is of the untamed Eros. Woman it is who must first die or be killed for the conflict between desire and *izzat* to end; any other solution, even if legally acceptable, simply will not do. This is well illustrated by the most popular love story of Muslim Punjab and, more generally, of northern India.

The Story of Heer and Ranjha

Once upon a time there was a wealthy landowner in the town of Jhang who had a beautiful daughter called Heer. The fame of her beauty had spread far and wide and there were many young men who came to her father to seek her hand. Finding none of them worthy of his beloved daughter, Heer's father dismissed them all.

One day Heer, who was in the habit of spending the hot days on a boat moored on the river, found a youth in the garb of a peasant fast asleep in the boat. Heer was angry at the intruder and roughly woke him up. The young man was contrite and told her that he had been turned out of his house by his brothers who thought him an idler since he was more fond of playing the flute than tilling the land. Heer was struck by the youth's delicate features and gentle bearing and asked him to play the flute for her. Ranjha—for that was the young man's name—did so exquisitely, pouring out all his youthful ardour and longing in the melody, and the two fell in love. Heer arranged Ranjha to be employed by her father as a herdsman. During the day, as he kept watch over the buffaloes grazing on the river bank, Heer too would give her companions the slip and join him, their love growing daily in intensity.

The affair did not escape notice for long and soon everyone

was talking about it. No one leaves lovers to their own devices, after all, for young love stirs envy and envy rumour, discovery and death. The gossip reached Heer's father, who decided to marry her off immediately—the only way to save the good name of the family. In spite of Heer's vehement protests she was wed to a young man of the Khera tribe who came in a big procession to fetch the bride and take her to their village. Grief stricken at the loss of her love, Heer was carried away. On the nuptial night she refused to submit to her husband, who went away, deluded into thinking that she would soon come around.

Among the women of the house was an unmarried sister-in-law who too was pining for the love of a man the family considered unfit for marriage, and she became Heer's confidante. In the garb of a beggar Ranjha came to the village where Heer lived, and, with the help of the sister-in-law, they devised a plan to end the lovers' cruel separation. One night the lovers escaped but were pursued and overtaken by the men of her husband's family who beat Ranjha and snatched away Heer. A crowd gathered. With both Ranjha and the husband claiming Heer, the pair was brought to the court of the governor who asked Heer which of the two was really her husband. Heer told the story of how she had never given her consent to the marriage and considered herself forcibly abducted rather than married. The governor gave his verdict that Heer was to be returned to her father who was ordered to marry her to Ranjha. The lovers were overjoyed and returned to Jhang under the governor's protection. Apprised of the verdict, Heer's father seemed to acquiesce. 'My son', he said to Ranjha, 'go home, make preparations and come with a proper marriage procession and Heer will be yours'. But the family's honour had been sullied and, as with Juliet's martyrdom, could only be salvaged by Heer's death. She was poisoned. When Ranjha returned at the head of the marriage procession he found that she was no more. Broken hearted, he did not take long to join her. Heer's grave became a shrine, especially for those who seek to remove obstacles to their love.

If, to men, the appeal of Layla, Heer and Sohni is of the 'good' woman, utterly devoted to the man unto death, repairing the damage caused by the 'bad' and fickle woman of a dominant collective fantasy, then their attraction for women in Islamic societies is of a different order. Faithful to a lover freely chosen rather than to their marriage vows, loving in secrecy and concealment yet without shame or guilt, these heroines are examples and ideals of the capacity for choice that is possible for women even under restrictive social conditions. The price for this subjecthood is indeed cautionary—death. Yet the reward is equally momentous—the promise of the immortality attained in becoming ensconced in the pantheon of love's legendary goddesses.

Love and Madness

The fascination of passionate love lies in its promise to resolve the inner paradoxes of two compelling and at times opposing erotic quests: the longing for oneness with the beloved, and the desire for sensual excitement, sexual possession and orgasmic release. Majnun in his madness embodies the first of these quests, and its terror. Seeking merger, he suffers (and comprehends) an elemental separation that both empties the inner world and destroys all ties to the outer.

At least this is how we, interpreters of a different era and ethos, respond conceptually, psychologically, to Nizami's ancient narrative. We do so, we hope, not through any harsh or reductive 'application' of psychoanalytic concepts, but rather by shifting back and forth between the levels of meaning contained in the epic's imagery and metaphors while attending to its intrinsic ambiguities. Under the special and protective conditions of art, Nizami makes the reader entertain the terror released when the urge to transcend the self by merging with the other—an urge otherwise held in check by the reins of ordinary life—tears loose from convention and is inevitably thwarted, foundering in what Shelley once called 'the lone and level sands'. Made palpable and awakened to full life through Nizami's poetic genius, pulsing through his verse, the poet's description of Majnun's 'separation anxiety' once 'the reins had slipped from the rider's hands' is no longer a matter of psychological abstraction or inference. Like the best of clinical work, as Joel Kovel has remarked, the artistic narrative too dislodges us from the reassurance of labels and so brings about a deeper appreciation, a personal knowledge of that ineffable psychic underside from which we otherwise turn away.[17]

Majnun's angst begins with the heart, that felt and metaphorical organ of love which can swell and burst with excitement, grow heavy with longing or break in disappointment. No longer securely anchored within the body, it 'had suffered ship-wreck; drifting helplessly in a boundless ocean; there seemed no end to the fury of the gale.' The body metaphor for passion, a sentimental cliché in all cultures, murmurs the visceral, coenesthetic origins of libidinal feeling in infancy, a time when the outer world is received through senses without discrimination as an inner reverberation. Thus emotional truth is always 'heartfelt'.

The oceanic and tempestuous metaphors are also riveting, especially in their context, and call up woman in her primeval aspect. Freud and Ferenczi likened her to the seas of our phylogenetic pasts, enclosing the globe before the ice-age—a desert is no doubt similar—forced us animals to encase our bodies and genitals in secure external envelopes. The seas are within us; rupture the protective membranes and we risk dehydration, somatically and psychically. The seas and the desert, images of a woman's swelling and fathomless body and of an evaporating bodily self, signal a profound psychic dislocation. Whether it is regarded as regressive or transcendent depends on the hearer's contextually bound bias—clinical or mystical. Yet, whatever the value attributed to it, the process harkens back to the eve of human consciousness.

The changes in Majnun's body-image are accompanied by a bitter impoverishment of the psyche as the multiple ties that bind him to others snap. This decay and denuding of the inner landscape, seared by a loneliness that can no longer be eased by anything real or loving—for example, in the efforts made by Majnun's father—is strikingly portrayed in depictions of Majnun's naked and wasted body endlessly wandering in the emptiness of the sands. It is indeed

as if his name has been torn out of the book of Life, and he had fallen into nothingness; as if he were no longer one of the living, and not yet one of the dead. 'Oh, who can cure my sickness? An outcast I have become. Family and home, where are they? No path leads back to them and none to my beloved. Broken are my name, my reputation, like glass smashed on a rock; broken is the drum which once spread the good news, and my ears now hear only the drumbeat of separation!'[18]

Majnun's fate intimates the shadow side of union. In the progressive dissolution of his identity, whose horror is matched only by the fascination of the total merger he reaches towards, Majnun's cries to Layla become the wrenching wail of the infant in chaos. It is a cry for maternal presence brimming with a soothing bountifulness, proffering the sustenance needed to save him from the psychic death of a rapidly disintegrating self and human relatedness.

I have fallen; what shall I do? Oh, my beloved, come and take my hand. I can endure it no longer, I am yours, more use to you alive than dead. Be generous and send a greeting, send a message to revive me. Bind me to you, wind again your tresses around my neck; they are torn, yet I remain your slave. Do something; help me! . . . Aren't we both human beings, you as well as I, even if you are a blossoming beech tree while I am a dry thorn bush?[19]

The crumbling of the mother's image shatters the very core of personal identity, which is reflected in it. It drains away that 'basic trust' and hope which are imparted through the 'mother's milk', to cement the edifice of the budding individual. Majnun in his madness (and Nizami in his poetry) recognizes this clearly:

If only your shadow had stayed with me, but even that you have taken away, and my heart and soul with it. What did I receive in return? What is left to me? Hope? A thirsty child may well, in a dream, see a hand offering a golden cup, but when he awakes what remains? All that he can do is suck his fingers to quench his thirst.[20]

More than any external threat, more than death itself, Majnuns madness captures what is perhaps love's greatest danger. Wrenched from self-possession , defenses of everyday life which have served well enough now weakened, the lover is once again vulnerable to the most primordial of anxieties, to what Freud called the mental helplessness encountered in the face of maternal loss. The birth of love brings with it, in a certain *deja vu*, intimations of its end. The loss of love glimmers darkly through the fiery exultation of the moment in which it is found. The beloved's image breathes fresh life and renewed death in our early inner mementos of the mother before she is defined as a distinct person in her own light.

All this has little to do, after all, with the fictional Majnun's relationship with what amounts to the mere shade of his mother. What we respond to is Nizami's artistic portrayal of a man seared by separation, a man mysteriously impotent to undo his basic solitude. In this the fascination of Majnun as a lover may be universal, irrespective of cultural or historical specificities, appealing to a state of mind that exists latently in all of us. The starkness, the drama, of Majnun's severed existence and his high pitch of precipitous mourning set in relief the grief felt by all expectant lovers.

Majnun's is at once a more primal and a more contemplative state than that of the more tempestuous and consuming Romeo. The preservation of Layla, to the extent that he denies himself erotic access to her, is paramount. He senses that in having her he will destroy illusion. He is the ascetic to Romeo's savage beast but a soulmate none the less, allied in an appreciation of life's essential dilemma and of man's instinctual nature. Romeo is the actor, Majnun the mystic, both servants, though, to infantile imperatives. Where Romeo proceeds under the delusion that he can possess what he desires or yields to despair at the frustration of this wish, Majnun anticipates and reflects upon a predestined utter disappointment.

Yet, as we know, Majnun also holds a special attraction for men in the Perso-Islamic world. In applying psychoanalytic techniques to a literary character we are, in fact, as Norman Holland asserts, applying them to his audience.[21] Majnun's truth, like beauty, lies in the eyes of the beholder. In other words we are suggesting that certain social-historical conditions make for a unique modal mother-son relationship in traditional Islamic societies. This, in turn, results in an unreliability of maternal-feminine representations in the men of Islam, predisposing them to extraordinary polar experiences of immersion and separation.

In much of the traditional Muslim society of the Near East, we are told, the relation of the child and the woman, powerful as it proves to be, tends to be disavowed or at least discredited.[22] The only world that the patriarchal culture deems real or worthy of notice is that of adult men. The first seven to eight years of a boy's life are spent exclusively in the orbit of his mother and other feminine caretakers. His attempts, significantly, to enter the men's domain generally meet with derision by the male adults who persistently spurn him and throw him back to the pleasures and perils of the mother-son dyad. Within the mother-child dyad the boy is the object of a woman's constant attention, concern and (sometimes unwanted) ministrations, intrusions which can be insensitive to his growing capacity for independent functioning. 'The Arab male child is oppressed by the father, he is smothered by the mother', may be an oversimplified view of this situation.[23] However, it does hint at a kind of maternal omnipresence and an absence of the graduated frustration provided by the 'good-enough' mother—a slower process, paradigmatic for the West, of psychological weaning which helps the child replace the real mother with her enduring representations. Such configurations inwardly compensate for her unavoidable shortcomings and absences and allow for a flexibility of relatedness, separate from mother's (or lover's) comings and goings.

Once the child is admitted to the privileged male world—the entry coinciding with his attendance of the *maktab*, the Koranic school—the exclusive 'maternalism' of his early years is abruptly replaced by an equally peremptory 'paternalism'. The boy is now required to repudiate completely the maternal-feminine world; everything that went before was childishness or womanish nonsense, the two equated by an adult male culture. The child is enjoined to adopt unreservedly the collective fatherhood's misogynist values. 'Growing up means forgetting childhood, wiping it out, and suppressing it. One becomes an adult in our traditional societies by scorning childhood and repudiating femininity', writes the Tunisian scholar Bouhdiba.[24] A thoroughgoing rejection of the maternal universe is demanded of the boy, a foresaking of Her who once mediated all his transactions and sustained him for so long with emotional riches. The repudiation must be perceived by the child as an outright betrayal of the mother. Could it be the guilt at this enforced treachery, when projected onto the mother—'It is not I who sever myself from mother but she who left me'—which gives the cultural fantasy of fickle and undependable women its emotional charge? And, further, could it not be an absolute rejection of her whom once we clung to which serves to ease the rupture? Devalued, woman lacks appeal, and the detachment from her is less poignant.

To return to our story from this excursion into cultural-psychology. Majnun's longing for union is so compelling that inspite of the progressive collapse of his identity he persists in it. It is erotic desire which he identifies as the biggest single roadblock in the path of union with Layla. Translated into the language of mother-son discourse in the culture, it is as if the son unconsciously blames his

separation from the mother and his (consciously longed for)
entry into the men's world on the fact of his maleness and
specifically on its primary expression—phallic desire. Such
desire not only divides and bifurcates what was originally
one, but has as its correlate the fantasized violence of sexual
possession which is felt to have no place in 'true' love. Majnun's attempt, or rather that made by Nawfal on his behalf,
to take possession of Layla through a war on her family and
tribe, symbolizes the destructive violence of the masculine
impulse and Majnun's own ambivalence towards it. To a certain extent Majnun agrees to and is even instrumental in the
eruption of hostilities—this show of bellicose manhood—but
he is loath to take part in the actual fighting. And once the
battles are over he punishes himself severely for having
acceded to manly desire's impetus, expiating his guilt by having himself chained by a woman and dragged around by her
like a wild animal on display. Coming to Layla's tent in this
condition he calls out:

Shackled, I stand before you, a rope around my neck, waiting to be
chastised. I know I have sinned, and my sin is so great that it can
never be forgiven.

I am your prisoner; you be my judge. Condemn me! Punish me as
severely as you like . . . It is my fault that your people have suffered.
In expiation I am beating my body with my own hands. Yesterday I
committed my crime, today I have returned in chains to suffer torture from you. Kill me, but do not reject me in my misery. How can
I plead innocence in front of you? *You are loyal, even when you
have abandoned loyalty; I am guilty, even when I am innocent.*[25]

In this tale of longing the father too represents an obstacle
to the son's quest for psychic unity with the mother. This
father, though, is not the oedipal counterplayer or rival of the
child's fantasy, met with in much of Western literature, one
who bars the son's sexual access to the mother in the service
of self interest. Rather, he is a figure who strives to push the
boy away from her, to draw the once androgynous and in-
dulged creature into the 'real' world of his adult male culture.

Thus in the father's conversations with Majnun he outlines the culture's vision of masculine identity and seeks to guide the son's entry into man's estate. Such a father is not a castrator or inhibitor but an initiator.

It is only after the father's death that Majnun 'succeeds' in renouncing altogether the claims of the masculine role and of phallic impulses. Willingly emasculating himself, he regains that psychic union with the beloved which is his true goal. It is a 'dual unity', moreover, which is sexless—lacking in erotic appetite as in any distinctions of gender. As Majnun says,

My love is purified from the darkness of lust, my longing purged of low desire, my mind freed from shame. I have broken up the teeming bazaar of the senses in my body. Love is the essence of my being. Love is fire and I am wood burned by the flame. Love has moved in and adorned the house, my self has tied its bundle and left. You imagine that you see me, but I no longer exist: what remains, is the beloved . . .[26]

Nizami describes Majnun's renunciation of violent sexual passions in images of his harmony with wild animals— 'reconciling wild ones with wild ones'— and is aware of the symbolism involved when, for instance, he remarks, 'Are animals not an echo of human being? They are what we make of them'.[27] The deep calm that now pervades Majnun as 'his eye no longer roamed over the night sky and his heart felt at home' is the prelude to a dream:

A tree grew out of the ground in front of him; quickly it reached great height and extended its crown towards the centre of the sky. Following its growth with his eyes, Majnun suddenly noticed a bird fluttering fearlessly through the leaves towards him from the farthest branch. Something glittered in its beak, like a drop of light. Just over Majnun's head, the bird let it drop. It was a jewel, which fell on to the crown of Majnun's head and remained lying there, a shining diadem.[28]

Nizami goes on to add:

Majnun's whole being was flooded by a feeling of happiness

such as he had not experienced for a long time. Did the bird of his soul take wing? Did not his body feel light, as if it could fly? Thus a dream may bring fulfilment at night to those who must live out their days without love.[29]

In some of his writings Freud repeatedly affirmed that invented dreams can be interpreted in the same way as real dreams, exemplifying his statement through the interpretation of the fictional dreams in Wilhelm Jensen's *Gradiva*.[30] He was of course aware that dreams in literature, unlike those in real life, were conceits rather than disguised wish-fulfilments, devices introduced to expedite the author's narrative—for instance, a prophecy required for the progress of the story or for a symbolic underlining of a theme. Moreover in essaying a fictional dream the vital element in disciplined dream interpretation—the dreamer's free associations to it—is absent. Nevertheless, with his view of the invented dream standing at a key intermediate point between real-life dreams and the creative imagination, Freud felt that if the dream could be convincingly placed in its context—i.e. related closely to the events in the text—then an interpretation was still possible. As far as the missing associations of the dreamer to his dream were concerned, the difficulty can be overcome by considering the fictional dreamer's impressions of the dream *after waking* and the feelings called up in its reproduction. The dream's latent content—or more precisely, its metaphorical import—might be further clarified by the substituting of the audience's or analyst's own associations in place of the dreamer's.

Majnun's dream occurs after the death of his father and in the climate of his growing sense of inner peace and harmony with his environment. Just before falling asleep on the night the dream occurs, Majnun in his prayer to God has reiterated his helplessness, ceded all claims to activity and the mastery of his own fate. In the manifest dream the passivity continues with Majnun lying upon the ground, looking up. In the latent dream content, however, both the passivity and the helplessness are reversed in the creation of a powerful self—a crowned king rather like the emperor of Romeo's climactic dream. The power is expressed in another dream image, of the tree growing into great height, its crown rising into the centre of the sky. The reference to the erections Majnun no doubt succumbed to in his sleeping moments is obvious. But so is the sense of grandeur achieved in defying them. He has succeeded in replacing and transfiguring the crude inflations of carnal lust with the grandiose self of the sexless baby. In its aftermath his sense is of a happiness long unknown to him, evident also in his reactions to the dream—the bird of soul taking wing, the body light, 'as if it could fly'. The father's death, we would suggest, has freed Majnun from oedipal fetters, possibly, but more probably from the demands of the male world on which he ·finally turns his back. Instead of being an outcast in this real world Majnun is an emperor in another, earlier terrain—the maternal-feminine universe in which most of us, at least for a time, have been emperors.

To conclude, in Layla and Majnun the stress is on separation and what psychoanalysts have deemed surrender, in this instance at once 'masochistic' and 'altruistic'. To us both Romeo and Majnun express pregenital desires, the imperious yet vulnerable erotic wishes of infancy. Our Western hero, though, does so through accepted convention and sexual consummation; Romeo is driven to seize, possess and devour his Juliet, offering up and consuming himself in the process. Majnun on the other hand abstains and abjures the beloved's physical presence so as to avoid destroying her through his omnivorous hungers.

Did we not already suspect the love story to undermine a culture's ideals we would have found Majnun's phallic surrender to a woman, in a tradition as manifestly male-centred as Islam, surprising. Like Romeo, the mad boy overturns the stereotypes of male dominance and womanly deference—universal notions to be sure, but accentuated in his era and area of the world. But more universally, in actively seeking infantilization, Majnun highlights the inference that the wish to be a babe in arms is as much a part of a man's erotic being as are his wishes to be a woman or, even more obviously, his desire to employ his penis in quest for union with the beloved.

All these seemingly contradictory wishes constitute a paradoxical unity at the hidden core of a man's sexual identity as he seeks to rediscover and reclaim in love's orgasmic encounters—with their frequent though transient crossing over of self and sexual boundaries—what is retrospectively felt to be paradise lost—the postpartum womb of life before 'psychological birth'. It is the latter-day phallic illusion of modern man which has denied legitimacy and reality to these wishes and has led us to oversimplify the erotic nature of man as a separate sexual being in abiding, conflictual, and perforce unrequited quest for union with a woman. /

CHAPTER FOUR

THE CLOISTERED PASSION OF RADHA AND KRISHNA

A psychoanalytic patient, a passionate man of twenty-four, found himself avoiding more and more the pleasure of intercourse with his girlfriend. Yet another of his symptoms was his inability to weep, much to his consternation, denting his image of himself as a romantic.

A dream brought to light one level of his terror, and desire. In it the patient dived with other children into a great gulf. He emerged as if uncertain of his body—of what lay beneath the neck—and found himself crossing his old school's soccer field, making his way not to the boy's but rather to the girl's changing room. In his associations he talked of the eerie feeling that, with penetration, he was welded to his lover, as if their pubic hair were somehow squashed, almost glued together. Her breasts, so delightful in their spongy round-ness, seemed to seep into his chest and become his own. Upon climaxing he felt, in an almost altered state of consciousness, that he was taking in her moistened vagina with his penis and found himself fighting off unnamed fears, becoming chilled and anxious. Of a sudden he remarked on his inadvertent refusal to weep, equating the watering of his eyes with the lubrication of a woman's genitals.

The analysand at last discovered and voiced what seemed his 'most secret' of wishes. He wanted to be as beautiful and bountiful as his lover; he wished to be a woman. Tasting the illusion, satisfying this surprising desire in the safety of the analytic space, he wondered whether he would re-emerge from a woman as a man—ambitious, powerful, rich?

After a pause the patient comforted himself with thoughts about the ubiquity of what had seemed an altogether idiosyncratic perversity. Perhaps his analyst 'knew' women in much the same way as he did. Had not the self-revelatory hero of Janet Malcolm's *The Impossible Profession*, the dreamy workmanlike amalgam portrayed by her as the 'typical' psychoanalyst, confessed the source of his failure to speak or write more? To do so, the hero of the book lamented, would be to symbolically fulfil a treasured but shameful wish—to parade before the gaze of others as a 'beautiful woman', and this before analysts who 'saw into people's souls'.

Another patient, in imitating an illicit love affair with the wife of a businessman for whom he worked, had crossed daunting social barriers of caste and class. The couple had secretly met on three occasions but had not yet become sexually intimate. His illness was preceded by a dream about the long desired moment of consummation. In it, as the would-be lovers finally embrace, he discovers to his excited horror that the woman has grown a penis which is rubbing against the wet lips of his newly formed vagina in a welter of unknown but exquisite sensations. Soon he felt strange changes taking place in his body: parts of it becoming soft and delicate like a woman's while others became even stronger and muscular. His terror began mounting when he began having 'visions' of Hindu gods and goddesses—Shiva and

Parvati, Krishna and Radha, Rama and Sita—in amorous embrace. The sensations and feelings of the gods and goddesses in intercourse, he felt, were being manifested in his own person, succeeding each other with a frightening rapidity.

It is some secrets of these patients—and of many 'normal' others—which we now address in the paradigmatic love story of Hindu India.

For an Indian—or, more exactly, a Hindu—the love of Radha, the beautiful cowherdess who later became a goddess for some cults, and Krishna, the youthful dark god who is the object of widespread devotion, is less a story remembered than a random succession of episodes seen and heard, sung and danced. Over the centuries their liaison has been portrayed in thousands of exquisite miniature paintings which have fixed the lovers in separation and union, longing and abandonment. The story is heard whenever we listen to the great vocalists of Indian classical music—from Kumara Gandharva to Jasraj—sing the devotional songs of medieval saints who in their poems sometimes watch and at others participate in the love-making as Krishna's beloved. The story grips our imagination every time we behold the animated expressions, flashing eyes and sinuous movements of an Indian dancer who (as Radha) dances her anger at Krishna's infidelities or (as Krishna) begs forgiveness for his impetuous dalliance. The affair is recreated each time a Krishna devotee participates in the communal singing of an episode from the story in a temple, and especially when he or she, possessed by the spirit of one of the lovers, feels impelled to get up and ecstatically dance the god or his beloved.

The Radha–Krishna legend, then, is not a narrative in the sense of an orderly progression whose protagonists have a shared past and are progressing towards a tragic or happy future. It is more an evocation and elaboration of the here-and-now of passion, an attempt to capture the exciting, fleeting moments of the senses and the baffling ways in which pleasures and pains are felt before the retrospective recollection which, in trying to regain a lost control over emotional life, edits away love's inevitable confusions. It is not tragic but tender, and, ultimately, cheerful.

The sybaritic tenderness enveloping the cameos of the lovers is striking. A long line of bards and balladeers, most of them indebted to the twelfth-century Sanskrit poet Jayadeva, who decisively shaped the legend's outlines, have often described the setting of their meetings. A Hindu needs only to close his eyes and 'remember' to see Vrindavan, an Indian garden of Eden, spring into existence. In the perpetual sunshine of the myth, distinct from the mists of history, a forest thicket of the banks of the river Yamuna awakens to life on a tropical spring day. The mustard fields at the edge of the forest, with their thick carpet of dazzling yellow flowers, stretch far into the distance. The air is redolent with the perfume of the pollen shaken loose from newly blossomed jasmine and bunches of flame-coloured mimosa flowers hanging round and heavy from the trees. The ears are awash with the humming of bees, the cries of cuckoos and the distant tinkling of bells on the necks of grazing cattle. The call of Krishna's flute comes floating through the forest thicket, further agitating the already unquiet senses, making for an inner uprising and an alien invasion. The story, aiming to fix the essence of youthful ardour, has an amorous rather than geographical landscape as its location; its setting is neither social nor historical but sensuous.

In the falling dusk, Nanda, Krishna's foster father and the chief of a community of cowherds, asks Radha to escort Krishna home through the forest. On the way, in a grove, their 'secret passion triumphs'. Radha's thoughts come to be absorbed by Krishna who, however, is unfaithful to her as he sports with other cowherdesses—hugging one, kissing another and caressing yet another dark beauty.

> When he quickens all things to create bliss in the world
> His soft black sinuous lotus limbs
> Begin the festival of love

> And beautiful cowherd girls wildly
> Wind him in their bodies.
> Friend, in spring young Hari [Krishna] plays
> Like erotic mood incarnate.[1]

Radha is jealous as she imagines the 'vines of his great throbbing arms circle a thousand cowherdesses'. But more than that, she is infused with all the confusing emotions of a proud, intense woman who feels deserted by her lover.

> My heart values his vulgar ways,
> Refuses to admit my rage,
> Feels strangely elated,
> And keeps denying his guilt.
> When he steals away without me
> To indulge his craving
> For more young women,
> My perverse heart
> Only wants Krishna back
> What can I do?

Solitary grief and images of love betrayed and passion lost, re-created in reverie, alternate and reinforce each other but seem somehow benign.

> My eyes close languidly as I feel
> The flesh quiver on his cheek,
> My body is moist with sweat; he is
> Shaking from the wine of lust.
> Friend, bring Kesi's sublime tormentor to revel with me!
> I've gone mad waiting for his fickle love to change.

The power of Radha's yearning works a change in Krishna. Of all the *gopis* (cowherdesses), interchangeable suppliers of pleasure and feelings of conquest, Radha begins to stand out in Krishna's mind as someone special who is desired in her uniqueness. In Maurice Valency's formulation, from the 'heroic lover' for whom no woman is exceptional and who simply desires a variety of amatory dalliances, Krishna becomes the 'romantic lover' impelled towards a single irreplaceable mistress.[2] The unheeding pursuit of pleasure, a bewil-

dered Krishna discovers, had been brought to a halt by pleasure's worst enemies—memory and attachment.

> Her joyful responses to my touch,
> Trembling liquid movement of her eyes,
> Fragrance from her lotus mouth,
> A sweet ambiguous stream of words,
> Nectar from her red berry lips—
> Even when the sensuous objects are gone,
> My mind holds on to her in a trance.
> How does the wound of her desertion deepen?

Having been the god who strove to please himself alone,
Krishna has become a man for whom the partner's well-being
assumes an importance easily the equal of his own. He discovers that he would rather serve and adore than vanquish
and demand. As a tale of love this transformative moment
from desire's sensations to love's adoration gives the story of
Radha and Krishna its singular impact.

It is a remarkable coincidence that three of the world's
best-known works of romantic love which occupy pivotal
positions in their respective cultures—Beroul's Tristan and
Isolde in Europe, Nizami's Layla and Majnun in the Islamic
world and Jayadeva's Geetagovinda in India—were all produced roughly at the same time: in the twelfth century.
Whether this represents happenstance, coincidence, or
springs from sociohistorical trends coalescing across the globe
is beyond our scope in this more *life* historical endeavour.
However, it is striking that the poetry of passion should pre-
date and possibly prefigure important cultural-historical
changes in Europe, India and the Middle East. It is as if the
unfolding discovery of each other portrayed in the love story
sheds light on what is fundamental to the human spirit.

To continue the story: hearing of Krishna's remorse and of
his attachment to her, Radha, dressed and ornamented for
love, awaits Krishna at their trysting place in the forest. She
lingers in vain for Krishna does not come. Radha is consumed
by jealousy as she imagines him engaged in an amorous en-

counter with a rival. When Krishna finally does appear,
Radha spurns him angrily:

> Dark from kissing her kohl-blackened eyes
> At dawn your lips match your body's colour, Krishna
> Damn you Madhava! Go! Kesava leave me!
> Don't plead your lies with me!
> Go after her, Krishna!
> She will ease your despair.

But, in separation, Radha and Krishna long for each other
with a mounting sense of desolation. Eventually, Radha's
friend persuades her to abandon her modesty and pride and
go to her lover.

> Your full hips and breasts are heavy to bear.
> Approach with anklets ringing!
> Their sound inspires lingering feet.
> Run with the gait of a wild goose!
> Madhu's tormentor
> Is faithful to you, fool.
> Follow him, Radhika!

In the full throes of a sexual excitement—when even her
'modesty left in shame'—Radha rushes to meet an equally ardent (and repentant) lover. Krishna sings:

> Throbbing breasts aching for love's embrace are hard to
>   touch.
> Rest these vessels on my chest!
> Queen love's burning fire!
> Narayana [Krishna] is faithful now. Love me Radhika!
> Offer your lips' nectar to revive a dying slave, Radha!
> This obsessed mind and listless body burn in love's desola-
>   tion,
> Narayana is faithful now. Love me, Radhika!

Once the ecstatic love-making has subsided momentarily in
an orgasmic release, a playful Radha asks Krishna to rearrange
her clothes and her tousled hair:

Paint a leaf on my breasts!
Put colour on my cheeks!
Lay a girdle on my hips!
Twine my heavy braid with flowers!
Fix rows of bangles on my hands
And jewelled anklets on my feet!
Her yellow-robed lover
Did what Radha said.

Jayadeva, legend has it, hesitant to commit sacrilege by having the god touch Radha's feet—the usual sign of a submissive lower status—was unable to pen the last lines and went out to bathe; when he returned the found that Krishna himself had completed the verse in his absence!

•

The fascination of Jayadeva's creation is, of course, also due to its musical form. Jayadeva set each canto of the love poem to a different musical mode (*raga*) and rhythm (*tala*). It is a work which succeeding generations have regarded a marvel of music as much as of language and meaning. And music, we know, that fine-tuned language of the senses, best captures the Dionysian—or rather, in our context, the 'Krishnanian'—spirit and sensual spontaneity of the erotic. The great Persian poet Rumi has aptly described the house of love as having doors and roof made of music, melodies and poetry. The sensibilities and pulse of lovers, and of others with either the potential for love or its haunting memory, can be reproduced in music with greater fidelity than in words since there is a direct rather than signified correspondence between musical forms and the forms of emotional life. Love is not *about* something: it *is*. Jayadeva seems to have intuitively known that (in Kierkegaard's words) 'the sensual wood is too heavy and too dense to be sustained by speech; only music can express it.'

The story of Radha and Krishna, as it has come down to us

today, differs from Jayadeva's version in only one significant respect. Jayadeva merely hints at the illicit nature of their love when he has an older Radha change from young Krishna's protective escort to become his lover, thereby also defying the authority and instructions of the chief of cowherds:

> 'Clouds thicken the sky.
> Tamala trees darken the forest.
> The night frightens him.
> Radha, you take him home!'
> They leave at Nanda's order,
> Passing trees in thickets on the way,
> Until secret passions of Radha and Madhava
> Triumph on the Jamuna riverbank.

Later poets, notably Vidyapati, who tend to focus more on Radha and her love than on Krishna, gave the illicit in the story a more concrete cast and a specific content. Radha is another man's wife and her liaison with Krishna, whatever its meaning in mystical allegory, is plainly adulterous in human terms. Radha is certainly not a paragon of womanly virtues detailed in Hindu texts; not does she come close to any of the 'good' or 'bad' mother-goddesses of Indian mythology and religion.

She is a more sophisticated character, more rounded and complex than a toddler's (or a Majnun's) dichotomous imagery would allow for. Radha is, indeed, a figure of the imagination of the boy just as he begins to discover his and his mother's sexuality. Rivals have just begun to enter the scene and have not yet been recreated as internal inhibitions, jaundicing any delight in the mother's eroticism. There is an unobstructed joy to the sensuality of this all-too brief era, a lack of self-consciousness about experimenting with its variations. In her passionate craving for sexual union with her lover and in her desperate suffering in his absence, Radha is simply the personification of *mahabhava*, a 'great feeling' that is heedless of social proprieties and unbounded by conventions.

Before continuing in our own interpretation of the

mahabhava of the legend, we must first briefly locate the love of Radha and Krishna in its cultural-historical context. As various scholars have pointed out, many different Indian traditions—religious and erotic, classical literary and folk—have converged and coalesced in the poetical renditions of the myth, especially Jayadeva's Geetagovinda, to give that particular work an allure that extends over large parts of the subcontinent.[3]

In India 'passion love' first appeared in the court poetry and drama of the so-called classical period of Hindu civilization, spanning the first few centuries of the Christian era. Earlier, in the epics of Mahabharata and Ramayana, love was usually a matter of straightforward desire and its gratification.[4] This was especially so for the man for whom a woman was an instrument of pleasure and an object of the senses (*indriyartha*)—one physical need among many others. There is an idealization of marriage in the epics, yes, but chiefly as a social and religious act. The obligation of conjugal love and the virtue of chastity within marriage were primarily demanded of the wife, while few limits were set on a husband who lived under and looked up at a licentious heaven teeming with lusty gods and 'heavenly' whores—otherworldly and utterly desirable at once, and most eager to give and take pleasure. Their Hindu pantheon is not unlike the Greeks' Olympus where gods and goddesses sport and politic with a welcome absence of moralistic subterfuge.

The Buddhist domination of Indian society which followed brought with it Buddhism's sombre view of life, in which the god of love was identified with Mara or Death. The new cosmology it imposed was not particularly conducive to developing a literature of passionate love. Nor did love enter through the backdoor of erotic mysticism. In the Therigatha, or psalms of notable sisters of the Buddhist order, marked by dutiful daughterly sentiments towards the Buddha, there is none of the eroticism of their medieval Christian counterparts who in their passionate outpourings conceived of Christ as a youthful bridegroom.

All this seems to have changed radically with the dawn of the classical period that spanned the first six to seven centuries of the present era. In the poetry and drama flourishing at the courts, love became a predominant theme, indeed one over-shadowing every other sentiment. It is a love that is both deeply sensual and moulded by mutual passion. The woman is as ardent as the man and initiates the wooing quite as often. Masculinity is not equated with seduction and conquest. Indeed the surviving poems of the few women poets show them to be even freer in their expression than their male counter-parts.

Yet, though one's 'ego' or self is not at stake, the verse depicts an eroticism that is narcissistic in spirit, more hedonist than impassioned. The Sanskrit poems and dramas are characterized by a playful enjoyment of love's ambiguities, a delighted savouring of its pleasures and a consummately refined suffering of its sorrows. Spontaneity, fervid abandon and exaltation are generally absent from this poetry. Apart from one or two notable exceptions, the rendering of love is on a miniature scale; corresponding to the paintings for which the culture is known. Short stanzas seek to freeze one or another of love's emotions; they are cameos yielding glimpses into arresting erotic moments. What is considered important—and this is the core of the Indian theory of aesthetics—is to capture the *rasa*, literally, 'flavour' or 'essence' or the mood, of a particular passionate instant, which can then be relished by the poetically cultivated connoisseur. The intensity of the mood is not enhanced through psychological depth but by the accumulation of sensuous detail.

Blurring the boundaries between internal feeling and external sensation, the poet seldom treats love as something ethereal or lifts from it a sentiment to be evaluated. Rather it is equated with a definite sensation or a feeling in its concrete bodily manifestation. As Barbara Miller remarks in relation to the Gitagovinda:

Passion is made palpable through the sensuous descriptions of movements and physical forms. Seasonal changes in nature and bodily signs of inner feelings are colored richly to create a dense atmosphere of passion.[5]

The emphasis, replete with developmental resources in the 'early genital stage' and its revival in pubescence, is on sexual self-discovery. The 'other' is a source of excitement and delight, enlivening the senses and the body with her image and aura. This 'other' is to be explored thoroughly, in enormous detail, and therefore she is not quickly abandoned. Yet her inner life or her past and future are not subjects of the entrancement; the impulse is not one of fierce monogamy.

For most modern readers who have an affinity for the personal and the subjective, the emphasis of classical Indian literature on love as a depersonalized voluptuous state, while delighting the senses, does not touch the heart. For those whose sensibility has been moulded by romanticism and individualism it is difficult to identify with the impersonal protagonists of Sanskrit and Tamil love poems. These are not a particular man or woman but man and woman as such—provided he is handsome, she beautiful and both young. The face of the heroine, for instance, is always like a moon or lotus flower, eyes like waterlilies or those of a fawn. She always stoops slightly from the weight of her full breasts, improbable fleshy flowers of rounded perfection that do not even admit a blade of grass between them. The waist is slim, with three folds, the thighs round and plump, like the trunk of an elephant or a banana tree. The navel is deep, the hips heavy. These lyrical yet conventional descriptions of body parts seem to operate like collective fetishes, culturally approved cues for the individual to allow himself to indulge erotic excitement without the risk of surrender or merger.

Now, a facet of the beloved woman's beauty is certainly impersonal in the sense that it is nature's gift, especially to youth, and its minimal presence is necessary for the glance to become a gaze, for the poet to wax lyrical. As Auden remarks, 'A girl who weighs two hundred pounds and a woman of eighty may both have beautiful faces in the personal sense, but men do not fall in love with them'.[6] For our tastes, however, the part played by impersonal beauty is receding in favour of a personal beauty which is more an individual than a natural or cultural creation. To borrow from the Brontës, 'beauty lies in the eye of the beholder', whose scrutiny sees in lustrous eyes windows to the soul and reflections of the whole. The lust evoked by looking at a woman in parts—and at the parts of a woman, as in most traditional Indian poetry—is for a mature modern man no longer solely determined by her conformity to a uniform cultural model. Rather it also resides in a feeling for her uniqueness in which even her flaws are cherished. It is now the fleeting yet characteristic trivialities—the narrowing of her eyes in a quizzical smile, the nibbling of the fleshy part of the lower lip when engrossed in thought—which fascinate and enthral the lover, the flash of aesthetic admiration superseded by the wave of adoration. In the verses of Shakespeare's great sonnet:

> My mistress' eyes are nothing like the sun;
> . . . .
> My mistress, when she walks, treads on the ground.
> And yet, by heaven, I think my love as rare
> As any she belied with false compare.[7]

A woman is a woman not out of her predictable construction but because she is herself, her limbs and features moved by her destined femininity. Appreciating her individuality goes hand in hand with what Jung, and later Mahler, termed the lover's individuation. Its attainment, relatively speaking, is a developmental milestone that brings to a close the early dyadic struggles of infancy and introduces the growing child to a world of 'whole objects or person', each with his or her complex attributes. Loving these people, a child or the adult proceeds beyond the self and its sensations for their own reflexive sake. To do otherwise, to reify sybaritics, is to deny the regressive and progressive thrusts of genuine passion.

Indian poetry becomes inaccessible, even boring, when its

early freshness begins to wilt under scholastic dictates, which become more and more compelling in the later centuries. Not unlike the cataloguing efforts of modern sexologists, Sanskrit poetics and 'erotics' began to define, analyse and categorize the many moods and situations of love. Lovers—men and women—were stereotyped according to the ways they approached and reacted to love. They were further divided and subdivided according to rank, character and circumstances, as well as by the different shades of their feelings and gestures. An initial revolutionary aesthetic fervour gave way to the bureaucratization of beauty. With its insistence on the 'appropriate' combination of types, feelings and situations, the scholastic steamroller gained momentum and, in its way, crushed the creative expression of passionate love as effectively as epic indifference or Buddhist disapproval.

From the sixth century onwards, first in the south and then in the north, another auspicious shift took place which led to a re-emergence of passionate love. As with most things Indian, the change originated in the religious sphere but then expanded to influence Hindu culture and sensibility in such a profound way that its reverberations are still felt today. Scholars have called the shift *bhakti*, the rise of devotional religions in rebellion against the petrification of contemporary Hindu practice. Drawing on conventions of the classical literature of love and using an existing pan-Indian stock of symbols and figures of speech, the *bhakti* poets none the less strive for spontaneous, direct, personal expression of feeling rather than a rarified cultivation of aesthetic effect and the 'emotion recollected' preferred by Sanskrit poets.[8]

Although linked to the heroine and hero of classical love poetry in many ways, the figures of Radha and Krishna are primarily products of the *bhakti* movement, whose principal mood has always been erotic. Here the culture has imprinted its particular stamp upon the sensual experience—in contrast to much Western poetry of sexual mysticism—though Radha and Krishna are not figures of erotic allegory. *Bhakti* extols possessing and being possessed by the god. For it sexual love is where the fullest possession, the 'closest touch of all', takes place. With this the creators and audiences of *bhakti* poetry seek to project themselves into Radha's love for Krishna through poems that recount all its passionate phases. *Bhakti* is pre-eminently feminine in its orientation, and the erotic love for Krishna (or Shiva as the case may be) is envisioned entirely from the woman's viewpoint, or at least from her position as imagined by the man. The male devotees, saints, and poets must all adopt a feminine posture and persona to recreate Radha's responses in themselves. Radha's passionate love for Krishna, raised to its highest intensity, is not an allegory for religious passion but *is* religious passion.[9] Jayadeva thus does not need to make a distinction or choose between the religious and the erotic when he introduces the subject matter of his poem by saying:

> If remembering Hari [Krishna] enriches your heart,
> If his arts of seduction arouse you,
> Listen to Jayadeva's speech
> In these sweet soft lyrical songs.

Befitting his status as the *adi-guru* (first teacher) of Radha–Krishna cults, Jayadeva, *knows* that the enrichment of the heart and the arousal of senses belong together. Moreover, this coincidence of knowledge and feeling is intimately tied to an illusion, or at least a crossing over, of genders.

The augmentation of passion, or, more specifically, the heightening of sexual excitement, is then the 'great feeling', the *mahabhava*, that pervades the Radha–Krishna legend. Radha incarnates a state of permanent amorous tension, a here-and-now of desire that carries within itself a future expectation of pleasurable release but . . . oh, not yet! Her concern is not with 'lineaments of gratified desire' but with their anticipation. Radha personifies an enduring arousal that does not seek orgasmic resolution, an embodiment of ideals elsewhere put into Tantric practices. Hers is an effort to reach the very essence of eroticism. As she herself says in one of Vidyapati's songs:

Through all the ages he [Krishna] has been clasped
To my breast,
Yet my desire never abates.
I have seen subtle people sink in passion
But none came so close to the heart of the fire.[10]

In her interviews with the temple-dancers of Orissa the anthropologist Frederique Marglin highlighted the fact that when these women talk of the love (*prema*) of Radha and other cowherdesses they do not mean a chaste, platonic love. Rather they refer specifically to the fantasy—conscious in this case but unconscious in many others—of unending and sustained sexual excitement.[11] The absence of *kama* or lust in Radha's love for Krishna does not mean an absence of desire, but simply of orgasm. The dancers, who seek to enact for themselves the tension and intensity of the mythical cowherdesses, explicate the distinction by stating that one of Krishna's names is *Acyuta*, 'the one whose seed does not fall.' Marglin writes:

What is the meaning of Krishna's retention of his seed? My informant delineated several levels of meaning. First, there is the testimony of everyday experience, in which sexual pleasure is only momentary. After orgasm the pleasurable erotic tension is gone; in such a manner one attains only temporary pleasure or happiness (*khyanika sukha*). Furthermore, by ejaculating one loses one's strength and becomes old. In this world, the world of *samsara*, pleasure is brief and one begets children whereas in the divine play of Krishna there is continuous (*nitya*) pleasure and no children. The *gopis* are not impregnated . . . The shedding of the seed has ulterior consequences, i.e. a birth. Krishna's erotic dalliances with the gopis has no ulterior purpose or consequence. It exists for itself, in itself.[12]

It is indeed a dwelling in the immediacy of excitement, a locking in of body and mind in total involvement.

Using classical conventions in which sexual excitement is denoted by certain bodily manifestations such as sweating and the bristling of hair (the mention of sexual organs and genital sensations were always crude and unacceptable), poem after poem seeks to convey the *rasa* of Radha's arousal. In giving central place to the body in the depiction of erotic passions—which are, after all, ideas which the mind would not entertain unless it were united to the body and dependent on it for its survival—the *bhakti* poets seem to intuitively recognize and affirm the truth of Auden's assertion that 'Our bodies cannot love: / But, without one / what works of love could we do.'[13] In Radha's excitement, produced by the anticipation of intercourse,

> She bristles with pain, sucks in breath
> Cries, shudders, gasps,
> Broods deep, reels, stammers,
> Falls, raises herself, then faints.
> When fevers of passion rage so high,
> A frail girl may live by your charm.[14]

While in the sensuous fervour of foreplay.

> There was a shudder in her whispering voice.
> She was shy to frame her words.
> What has happened tonight to lovely Radha?
> Now she consents, now she is afraid.
> When asked for love, she closes up her eyes
> Eager to reach the ocean of desire.
> He begs her for a kiss.
> She turns her mouth away
> And then, like a night lily, the moon seized her.
> She felt his touch startling her girdle.
> She knew her love treasure was being robbed.
> With her dress she covered up her breasts.
> The treasure was left uncovered.[15]

At first persual the large number of Radha–Krishna poems that describe the near harrowing effects of their separation on Radha do not seem to support the contention that sexual excitement is the central emotion and its generation their chief object. Much of the content of the separation poems, however, consists of Radha's recollections of their erotic pleasure—an effort to retain expectancy through reminiscence. Further, in romantic literature around the world, the division of lovers has been a well-known device for whetting erotic hunger. In life, as in art, turnings in the path of love's fulfilment have always been found necessary to swell the libidinal tide. Separateness and union are not different categories of love, as the convention of Indian poetics would have it, but are merely different phases of the cycle of love, both intimately connected through the workings of desire. The lover's and the poet's dwelling on apartness represents his or her renouncing a possession that would deflate desire. Erotic passion, in de Rougemont's anthropomorphic formulation, always invents distance in order to exult itself more completely.[16] Below the surface sadness lies the lover's *need* to create impediments to the enjoyment of their love, to *deliciously* postpone delight, to suspend ecstasy in time, make it all last forever.

Sexual excitement is also a mental state, the product of those fantasies wherein, as Robert Stoller has pointed out, one oscillates between an anticipation of danger and the expectation of replacing danger with pleasure.[17] The major fantasies, largely unconscious, which are reflected in the trembling attraction of Radha's love for Krishna, are decisively formed and coloured by the theme of a forbidden crossing of boundaries.

First, in the pervasive presence of the adulterous in the narrative there is an illicit transgression of moral limits. Second, in striving to entertain the erotic feelings and sensations of the other sex, a lover would violate his primal sexual demarcation as a male. Furthermore, the arousal provoked by these fantasies is both preserved and brought to pitch by the stealth and secrecy in which the crossing of such bounds takes place.

The most obvious manifestation of the illicit, involving the crossing of boundaries set by social mores and norms, is found in the adulterous and later accounts which saddle Radha with a husband, throwing in a mother-in-law for good measure. These persistently underline the adulterous nature of her love for Krishna. There was, of course, much theolo-

gical uneasiness regarding this circumstance. Some commentators went to great lengths to explain why, since Krishna is
god, he could not have actually coveted the wife of another.
Others strained to prove the contrary, explaining that precisely because Krishna is god he is not bound by normal human
restrictions. In the end, and perhaps inevitably, the community's quest for pleasure triumphed over its theological scruples
in firmly demanding that the mythical lovers be accepted as
unambiguously adulterous.

The identification of the adulterous with the thrilling and
romantic is common enough in the Western literary tradition,
evident in the etiquette of Aquitaine and the novels of our
own day. But in the Indian context the link is possessed of a
special resonance since there the dichotomy between the conjugal and the adulterous had remained sharp and charged with
tension over many centuries.[18]

In the ritual sphere the god and goddess of sexual love have
always been segregated from deities who preside over marriage and fertility. Even today in India the so-called 'love
marriage', almost a contradiction in terms and the subject of
much excited gossip when it occurs, is mostly met with in the
fantastical world of movies and is generally deemed a daring
Western import of the urbanized and presumably licentious
upper classes.

As far as legalities are concerned both the conventions and
the laws about adultery have been and remain extremely
strict. The epics considered adultery as one of the five great
sins for which there is no atonement—the others are the murder of a Brahmin, the slaying of a cow, unbelief and living off
a woman—and warned against its frightful consequences:

In all castes a man must never approach the wife of another. For
there is nought in the world which so shortens life as that the man
on earth should visit the wife of another. As many pores as are on
women's bodies, so many years will he sit in hell ... He that
touches another man's wife is born as a wolf, as a dog, as a jackal,
then born as a vulture, a snake, a heron, as also a crane.[19]

In mythology, too, the adulterous woman at least, rarely escapes the consequences of her actions. Ahilya, the wife of a sage, who was more a victim of Indra's (the king of the gods') lechery and less an enthusiastic participant in their short-lived revel, paid dearly for her unwitting lapse. Parshuram commanded by his father, killed his own mother who, when out bathing, caught sight of a handsome king sporting with his wives and was 'unfaithful in her heart.' Even today we know from clinical practice that in most sections of Indian society adultery is rarely a matter of casual, commonplace liaison. Its mere contemplation is a momentous psychological event for a woman, provoking moral dread.

In contrast the poets and litterati of the classical period, who have exercised a great influence on subsequent cultural attitudes and sentiments, at least of the upper castes, generally scorned the Hindu marriage as a pre-eminently social and religious duty. They saw in marriage a deadly foe of the great feeling to which they—as indeed most poets—have always aspired. In writing with nostalgia of scenes of love unhampered by matrimony, or in lamenting the disappearance of love with marriage, the poet's scorn of conjugal love was unremitting.

> Where the moon is not inveighed against
> And no sweet words of the messenger are heard
> Where speech is not choked with tears
> And the body grows not thin;
> But where one sleeps in one's own house
> With he who owns subservient to one's wish;
> Can this routine of household sex,
> This wretched thing, deserve the name of love?[20]

The poets, then, and especially the females of this artistic species—Vidya and Bhavakadevi for example—idealized the rapture of the illicit liaison.[21] In counterpoint to the damnation heaped upon her in religious and legal texts, the adultress was assured of the poet's admiration.

In the poetic and dramatic conventions, for instance, there

are three kinds of women: the courtesan (*veshya*), the wife (*svakiya*), and the 'other woman' (*parakiya*). The other woman is further subdivided into two kinds: the unmarried young girl (*kanyaka*) and the married woman (*parodha*). In an obvious 'oedipal' allusion, it is the *parodha*, the other man's wife, who best embodies the principle of eros (since, risking much, she has the most to lose) and is therefore considered the most desirable lover. As one Sanskrit poet writes:

> So there are
> women who attract with
> their loose ways
> prostitutes
> and there is the deep shyness
> of one's own wife
> the most beautiful and most
> graceful showing
> her love
> opening flower
> but who in this world can
> fill one with joy
> like another man's wife
> loving with naked breast.

In contrast to classical poets who stressed the frank elation, the incomparable 'joy' of loving another man's wife, the *bhakti* cults gave more exalted reasons for making Radha an adulterous *parakiya*. For them the adulterous was symbolic of the sacred, the overwhelming moment that denies world and society, transcending the profanity of everyday convention, as it forges an unconditional (and unruly) relationship with god as the lover. Stirring our sense of the essential instabilities and disorderliness of passionate love, Radha would sing:

> At the first note of his flute
> down came the lion gate of
> reverence for elders,
> down came the door of *dharma*,

my guarded treasure of modesty was lost,
I was thrust to the ground as if by
a thunderbolt.
Ah, yes, his dark body
poised in the *tribhanga* pose
shot the arrow that pierced me;
no more honour, my family
lost to me,
my home at Vraja
lost to me.
Only my life is left—and my life too
is only a breath that is leaving me.[22]

In imparting adulterous love elements of the divine, the *bhakti* poets went even further than the troubadours of medieval Europe who had equated it with 'true' love. In the legendary decision taken at the so-called Court of Love in Champagne in 1174 it was maintained:

We declare and affirm, agreeably to the general opinion of those present, that love cannot exercise its powers on married people. The following reason is proof of the fact; lovers grant everything, mutually and gratuitously, without being constrained by any motive of necessity. Married people, on the contrary, are compelled as a duty to submit to one another's wishes, and not to refuse anything to one another. For this reason, it is evident that love cannot exercise its powers on married people.[23]

Both the Indian sanctification and the European romanticization of extra-marital love distract attention from its 'real' fascination: its obviation of many factors that promote sexual anxiety and consequently inhibit desire. The structure of the adulterous, so far removed from the mundane, the long-term 'dream of safety' and dependability of the conjugal relationship, may not be so easily subject to the steady erosion wrought by oedipal taboos which, in a marriage, often come to attach themselves to the partner. In other words, lacking in defensiveness, the adulterous relationship is relatively free of those instances of impotency or frigidity in marriage that involve a transference to the spouse of unconscious sexual attitudes and prohibitions entertained earlier towards the parent of the opposite sex. Freed of inner taboos the adulterous situation yet partakes of its delightful excitement, with the betrayed spouse serving as an *outside* impediment, both regulating erotic intensity and, in so far as he or she is an obstacle, enhancing it. Reliving the thrills of oedipal fantasy, the adulterous lover does not confront the parent's image or injunctions in the person to whom he or she makes love. In this adventure taboos have been cast by the wayside and are not everyday matters.

In the Indian case there is an additional consideration. The hierarchical dictates of the family call for male supremacy within marriage. The adulterous, in contrast, is free of all distinctions of relative status between man and woman. Radha can address Krishna as '*tu chora*' (You thief!), which would be unthinkable for a wife, who is constrained to use the most respectful form of second person address when speaking to her husband—a proscription which is hardly conducive to sexual abandon in the 'master['s] bedroom'. Furthermore, the clandestine life of the adulterous is composed of snatches of stolen time, rather than long periods of coexistence. This mitigates demands for intimacy on levels other than the sexual. The body, shackled by social and moral restraints and enmeshed in a web of unconscious expectations and attitudes from the past, glimpses in the adulterous a promise of newfound emancipation and expansiveness. Therein it is liberated by the spontaneous, vivid, if transient, encounter.

Besides the adulterous overthrow of social convention, indeed facilitated by this very circumstance, the crossing of individual sexual boundaries provides the other major source of erotic excitement in the artistic treatment of Radha and Krishna. We are either men or women, after all. We have known this to be an intractable fact of life since we were two and a half years of age when our core gender identity becomes fixed. Thereafter we grow up in an established social milieu which affixes to gender sex roles that seem to emanate from our bodies, our penises and wombs, and all those secondary sexual characteristics that go along with them. Can all this be changed, should it—when it is the distinctions of sex that impel and permit man and woman to come together? To these questions the Indian love poetry and art respond with a resounding yes. And they do this within an elaborate mythological tradition rather unknown to the West, whose deities have always tended to be more prosaically human than otherwise.

In painting, the depiction of this crossing ranges from the portrayal of the lovers in the traditional Orissa school, where they appear as one androgynous entity, to some of the paintings from the Himalayan foothills where Radha and Krishna are dressed in each other's clothes, or Radha is seen taking the more active 'masculine' role in coitus. In poetry, Sur Das would speak in Radha's voice:

You become Radha and I will become Madhava, truly Madhava; this is the reversal which I shall produce. I shall braid your hair and will put [your] crown upon my head. Sur Das says: Thus the Lord becomes Radha and Radha the son of Nanda.[24]

The inversion of sexual roles is all the more striking in the depiction of their intercourse. The poet Chandi Das praises as beautiful 'the deliberate, sensuous union of the two / the girl playing this time the active role / riding her lover's outstretched body in delight,'[25] while Jayadeva gives voice to what are normally regarded as 'feminine masochistic' sexual wishes when he has Krishna sing:

> Punish me, lovely fool!
> Bite me with your cruel teeth!
> Chain me with your creeper arms!
> Crush me with your hard breasts!
> Angry goddess, don't weaken with joy!
> Let Love's despised arrows
> Pierce me to sap my life's power![26]

It was only under the influence of nineteenth-century Western phallocentricity, one of the dubious intellectual 'blessings' of British colonial rule, that many educated Indians would become uneasy with this accentuation of femininity in a culture hero. The great Bengali writer Bankim Chandra Chatterji, the proponent of a virile nationalism, would write of the Gitagovinda:

From the beginning to the end, it does not contain a single expression of manly feelings—of womanly feelings there is a great deal—or a single elevated sentiment . . . I do not deny his [Jayadeva's] high poetical merits in a certain sense of exquisite imagery, tender feeling, and unrivalled powers of expression, but that does not make him less the poet of an effeminate and sensual race.[27]

In the *bhakti* cults, where the worshipper must create an erotic relationship with Krishna, the transcendence of boundaries of gender becomes imperative for the male devotee, who endeavours to become as a woman in relation to the Lord. In his case the violation of the biblical injunction 'The woman shall not wear that which pertaineth unto a man, neither shall a man put on a woman's garments' is far from being an 'abomination unto the Lord thy God.' In *bhakti* Krishna not only demands such a willing reversal from his male worshippers but is himself the compelling exemplar. Consequently, tales of Indian saints who have succeeded in feminizing themselves are legion. To give only two illustrations: the fifteenth-century Gujarati saint Narsi Mehta writes,

I took the hand of that lover of *gopis* [Krishna] in loving converse . . . I forgot all else. Even my manhood left me. I began to sing and dance like a woman. My body seemed to change and I become one of the *gopis*. I acted as go-between like a woman, and began to lecture Radha for being too proud . . . At such times I experienced moments of incomparable sweetness and joy.[28]

A. K. Ramanujan tells us that the voice of the Tamil saint-poet Nammalvar, who wrote 370 poems on the theme of love, was always that of a woman: Krishna's beloved, the girlfriend who consoles and counsels, or 'the mother who restrains her and despairs over her daughter's lovesick fantasies'.[29] Nammalvar's love poems alternated with other subjects and a thirteenth-century commentary explained these shifts: 'In knowledge, his own words; in love, a woman's words'.[30] A legend has it that Amaru, one of the earliest and greatest Sanskrit poets of love, was the hundred and first incarnation of a soul which had previously occupied the bodies of a hundred women.

Narsi Mehta, Nammalvar, and countless other unknown devotees of the Radha–Krishna cults, bear testimony to the primal yearning of men, ensheathed and isolated by their 'phallic' masculinity, to yield their heroic trappings and delight in womanliness, woman's and their own. These universal wishes are distinct from the pathological cases where similar fantasies and feminine behaviour might well be a manifestation of 'homosexual libido', a retreat from phallic masculinity into anal eroticism. In other words some of the devotees may indeed be closer to Freud's history of the paranoid Schreber, the psychotic German judge who was convinced that he was being transformed into a woman in order to become God's wife and give birth to a whole new race of men.[31] Like Schreber, these devotees too may be defending against their fear and unconscious belief that they have been emasculated and consoling themselves with femininity as a compensation.

Yet for most of the worshippers and the saints, as for the rest of us, the wish to be a woman is not a later distortion of phallic strivings but rather another legacy from our 'prehistoric' experience with our mothers. Indeed this ambisexuality, the play of masculine and feminine, probably represents the acme, the climax of pre-oedipal development before castration anxiety and guilt enter to limit and dull the sexual quest.

The mother has figured early on as the omnipotent force of a parental universe, making things, including fathers and other males, materialize as if at will. It is she whose breast and magic touch have long ago soothed the savage instinctual imperatives, she whose fecund womb seemed the very fount of life. Such maternal and feminine powers are earthly yet mysterious and transcendent, undiminished by the utter sensuousness in which they are manifest. As the little boy grows towards manhood and assumes his predestined masculine role in society, he may come to exaggerate the brittle and rather obvious puissant attributes of the phallus and disparage those who do not possess it. Notwithstanding what has been termed his 'masculine protest', what he does not have gnaws at a boy, at a man. In the veil of night, or in the veil drawn over consciousness in the ecstasy of religious possession, he would gratefully surrender his penis to the vagina and the woman who possesses it—that is, so long as he does not lose it forever.

Krishna's erotic homage to Radha conveys something of the aching quality of the man's fantasy of surrender at the height of sexual excitement. He longs to be smothered and penetrated by the woman's breasts as he himself willingly shrinks in his mind's eye. Every genital fibre is attuned to the welcoming wetness his eyes cannot see nor know from within, straining even as he finally expels his seed from his self, an emissary journeying deep into the lover's internal dark continent, still forbidden to him. The thrusting penis, man realizes once again, can never take or hold the woman. It merely enters her territory and touches her portals, only to shrivel and all too rapidly to be withdrawn. Did it not provide a recurrent bridge to her, man would gladly cede his crude organ and castrate himself to be one with the beloved—at least for a moment of bliss. The 'secret of men', gods included, to borrow from Bruno Bettelheim, is that they want to be that which they cannot have: Woman.

The profusion of the imagery of darkness and night—in the meetings of Radha–Krishna—as indeed in the trysts of Romeo and Juliet and of Layla and Majnun (or, for that matter, Tristan and Isolde)—underscores the secret nature of these fantasmagoria and illusions of the soul. The paintings show Radha and Krishna surrounded by darkness while they themselves are lit by a sullen glare from the sky. They portray the lovers enclosed in a triangle of inky night while around them the rest of Vrindavan's inhabitants unconcernedly go about the day's tasks. These are visual metaphors for a sensualism which is simultaneously hidden from the world and from the lovers' awareness. For Radha, as for Juliet, night and darkness are excitement's protectors, silence and secrecy its friends. Shrill disturbances to these servants of nature's erotic cycle are to be avoided: 'Leave your noisy anklets! They clang like traitors in love's play / Go to the darkened thicket, friend! Hide in a cloak of night!'[32] In a Basholi painting from *Rasmanjari* the text describes the seated lovers thus: 'Fear of detection does not permit the eager lovers' gaze to meet. Scared of the jingling sound of armlets they desist from embracing. They kiss each others' lips without the contact of teeth. Their union is hushed too'.[33] Many other portraits of Radha reveal that it is not only other people who must remain unaware of her sexual arousal. Radha, too, when in a state where 'love's deep fantasies / struggle with her modesty',[34] would fain ignorance of her true condition, as if it were a secret another part of her self must not admit to knowing. It is given to the poet to perceive correctly her struggle.

> Words of protest filled with passion
> Gestures of resistance lacking force,
> Frowns transmuted into smiles,
> Crying dry of tears—friend,
> Though Radha seeks to hide her feelings
> Each attempt betray's her heart's
> Deep love for demon Mura's slayer.[35]

Identifying with Radha's pounding breast as she steals out at night to meet Krishna, other poets graphically describe her fear while merely hinting at the suppressed thrill of her sortie, her arousal sharpened by the threat of discovery. They give us images of storm, writhing snakes, scratched and burning feet.

O Madhava, how shall I tell you of my terror?
I could not describe my coming here
If I had a million tongues.
When I left my room and saw the darkness
I trembled:
I could not see the path,
There were snakes that writhed round my ankles!

I was alone, a woman; the night was so dark,
The forest so dense and gloomy,
And I had so far to go.
The rain was pouring down—
Which path should I take?
My feet were muddy
And burning where thorns had scratched them.
But I had the hope of seeing you,
None of it mattered,
And now my terror seems far away . . .
When the sound of your flute reaches my ears
It compels me to leave my home, my friends,
It draws me in the dark toward you.[36]

We imagine that on hearing Radha's plaint, Krishna, whose gaze into the recesses of the human heart is as penetrating as it is compassionate, smiled to himself in the dark. He would have surely known that the strains of his flute, like that of Pan's before him, are the perennial and irresistible call of the human senses caught up in the throes of love.

And what do darkness and night mean to Krishna as he passively offers himself to Radha's embraces? Here, too, only under the cloak of night does the Lord reveal the deepest 'secret of man'—that he, too, would be a woman. In the night, in the jungle, visual and discrete modes of perception are replaced by the tactile, the visceral, and the more synesthetic forms of cognizance. Representations of the self and beloved fade and innermost sensate experience comes to the fore. As the illusion of bodies fused, hermaphroditic, it fostered, the fantasies around womanliness and sexual excitement feed each other, and Krishna 'knows' Radha not with the eye but with the flesh.

Night's curtains never completely part in this gentler story, whose protagonist, moreover, is a god able to withstand and transcend such protean changes. Hence the lovers survive, and tragedy is averted. Undiscovered, they remain unseen by the eyes of inner vigilance—by castration terror, by ambivalence, or, worst of all, by guilt.

PART II

EROS ADULTERATED

In earlier chapters we have considered those myths of first love that have helped shape their cultures' images of erotic passion, informing the fantasies and conduct of youthful lovers and the retrospective ideals of those past their libidinal prime. These love stories tell us of the burning torment, transports and secret dreads that lurk within an amorous dyad.

We turn now to triads—to those proverbial eternal triangles which arise when passions challenge generational prerogatives and the normal rules of succession and possession. Resonating with the more internal triangles that govern all inner life, these are tales not so much of madness and instinct unchained but of conflict and multiple ambivalence. Having gazed upon the play of passion per se, we see in what follows a greater emphasis on its collision with more intimate and internalized constraints. Not that our young lovers have been free of this: it is only that the couples or triads now in question find their desires shaped by the forces that inhibit them.

In psychoanalytic parlance we are now ushered into the age of Oedipus. The first of our chapters elaborates upon the power plays transpiring between fathers and sons, in which women figure more as tokens for 'phallic narcissistic' conquest and domination than as primary sources of (sexual) attraction. In the Persian story of Vis and Ramin, in the Indian legends, and indeed in the myth of Oedipus, parricide and filicide loom as the great dangers.

In the chapter that follows, the story of King Mark and Tristan and Isolde speaks of the ambivalence and the deep love between fathers and sons, tender but at times sensuous as well. It tells of the remorse and mourning when the lure of woman's magical sexuality divides the devoted young man from his patron. In the wake of this loss, as in *Hamlet*, both threatened castration and father love become internalized in the form of guilt. The embrace of conscience paralyses the son from pursuing desire and, with it, any impulse. The threat now is of an unremitting compunction, a 'mind dagger' thrusting home again and again the fact that in transgressing moral bounds, even in the mind's eye, one is unlovable. This becomes all the more poignant when in adolescence, as in *Phaedra* and in an Indian tale, the young man is lusted and longed for by the very older woman he has fought so hard to give up. Now danger does indeed become reality, an electrifying and stunning possibility whose realization can destroy the social order together with all its participants.

CHAPTER FIVE

KINGS AND CUCKOLDS: PASSION AS POWER

Gods find it easier to change their sex with impunity than mortal men. Often enough, the latter assert their masculinity in bold yet brittle attempts to wrest themselves from the persistent hold of femininity and their own structureless origins in it. For such men, women serve as the trappings of and mirrors for the phallus, the man's sensual pleasure incidental to his self-love. It is power, not so much women, they would seize from their fathers.

One psychoanalytic patient, uncertain of his manhood, described lifting his girlfriend upon his loins and wielding her body as an enlargement and embodiment of a penis that he felt was still little and childish, set against his bulk. He engaged his analyst in an ongoing rivalry, imagining him as a stud servicing a stable of women patients parading through the consulting rooms. His was not a quest for coveted oedipal treasures but for manly empowerment. Attending his associations, the clinician's stream of consciousness drifted to the primitive displays of the three- and four-year olds in the local playground. Bathed in the ever watchful eyes of their mothers, they zoomed about in ersatz combat with each other, sticks and spears held between their legs to extend and amplify their anatomy. He recalled the description of an Indian maharaja during the early part of this century who, on his birthday, would walk through his capital city at the head of a procession stark naked, his majestic organ pridefully erect to its considerable glory.

Three-year-old boys, an analytic patient in the throes of a 'controlled regression', a pretentious maharaja of yesteryear— they are easy enough to take with an understanding smile. But when a boy emerges into manhood, in the full glow of youth's energy and power, he poses a threat to our collective fatherhood teetering on the edge of aging and decline. The phallic thrust of a masculinity now on the rise runs afoul of the older overlord's claim to unflagging vigour and, beneath this, to immortality. At some level and in some measure, as generations cycle through human history, a deadly confrontation is inevitable—especially when a woman lurks among the spoils of combat. Woman, after all, with her access to immortality through sex and procreation, holds the keys to the kingdom.

The narratives in this chapter—the Persian story of King Moubad, Vis and Ramin, the Indian legends of patriarchs, gods or kings, lusting after their daughters and coming up sharply against their sons, and even the famed myth of Oedipus—introduce us to triangles in their more primitive aspect.

The triangles, we should emphasize, are not the so-called straightforward 'oedipal triangles' seen from the vantage point of the 'son' alone. Such a delimited focus, almost ninety years after the discovery of the Oedipus complex, would amount to a stereotyped exercise which can only tread a well-worn path, confirming all we have come to anticipate along the way: the son's urge to unite and bind with his mother: his wish for sexual union with her; his would-be exclusion and destruction of the possessive father; and, lastly, his Hamlet-like proclivity for revenge on the incestuous object who had given herself instead to the rival patriarch. Even the story of Oedipus itself, to which we shall turn at the conclusion of this chapter, violates such linear expectations.

For one thing, sexual rivalry between father and son in the Islamic and Hindu tales does not necessarily hit upon the mother as the prime object of desire, at least not manifestly. The battle centres on daughters and their surrogates. When Freud, in illuminating the importance of the Oedipus complex in literature, gave the examples of *Oedipus Rex* of Sophocles, Shakespeare's *Hamlet* and Dostoevsky's *The Brothers Karamazov*, he seemed oddly not to heed the fact that the struggle between father and son in the last of these has a different quality from the one that grips the souls of male protagonists in the first two stories.[1] Gruschenka clearly belongs, if she 'belongs' to anyone, to the son, Dmitri, and it is the father, Fyodor Pavlovitch, who would entice her away from the son. Further, the struggles between father and son for a woman, who generationally if not legally belongs to the son, is in fact a favoured theme in the non-Western legends of love. Structurally so similar to other oedipal narratives, these reveal a shift in focus from the son's incestuous wishes towards his mother to a father's illicit desire for his daughter. The obscurity of the object of desire in our Persian tale for instance, the ambiguity of whom Vis really 'belongs' to, the 'father' or the 'son', contributes to its enduring fascination and evocative power.

King Moubad, Vis and Ramin

The story of Vis and Ramin as narrated by the eleventh century Persian poet Fakhr-ud-din Gurgani begins with the great feast given by King Moubad. In this spring banquet, which parallels the festival of King Mark in *Tristan and Isolde* and the opening gambit of many other Western and Eastern heroic epics, there are many noble lords, ladies, princes and lesser kings and queens from all over the realm. Moubad, a generous and open-hearted king, much given to the pleasures of sport and wine, espies Shahru, a queen from a distant province.

He asks her hand in marriage. Shahru pleads her age since she is, after all, in her late twenties and has borne many children—reasons for refusing the king's chivalrous offer. 'My beauty made slaves of kings, my scent brought the dead back to life', she says,

but now my life has reached its autumn days, the spring of beauty has deserted me. Time has scattered yellow flowers on my cheeks and mixed my musk with camphor; abstracted the glow of beauty from my face, bent the crystal cypress of my figure. The world piles shame and humiliation upon every old person who plays at being young![2]

Age and erotic accessibility are, clearly, culturally and historically relative.

Moubad courteously demurs but concedes the correctness of her point of view—though in his dotage he will himself do otherwise. He asks, 'Now if you will not be my mate and lover, give me a daughter born of you. Since the fruit will surely be like the seed, your daughter will be jasmine-bosomed like you'. It is interesting, indeed, first to fall in love with a mother and then to court a daughter unseen as her younger proxy. Shahru replies that of her many children there is not one daughter among them. She, however, swears a solemn oath that if a daughter is ever born to her, Moubad alone will be her son-in-law.

After a few years a daughter is indeed born to Shahru and is named Vis. Immediately after her birth her mother gives Vis to a nurse who takes her away to her own home in a distant city. The nurse brings up Vis with great care and tenderness, as she does Ramin, the infant brother of King Moubad. For the first ten years of their lives Vis and Ramin are raised together like brother and sister before Ramin goes back to the palace of Moubad.

Vis grows up into a divinely beautiful yet imperious girl 'whose body was of silver, but whose heart was of steel'. The nurse's description of the girl once again echoes Persian and Islamic ambivalences towards the woman who is reputedly composed of 'the hardness of a diamond, the sweetness of honey, the cruelty of a tiger, the warm brightness of a fire, and the coolness of snow.'[3] The nurse writes to Shahru asking her to take her daughter back. Vis returns to her family. Her mother seeks to arrange a quick marriage for the girl but cannot find a suitable match. She takes recourse to a social convention alien to the modern sensibility:

Since I do not know of a husband for you in the wide world, how can I give you to someone less than a husband? There is no mate in all Iran worthy to be your spouse except Viru, who is your own brother. Be his mate and make your family glorious, and make my days happy by this union. Viru's worthy sister shall be his wife, our bride shall be our fair daughter.[4]

When Vis hears these words, 'passion welled up in her heart, her silence signified consent. Not a word either way did she say to her mother; for love of her brother was in her heart'.[5]

The uncomplicated way in which sexual love between brother and sister is treated here follows from the cultural tradition of ancient Iran. As in ancient Egypt, the 'royal marriage' of brother and sister in the ruling dynasties was a norm rather than an exception. To contemporary psychoanalysis what is 'royal' in brother–sister incest are its symbolic reverberations, above all the underlying fantasy of an erotic self-completion, one which elevates the individual above and excludes him or her from the rest of the world. The sibling is not a dangerous 'other' to whom one may unwittingly become vulnerable through the promptings of normal erotic desire but a safer part of the same self. Epitomized in the fantasy of love between twins, the brother and sister are the male and female versions of the same superior. 'I'.

Then too, there is promised a special sanction of sensual desire and sexual union within family confines—so long as the generational power structure remains undisturbed. Here the transgression of the incest taboo is lateral rather than lineal, though it partakes of the thrills that would accompany violating the latter. Thus, the clinician is all too familiar with the associative pathways that lead from virtually universal adolescent dreams of sibling sex into the unconscious, and therein to the forbidden parental guardians.

While the wedding is being celebrated Moubad's messenger suddenly appears on the scene to interrupt the festivities and remind Shahru of her promise. Shahru is in a quandary, ashamed to break her covenant yet loath to keep a rash promise made many years ago. Vis takes matters into her own hands and sends Moubad this message:

Your mind had become addled from old age . . . You would not have chosen a young bride from this world, but would have sought out provision for the next! Viru is alike my husband and brother, while worthy Shahru is my mother; my heart is glad in the one, joyous at the other. While I have in my embrace a fruitful cypress, why should I seek a dry and barren plain? . . . I shall sort with my brother like wine and milk: I do not wish old Moubad in a foreign land. Why should I reject a youth for an old man? I speak frankly, and do not keep this secret in my heart.[6]

Incensed at the answer and the gratuitous insult to his manhood, Moubad gathers an army and marches to the country of Vis and Viru, determined to hold their mother to her promise by dint of force. In the battle, Vis and Viru's father is killed. However, Moubad is defeated and is on the point of retreat when another general, taking advantage of the situation, attacks the province. Prince Viru hurries to meet this new threat. The marriage to his sister, because of her menstrual period during the wedding and the war with Moubad after it, remains unconsummated.

Hearing of Viru's departure, Moubad retraces his steps and once more appears before the walls of the city with the remnants of his army. He sends Vis the following message:

I have come here for your sake, for I have become crazed with love for you. If you will become my true lover, many a desire will be fulfilled for you at my hand. I shall swear you a lover's oath today that henceforth we shall be two heads with but a single soul. I shall follow every ambition with an eye to your pleasure, say all I have to say at your command. I shall bring you the key of the treasures, make over to your hand all, great and small. I shall keep you supplied with such wealth of gold and ornaments that moon and sun will envy you . . . As long as life inhabits my body, I shall hold you equal to my very soul.[7]

Once again Vis spurns the old king's offer of wealth and power while she mocks his age, calling him the 'doddering Moubad'. She calls, furthermore, on an authority greater than his. 'If I break faith with him [Viru] in love', she replies,

what excuse shall I make on the other side before the Creator? I, young as I am, fear the Creator; are you not afraid who are an impotent old man? If you are wise, fear the doom of the Creator: for this fear is nothing to old men! The Lord of the World has vouchsafed to me ornaments and brocade and coin in plenty; do not seek to subvert me with ornaments . . . Not even my brother, who is my chosen spouse, has thus far gained his desire of me. How are you, an outsider, to gain your desire of me, even were you sun and moon? I have not given my silvery body to my brother, with whom I was born of one and the same mother. How, then, shall I give it to you, simpleton, at whose hand my homestead has been ruined?[8]

The love-crazed Moubad is delighted by this message from Vis, for what he fastens upon in her words is not her aversion for him but the fact that she is still a virgin. Her innocence remains untainted and is therefore rejuvenating. He calls his two brothers, Zard and the youngest one, Ramin, for consultations on how to proceed further.

Ramin, who had grown up with Vis and has been secretly in love with her all this time, tries to dissuade Moubad, who has been *like* a father to him, from pursuing her. 'Only through much disaster will you attain her', he says,

> and once you have attained her you will not support the disaster she brings in her train. An even greater problem which confronts you where Vis is concerned is the fact that you are old, while that charming maid is young. If you must take a mate, take one other than her; youth to youth, old age to old age. Just as someone young is your aim, she too should have just such a one. You are December, that sweetheart spring; a hard matter indeed to unite the two.[9]

Age violates youth, and not the contrary.

In *Vis and Ramin* we have stressed the metaphorical equivalence of the relation between eldest and baby-brother, and that between a father and his son. But the displacement is also significant in attenuating what would otherwise be an unthinkable breach of family law. It permits ambivalence and ambiguity and allows an ongoing generational dialogue, with all its twistings and turnings, in dramatic action.

Ramin's advice does not dissipate Moubad's aged ardour but rather fuels it all the more with the promise of revitalization. Or, as Gurgani writes:

> A heart full of love is not susceptible of health; blame but increases its fervour. When a heart is corroded with love, reproach only fans its fire. Even should a cloud rise from the world and stones rain from it instead of reproaches, the lover would not fear the stormy rain, even were spears to replace the stones. Everything which provokes blame is a fault, save the pursuit of love, which is a virtue. A critic by his remonstrance will not wash desire from the heart of a lover. Desire is like fire, remonstrance the wind; and what does wind do when it blows on fire?[10]

The forces of passion, and specifically desire, are closer to their animalistic reserves than those of scruples, primitive though our superegos may be. The self interest and pride of others are, however, also motives to be reckoned with. The other brother, Zard, more genuinely attached to the king's suit and of a practical nature, advises Moubad to send costly presents, money and jewels to Shahru. The tempting wealth, together with Shahru's own guilt at breaking her oath, he surmises, will persuade Shahru to yield her daughter to the king. His conjecture proves correct, and Moubad is successful in carrying away a lamenting Vis.

Ramin, who is a part of the escort, sees the face of a grown up and womanly Vis for the first time and is assaulted by the full force of erotic passion:

He fell from his horse as mighty as a mountain, like a leaf that the wind rips from the tree. The brain in his head had begun to boil from the fire in his heart; heart had fled from body and sense from head ... The rosy cheeks had turned the colour of saffron; his wine-coloured lips blue as the sky. The hue of life had deserted his face, the insignia of love appeared there in its stead.[11]

Once more the hero is unseated and laid low by woman's allure. A major characteristic of Persian poetry, and the poetry of other countries it has influenced, is its pre-eminence in the depiction of the torments of unslaked desire, unfulfilled longing and unrequited love, all tributes to woman's riveting, indeed ruthless, sensual power. Gurgani's description of a distraught Ramin, beside himself for the love of Vis, is one of the many such depictions of love's suffering in the story, a theme that became a major focus of later Persian poetry and one that stands in opposition to defensive misogyny.

Vis is grievous over the separation from her brother and husband, Viru. 'Whenever she saw Moubad she rent her body in place of her garments: she would not hear the words he spoke nor show him her fair face. She turned her beautiful face to the wall and sent a flood of tears of agony from her eyes down her cheeks'. Her suffering is in its turn exciting.

'Thus she was, both on the journey and in Marv; the King had no joy of her even for a day; the face of Vis was glorious like a garden—but a garden whose gate is shut tight ...'.[12] The face, as psychoanalyst Phyllis Greenacre has underscored, is the mirror of the genitals. Gazing on it, man beholds the mother of the infant at the breast, the unseen parts of the mother of five-year-old boy's Oedipus complex and the radiant woman wooed—all are of a piece.

The nurse learns of the plight of Vis and how the king had abducted her, and travels to Marv, the royal abode, to be with her former charge. She tries to console Vis and advises her to enjoy whatever life has brought her, extolling the pleasures of sensuality and sexual intercourse with a man. Vis, however, is adamant in her steadfastness and sorrow:

Your words are like fruitless seed: my heart is sated of scent and colour; I shall not don raiment nor sit on a throne. Sackcloth is my raiment, dust my throne, and pain and sad sighs my courtiers; neither will Moubad have joy of me nor I renown of him. As I was a palm without a thorn with Viru, now I am a thorn that will not bear dates. If I must have a husband for the sake of desire, it suits me better to be free of desire. Since in the event he missed his desire, may no one else enjoy desire of me.[13]

What Vis wants from the nurse is to contrive a spell that would render Moubad impotent for a year so that he would leave her alone. The nurse reluctantly agrees and prepares a talisman which she buries in the moist earth near the bank of a river. As long as the talisman remains wet, Moubad will be impotent. After a year the nurse hopes Vis will be reconciled to Moubad. She then only needs to burn the talisman, for 'the moment fire burns the clasp of the talisman, the candle of manhood burns again'. Unfortunately for the king, there is a flood in the river that washes the talisman into the sea and Moubad is left impotent for life. Even if he were to possess her he cannot penetrate her, such is the awesome power to invite, soothe, engulf and emasculate in the ocean that is woman.

Ramin, in the mean while, is suffering as he indulges mightily the full panoply of lover's sighs, 'blood-stained tears' and sad songs of separation. Meeting the nurse in the garden and addressing her as 'mother', he beseeches her help. The nurse has fond memories of the little boy but is still reluctant to help him win the love of Vis. Ramin, however, decides the issue by taking her in his arms and 'gaining his desire of the nurse'. The nurse's former cold words now grow warm in the heat of another thinly disguised seduction of the parent. Transported by the near incestuous liaison into another realm of awareness and moral sensibility, an aged child of passion herself, she promises to exercise all her considerable skills in helping Ramin to win over Vis. As Gurgani, reflecting on the reigning orthodoxy of love relations of his time, comments, 'when one has once gained one's heart's desire of a woman, it is for all the world as if one has placed a bridle on her head'.[14] As with Vis in the scene to come, sex vanquishes the older woman and liberates the truth of her womanly nature. No longer is Ramin her little boy.

The nurse now begins her campaign to persuade a reluctant Vis to meet Ramin. Using spells, flattery, cajolery, lyrical descriptions of sexual pleasures and extolling Ramin's charms of body and mind, she overcomes Vis's compunction and arouses in her a curiosity about Ramin. They finally meet, when the king is absent on a journey, and become lovers.

Gurgani's description of their first love-making reflects the culturally heightened phallocentric conception of sexual intercourse in which the man enacts the conquering hunter and the woman his hapless prey. Woman's virginity is depicted as a treasure which the man covets and loots. In the sexual act the haughty Vis is laid low, her power now wrested from her by a mighty male overlord. Violence and martial brutality of sorts permeate the poet's imagery.

As he pranced in the lights of happiness he put the key of desire in the lock of happiness: his delight in the lover grew the more when he saw the seal of God was as yet intact upon her. He pierced that soft pearl of great price; seduced a saint from her virginity. When he drew the arrow from the wound, target and arrow alike were covered in blood. Vis of the rosy limbs was wounded by the arrow, her heart's desire was realized in that wounding. When both had slaked their desire their love grew apace; they remained in this wise for two months, enjoying only happiness and their hearts' desire.[15]

Her illusory phallus is stripped from her by the man, who finds his way to her 'true' femininity. In the androcentric fantasy at least, a woman as lover is at last impelled to yield herself up to her own masochistic wishes and enslavement to her lover's and her body's will.

Moubad, whose journey has taken him to the country of Vis, writes to Ramin that he misses his company and, as yet unaware of their liaison, requests him to bring Vis along with him. The lovers journey to the king's court where they contrive to go on meeting secretly. One day, when the king is asleep with Vis in his arms, the nurse comes to tell Vis that Ramin is going away for a month on a hunt and she should hurry to meet her lover before he leaves. King Moubad, awakening, hears the nurse and is furious at the betrayal. He summons Viru and asks him to discipline the nurse and chastise his sister, for he cannot trust himself in the rage which overtakes him:

If I have to discipline them I shall do them harm beyond all bounds. I shall burn the eyes of Vis with fire, then impale the nurse on the stake. I shall banish Ramin from this city and never mention his name again. I shall make a clear sweep on the shameful world and cleanse my soul of the shame of all three.[16]

Vis, though, is unrepentant and, in the presence of her husband and brother, boldly proclaims her love for Ramin.

Ramin is my choice in the two worlds, soul of my body, soul of my very life; he is the light of my eyes, my heart's ease, my lord, lover, sweetheart, friend. I have life only for the sake of love. I shall not relinquish loyalty and love for Ramin till I lose my life . . . Ramin is dearer to me than Shahru, dearer to me than Viru. I have told you my secret openly; be wrathful or merciful as you please. Kill me if you will, or hang me; I neither have abstained from Ramin nor ever shall.[17]

King Moubad, rage and bluster as he will, cherishes both Vis and Ramin as Mark does Tristan and Isolde. Nor can the

Persian patriarch really bring himself to harm either one of them. He sends Vis away to her mother's home. When Ramin begs the monarch's permission to go on a hunting trip to the country of Vis and Viru, Moubad is not fooled regarding the purpose of the journey. But he is rendered helpless by affection. 'Go now wheresoever you will, ill omen and sinister fortune your companion; your road full of snakes and the mountains you traverse full of leopards', he says and adds:

You have sacrificed your life to Vis; she too dies of longing for you. This evil nature will leave you at death, but by its means hell will materialize before you. My words are today by way of advice to you; bitter, like wine, but for your good . . . See that you do not count these words as sport; one does not sport with a marauding lion! When a cloud comes, do not fight with its rain, but with all speed arise from the track of flood.[18]

Ramin assures Moubad that he does not intend to see Vis and expresses all the proper dutiful sentiments towards him. He then leaves Moubad and promptly rejoins his beloved in her city where they remain together for seven months.

From now on the tale is of the lovers' deceptions of Moubad, deceptions of which the king is all too acutely cognizant. Yet Moubad remains paralysed by love, unable to cut through the tangle of his feelings of affection and rage towards the impulsive lovers and to act. He threatens, offers bribes, asks the pair to swear oaths that they are not deceiving him, locks up Vis when he goes away on his military campaigns, but all this is to no avail. The lovers swear their loyalty to him but cannot resist the imperious behest of their desire. Vis escapes from locked rooms to be together with her lover, and once, reminiscent of the parallel episode in Tristan and Isolde, substitutes the nurse in the regal bed while she goes to be with Ramin at night. Similarly, Ramin climbs cliffs to break into guarded castles and feigns illness when out on hunting expeditions or military campaigns with the king so as to secretly return to his beloved. Moubad is clarity itself in the diagnosis of his condition yet powerless to change it.

His, we conclude, is the shameful infatuation of the old man and the father's guilt at being stirred by a daughter's beauty. Indeed the story of Vis and Ramin is not theirs but Moubad's tragedy.

Alas for my fate! I have squandered army, treasure, and chattels without number, all for the sake of my heart; now I am bereft of sovereignity and heart. I am far from both heart and lover; far better to die on such a day! As soon as I take one step to seek her it is as if a limb drops from me. My distress has become manifold since my very soul has deserted me ... Let love be unsuitable for old age— but why must I have this love together with all this pain? This pain would make a child a doleful old man; see, then, to what an old man will be reduced. I chose an angel of paradise out of all the world and came face to face with hell in separation from her. The more I recall her cruelty and tyranny in my heart, the more love and devotion for her increase in me. The more I count her faults, the worse I become; you would swear I love her faults. Before I became a lover I was powerful, keen-sighted, and knowing in my own affairs. Now in love I am weak as water; I have grown to be unable to know even when I see! Alas, my reputation for sagacity! Alas, my tribulation in the ways of love! The wind has suddenly blown away all my endeavours; fire has forthwith fallen upon my soul. My heart has become blind from love and sees none of this world's desire.[19]

If Moubad, more sinned against then sinning, is often the object of the lovers', the author's and his own scorn, it can only be due to the deeply rooted conviction, shared across cultures, that erotic love is the sole preserve of youth and that passion's fires have no place in wintry bodies and tired old hearts. Until very recently, for example, Indian and European literary conventions demanded that the love of an older man for a girl, 'young enough to be his daughter', be an occasion for derisive hilarity or unmitigated ridicule. Through the centuries Moubad's self-loathing has been echoed by many others who have found themselves unable to quench the rekindling of erotic excitement which an infatuation of their waning years has brought them. The seventh-century Indian poet, Mayura, for instance, in his stanzas to a young girl,

vividly captures this combination of passion's drivenness and
the twinges of self-disgust:

> Rearing the green flame of his tail, the
> peacock casts the hen beneath him in the
> dust of the King's walk. He covers her,
> and we can hardly see her. She cries and he
> cries; and the copper moons in the green
> bonfire of his tail die down; and I am an
> old man.
>
> Old maker of careful stanzas as I am, I
> am also as the fishmonger's ass and smell
> to you in riot. He is insensate and
> does not care though the Royal retinue be
> passing. He climbs and is not otherwise
> contented. And he brays aloud.
>
> Once I told my king that night had
> fallen, and he said: 'It is as yet noon.'
> But I insisted, proclaiming: 'Night has
> descended in long shadows, because that
> woman has let fall her most heavy hair.'
> And he said: 'You are an old man, Mayura.'
>
> For now I break branches out of my
> path, seeing that the palms of your feet
> are red. The rain scent of the coupling
> of the trees comes again to the poets'
> assembly, and your hair is nightfall, and I
> am an old man.[20]

In the West, too, poets and playwrights from Chaucer to
Moliére to Shaw and O'Neill have offered similar tragicomic
renditions of elderly eroticism.

Vis and Ramin are often clear sighted about the blindness
of their passion, which they call demonic, and the dangers to
which it exposes them. Yet they too are unable to escape their
and all lovers' fate, a fate which strips them of all choices except the one dictated by passion. Vis, for instance, is quite
aware of her own ambivalence towards Ramin but feels im-

pelled to act as if her love for him was indeed blind. As she says to the nurse,

Even if Ramin be all beauty and grace, you yourself know how apt a seducer he is; he has no stock save of sweet oratory; he does not seek righteousness in love. His tongue has all appearance of sugar; but his nature is colocynth at the time of trial. I am involved with my lover in a hundred ploys, all in vain; at the time of love, surrounded by a hundred lovers and without a lover. I have lover, husband, and brother; at the hand of all three I burn in fire. I have become famous for taking husbands. I have suffered pain in the pursuit of love. My husband is not as other women's husbands; nor my lover like the lovers of the fair. Why must I have a husband and lover who cause my soul pain and distress? Had my fortune aided me, my sweetheart would have been none but Viru. Neither Moubad nor Ramin would have been my mate; nor would friends with enemies' ways have been my portion. One in feud against my life, like grief, another like stone and glass; the tongue of one does not bear out his heart; both tongue and heart of the other are cruel.[21]

Ramin, for all his passion for Vis and the flowery speeches professing his undying devotion, is neither insensible to the charms of other women nor unaware of the dangers of his love of Vis. At the transition point between the heroic and the romantic lover, Ramin regresses to the 'heroic' mould when he seeks and accepts the counsel of the sage Bihgu, who outlines for him the Islamic culture's pragmatic version of the 'heroic' lover:

You have enjoyed the desire of your heart from Vis; have plucked the fruit from the branch of love. Even if you see her for a hundred years she will be the same; she is no *huri* of Paradise not yet the moon in the sky. If you seek you shall find a thousand superior to her in beauty and purity. How can you dissipate life and youth with one woman in this profitless manner? If you take another lover, you will hold your bond as naught in your heart. You have known no sweetheart but her in the world; this is why you have chosen her before other beauties. You deal in stars, for you have not known the moon! Expel desire from your heart that has lost its way, try a road of your own; with your brother you hold in victorious sway the

wide world from India and China to Byzantium and Barbary; it is
not as if there is no other land but the march of Khursasan, or no
other sweetheart but Princess Vis; seek out an abode for yourself in
another quarter, seek out a silvery-blossomed beauty from every
city.

Review all the beauties till you find a sweetheart fairer than the
moon; a beauty such that beside her fair face Vis will slip from your
memory. Enjoy fortune and life: ever slake your desire of this
world.[22]

Not a Christian chastity but rather a man's phallic promiscuity presents itself as the cure for passion's poison: an utter surrender to possessive desire as an antidote to the unquenched
longing for a unique and irreplaceable woman.

Ramin follows the sage's advice and goes away to the city
of Gurab, where he meets and falls in love with Gul, whom he
marries. Vis is disconsolate and writes ten letters to Ramin be-
moaning the pain of separation and expressing her longing for
their union. Ramin is quickly sated with Gul and returns to
Vis.

After initial recriminations, the lovers are together again
and with the help of the nurse plan to usurp Moubad's
throne. While Moubad is away on a hunt, Ramin makes himself the master of the king's treasure after killing his elder
brother, who was guarding it. Before Moubad can react to
this fresh offense, he is killed by a wild boar, a recurring symbol, perhaps, of an instinctual greediness fatal to lovers.
Ramin ascends the throne with Vis as his queen and they rule
Iran for eighty years. Sensuality, conquest and the survival of
the fittest, of the young rather than ethical niceties or just re-
wards, reign with them.

Power and Love in India

In the Indian literature too, rivalry between father and son
centres on a father's incestuous attempt to defy generational

barriers rather than the son's wishes for sexual union with the mother. The Indian mythical imagination illuminates currents submerged and plumbed only psychoanalytically in Western and Middle Eastern counterparts. For these reasons, and in the absence of any single epic, we will overview the starker Indian variations of the father–daughter motif rather than adumbrate one otherwise obscure legend.

In myths and folktales undisguised sexual relations between father and daughter have been a subject of great interest and elaboration, surpassing by far the preoccupation with other incestuous pairings. The earliest creation myths, for instance, are mainly of father–daughter incest. These, along with later myths and folktales, share certain common features.

Significantly, the 'unnatural' lust is the father's alone. Rarely, if ever, does a daughter reciprocate or submit quietly to the father's sexual advances. The daughter generally tries to dissuade the father by appealing to his sense of propriety, pointing to this particular desire's incompatibility with *dharma*, the 'order of things'. Manasa's words to a lustful Shiva in the *Manasamangal* are typical of the daughter's entreaty: 'I am called Padma and you are my father, worshipped throughout the world. It is not proper for a father to ravish his daughter. God of gods, will you do this evil thing? If you ravish your daughter, Hara, you will suffer great shame'.[23]

In the oral folktales, whose point of view is perhaps more forcefully feminine than the one expressed in the more 'masculine' literary myths of a patriarchal culture, the daughter must actively guard her chastity through flight or stratagem. Thus in a Tamil story a king who wants to marry his four beautiful young daughters asks his ministers to make the necessary arrangements:

The ministers think he is mad, but humour him by saying that they would take care of it. Then they rush to the daughters with the bad news; the resourceful daughters pray to the goddess Parvati who transports them into a sealed lacquer palace in the heart of a jungle—a seven-storied palace, with living quarters on the first, and food and clothing of every kind stored up in the six upper stories to last several years. The palace has no doors or windows: a good image for virginity, indeed. Several years later, a prince strays into the jungle and hears strange music which lures him to the sealed palace, and it opens miraculously to let him in. He falls in love with all four of them and marries them. The young women's virginity was offered only to the rightful young man, after being denied to the incestuous father.[24]

In the folktales, more 'esterocentric' as they are, the mother (or her substitute—the goddess or the wise old woman) is a secret albeit passive helpmate, aiding the girl in guarding her virtue without openly confronting the father's power or arousing his ire. In the patriarchal myths, she is, in contrast, wholly absent. In these the resistance to the father's wishes is generally provided by sons, who serve to build the third side of the triangle. Like the counsellors to the king, however, they are mostly reduced to impotent entreaty as they appeal to their sire's rather tenuous sense of propriety: 'What is this disgusting act you are bent upon, to wish to enjoy your own daughter?'

In both the myths and the folktales, strikingly, a father is not merely blinded by lust but endeavours somehow to justify his contemplated transgression. Anticipating accusations of impropriety, he supports his amorous case on the basis of *property*. In the myths, the daughter is born, Minerva-like, of the father's body without the collaboration of a mother, and is thus solely and irrevocably his: the father literally creates the daughter out of his own substance. In one version of the Manasa myth, quoted by the anthropologist Ralph Nicholas, 'Dharma first gives birth to the Hindu trinity of Brahma, Vishnu and Siva, who establish themselves in meditation at three places on the seashore. Not seeing the faces of his three sons, Dharma's mind became sad, and he sighed a long breath. The birth of Manasa took place out of the exhalation; she arose sitting at Dharma's left side'.[25] Manasa is born androgynous, and it is the father who not only gives her the breath of life but also her sex by parting with his fingernail, 'the path where blood flows'. When Dharma determines to marry his daughter he first asks his sons the question: 'Is there any fault in enjoying the results of one's own effort?' The divine sons reluctantly agree that there is no fault in this.

In the folktales, the father's property rights are not those of the God-Father but are comparable to the mandate of a king reigning over his domain. In the Tamil tale mentioned earlier, when the king desires his daughters he first asks the family and the counsellor, 'If I have something precious, should I enjoy it myself or give it away?' In another Kannada tale, also narrated by Ramanujan, a king who falls in love with his youngest daughter asks his wives and counsellors, 'If there is a lovely thing born in my kingdom, to whom does it belong?' 'Of course, the best horses, elephants, pearls, precious stones and the loveliest women in a kingdom belong to the king', they answer.[26]

Daughters and all women in these narratives, as in those of Tristan and Isolde, and Vis and Ramin to some extent, are at one and the same time devalued and idealized. For the psychoanalyst, paradoxes like these point towards the narcissism of a possessive overlord who would rather enhance than expand his self.

Inherent in the myth of creation and ownership of the daughter is the longing for a woman who is totally complementary to the man and has no independent existence or wishes of her own.

The daughter is simultaneously the soul-mate, the idealized child-bride (and child-whore), female companion, and the good, nurturant mother. She is the girl-woman who is exquisitely responsive to the father's needs of the flesh and the spirit, simultaneously fulfilling his infantile longings and adult desires without making any threatening demands of her own. She is also the father's feminine and, to a male, passive and childish self.

The fantasy is vividly captured in the massage scene of the

Tamil tale which leads the king to fall in love with his four daughters:

One day the daughters are watching from the balcony while a clumsy tone deaf masseur is patting oil into the king's body with all the wrong rhythms. The daughters disgusted with the unmusical performance, come down from the balcony, dismiss the lout, and proceed to give the delighted father an oil bath, all four of them massaging and patting oil into his limbs in pleasing rhythms, conducting a very orchestra of touch.[27]

After the bath the king is filled with desire for his daughters.

In the myths, to fulfil his aching longing for the daughter, worshipful like a little girl yet ever-present like the mother, the father is prepared to pay the price of losing his creative paternal powers and his exalted status. In an (unconsummated) incest myth from the Matsya Purana—

When Brahma began his work of creation, the goddess Gayatri appeared in the form of a girl from one half of Brahma's body, who mistakenly took her for his daughter. Seeing that form of exquisite beauty, he was fired with love ... the sons of Brahma, taking Gayatri for their sister, expressed indignation and contempt ... Gayatri began to circumambulate him in reverence ... he felt shy of turning his head in her direction, as his sons were close by. He therefore created four heads, each facing one of the directions, so that he might see her undisturbed. Seeing Brahma in this state, Gayatri went to heaven, and as she journeyed upward, Brahma put a fifth head on top ... After this Brahma lost the powers that he had acquired by asceticism.[28]

Besides its roots in the unconscious wishes and desires of individual fantasy, the conception of the daughter as the sole creation and possession of the father also reflects the reality of traditional Indian social structure. In India, as in other patriarchal societies, the general notion of women as the property of men has shaped and permeated the organization of social relations between the sexes. The informal realities of the situation may have varied in different regions and at different periods of history. Formally, however, men's sexual authority over women has been consistently formulated in terms of depersonalizing property rights, though sometimes with the addition of the typical Hindu concern around purity and pollution. 'A wife and a cooking vessel should always be carefully preserved, for they are consecrated by the touch of the owner and desecrated by the touch of others'.[29] As in the Biblical injunctions contained in Leviticus—and pointed out by Judith Herman—it is clear that incest violations are not offenses against the women taken for sexual use but against the man in whom the rights of ownership, use, and exchange are vested.[30] As far as father–daughter incest is concerned, 'Every man is thus expressly forbidden to take the daughters of his kinsmen, but only by implication is he forbidden to take his *own* daughter. The patriarchal God sees fit to pass over father–daughter incest in silence.'[31] The silence is also shared by the Indian lists familiar to us which have enumerated prohibited sexual relations. For instance, one of the longest such inventories says:

If a man has sexual intercourse with any of these women: sister, mother, mother's sister, mother-in-law, a wife of a paternal uncle or of a friend or of a pupil, a sister, sister's friend, daughter-in-law, the wife of one's Vedic teacher, a woman of the same *gotra*, one who has come for protection, a queen, an ascetic woman, one's wet nurse, a woman performing *vrata* (religious ritual) and a brahmana woman, he becomes guilty of the sin of the violator of the guru's bed [i.e. incest]. For that crime no other punishment is laid down except that of the cutting of the penis.[32]

Indian injunctions against incest differ from their Western counterparts in that they extend beyond prohibitions of sexual intercourse with kinswomen. Central to the Indian view of incest is its definition as a sexual offense against a 'weighty' (guru), elder male. Incest is *gurutalpabhigamana*, the 'violation of the guru's bed'. The concern seems less with the son's forbidden sexuality within the family than with the clash between different generations of men over sexual rights to younger women. The Hindu version of Darwin and Freud's 'primal horde' has filicide rather than parricide as the outcome of the generational conflict over access to women. In most Indian myths the father's protagonist is initially not the individual son but a band of brothers. Parricide as a filial response to the father's encroachment on a son's prerogatives is an extremely rare denouement, and the following is more the exception than the rule:

> Prajapati, the father of the gods, the creator, cast his eyes upon his own daughter, desiring 'May I pair with her'. So saying, he had intercourse with her. This was a crime in the eyes of gods, who said, 'He is guilty who acts thus to his own daughter, our sister: pierce him through'. Rudra aimed at him and pierced him. Half of his seed fell to the ground.[33]

A son may remonstrate with his father or else simply acquiesce to his wishes. The culturally favoured reaction, however, is for the son to renounce actively his own sexuality. His thus becomes a self-castration that sacrifices to the father the son's right to sexual activity and generational ascendancy.[34]

Two of the most popular illustrations of this theme are the myths of Bhisma and Yayati from the Mahabharata. Though these myths are constituted of a complex sequence of events, with many interwoven themes, their central episode which the culture 'remembers' again and again in its literary and artistic creations is the son's sexual self-sacrifice.

The king Santanu, Bhisma's father, falls in love with a fisher girl. He goes to the girl's father to ask her hand. The fisherman agrees to the match on condition that the son born to his daughter inherit the kingdom. Santanu cannot give his consent to this condition. He returns to his palace where he sinks into a depression born of an old man's unfulfilled passion for a young girl. Bhisma, on coming to know the reason for his father's grief, goes to the fisherman. Bhishma promises both the renunciation of the kingdom and of sexual life that could result in a progeny threatening the rights of the sons born to the fisher girl. 'Then on his father's behalf he said to the famous maiden, "Ascend my chariot, mother. We shall go to our house." ' Bhishma then brings the girl to the capital of his father's kingdom and hands her over to Santanu who bestows the boon that death would come to Bhishma only at his own bidding.[35]

King Yayati, cursed by a sage to suffer old age, wants to live a life of sensual pleasure and asks his five sons, one after another, to give him their youth for a thousand years. The elder sons refuse and are cursed by the father. Puru, the youngest son, agrees: 'Sir, I shall do as you say. I shall take on, O king, your guilt and old age. Take my youth from me and enjoy the pleasures you are seeking. Covered with your old age and wearing your aged body, I shall live as you say and give you my youth'.[36] Puru is blessed by the father and later inherits the kingdom.

If the power of Freud's Oedipus complex is derived from the son's guilt over a fantasized and eventually unconscious parricide, the 'Bhishma complex' is charged with the dread of filicide. In stressing the father's envy—and thus the son's persecution anxiety—as a primary motivation in the father–son relationship, Indian culture inverts the psychoanalytically postulated causality between the fantasies of parricide and filicide. The Bhishma solution of symbolic self-castration deflects the father's envy and the son's primal fear of annihilation at his hands, while at the same time it provides a way of keeping the bond of affection between father and son intact. An enduring genital inhibition and a renunciation of all competitive feelings with the father seem to be the typical Indian solution of the 'Bhishma complex'.

A Return to Oedipus the King

The story of Vis and Ramin and Indian myths and folktales in the same vein are as much about fathers as sons, as much therefore about rivalry and violence as about sex. But, then, too, so is the legend of Oedipus himself, a parable which Erich Fromm once suggested had less to do with incestuous yearning or the erotic *per se* than with a patriarchal power struggle and the violence of parents towards children.[37]

Laius and his son Oedipus were direct descendants of Cadmus, founder of the city later named Thebes. As in the famed curse upon the House of Atreus, Cadmus's line also had been blighted by crimes against nature. With these as a background the terrible tragedy which was to consume the father and his legendary son was played out. These original sins involved not fathers at first, but rather mothers and sons. In so far as they set in relief the relations then prevalent between them, they may help explain the filicidal disposition of the father.

Mount Cithaeron, near the city of Thebes, on whose slopes Oedipus, fresh from the womb, was left to die, had witnessed a breach of parenthood, a crime against nature, long before the infant's birth. King Cadmus had several daughters, among them Semele and Agave. Semele lay with Zeus, their union producing a son, Dionysus, the ambisexual sybarite of the Greek pantheon. The Thebans disputed Semele's claims to divine insemination, and when she was killed by lightning because of her wish to see Zeus—the father—in his true form, her son Dionysus was denied his birthright, the status of god. Orphaned and forced to wander Greece (like Laius and Oedipus after him), Dionysus returned to Thebes to exact his revenge. His hedonism and demonic charisma infected the city's women, who became his Bacchanalian followers or Maenads.

Among the women was Semele's sister Agave. Agave had a son, the Theban prince Pentheus. Straining in his display of martial masculinity, he energetically persecuted Dionysus' crazed disciples in an effort to suppress their bisexuality, lustfulness and savage abandon. But Pentheus's vain war with instinctuality came to a hideously ironic conclusion. According to Euripides' *Bacchae*, intrigued by the Dionysian mysteries in spite of himself, dressed in women's clothing, Pentheus spied upon the Maenads. Having mistaken his golden wig for a lion's mane and him for a cub (the paranoid distortion is telling), Agave and the other women murdered him, dismembering the body and ripping off Pentheus's head. Hence Thebes's first filicide at a mother's hands. Agave's Dionysian filicide, which figures as the first horror in the House of Cadmus, may be symbolic of the relations then prevalent between mothers and sons.

Where Oedipus was able to solve the Riddle of the Sphinx, the mystery of life, it seems that Pentheus may have succumbed because of his ignorance of his own instinctuality, specifically his bisexuality. Disavowing desire, he fell prey to what analysts would later describe as the emasculating, murderous power of the 'preoedipal' and 'phallic' mother. In her grasp this first son was effeminized, castrated, and destroyed.

But Oedipus escaped her reach, only then to fall victim to an indifferent mother and, above all, to an ignorant, weak, authoritarian, and by all accounts homosexual, father. He was a father who had much in common with his would-be forebear, Pentheus.

As a baby, Laius himself had been subjected to abandonment and persecution. His father, Labdacus, the ruling Theban king, died when he was one year old, leaving Laius to the care of his mother. When his uncle usurped the throne Laius was expelled and forced to wander Greece before he could return to Thebes to reclaim his kingship.

Laius's life as a boy with his mother is an uncharted chapter in the legend, of course. What happened after this, in Laius's adulthood, however, is well known, having been chronicled by poets and dramatists, and indicates that he carried common practice beyond the bounds. While visiting Piza, Laius kidnapped and sodomized Chrysippus, the beautiful illegitimate son of his host, King Pelops. The eroticism of the act, the pedophilia proper, was not a crime in the Hellenic scheme of things: but violation of hospitality, overbearingness and violence were; Laius's kidnapping and rape were bonafide transgressions.

They infuriated the father, Pelops. He cursed Laius, and the gods condemned him to remain for a long time childless and/or then to be both murdered by the son he eventually conceived and replaced by him in his wife's bed. The versions vary somewhat. Thus, the famous oracle, sealing the destinies of father and son, did not spring into being as a matter of chance. Rather, it bespoke revenge—a retaliation for violations perpetrated by the man so caught up in his self and his sadomasochistic assertions of it that he is oblivious to a boy's needs. Oedipus is fated to *avenge* Chrysippus, his alter ego. Laius must die; such is his generational fate.

Not all fathers hate and maim their sons. Not all sons rise up to degrade or kill patriarchs. These are only partial developmental fictions, and, as we have seen, even the imperious Moubad struggles mightily with his ambivalence.

Fathers and sons also love each other. This love makes poignant a son's predestined challenge to the father's authority and converts desire, so natural at the dawn of one's love, into torment, or, at the least, 'tragic bliss'. In the next chapter we turn to the ambivalence between fathers and sons, to the qualities of regret and to the harsh pangs of conscience suffered because of increasingly unknown crimes of the heart.

CHAPTER SIX

THE CONSCIENCE OF THE KING

Any interpreter of a legend of love perforce imposes his or her preoccupation on narratives which yet live on in their own right and thus defy reduction to a single theme. Is the Tristan and Isolde tale about young love, adultery, or about the interplay—one vibrant with theological resonances—of love and death? Or does its abiding allure owe itself to a synthesis of all these and of yet other less obvious elements?

Like Romeo and Juliet, the story of Tristan and Isolde has been retold many times. In different historical eras its various narrators have naturally exploited the plight of the lovers according to the place granted to Eros in their era and culture. In the process reinterpretations, aesthetic and philosophical, have happened upon the hidden and repressed determinants of the reigning ideology of love. Thus, for instance, against a backdrop of the twelfth-century age of courtly love, with its exaltation of the erotic and of the spiritual benefits arising from being in the state of pure love, the poet Beroul emphasized the *tragic* bliss of the lovers—the sublime loss, the pain and bitterness of passion freed from the confines of sanc-

tioned marriage. In contrast, nineteenth-century Romanticism, with its official canons of sentimental monogamy and
love's permanence, the clinging vine of nature and the essential chastity of women, would none the less uncover the darker underside of its own ideology of Eros in Tristan and
Isolde's undeniable sensuality, adultery and the volatility of
passion.

The current ideology of love has been most influenced by
psychoanalysis, which, at its inception and in its heart still, is
an inquiry into sexual desire. Freudian man expects that we
look for the most profound truths about love and the lover
not in the higher planes of human spirituality but in the infer-
nal regions, in the nether world of desire's domain, ultimately
in the unconscious. The cultural vigour of psychoanalysis, in
fact, is rooted in the idea, as Foucault puts it, that 'truth' itself
resides in the depths of sex.[1] What distinguishes the
psychoanalytic proclamation is its insistence that desire takes
root in infancy, grows secretly within the family and has as its
first objects the child's tender caretakers. The progressive detachment of sexuality from its incestuous origins is seen to be
the fundamental task of every life. Indeed the negotiation of
this disengagement from the past exerts far-reaching effects
on how the individual contends not only with subsequent
forks in the pathways of desire, but, for that matter, with all
of life itself.

In the fundamental and, to the uninitiated, perverse spirit
of our classic psychoanalytic enterprise, we would discern in
the legend of Tristan and Isolde and in the tragedy of Hamlet
the Dane, as we have in Vis and Ramin, vagaries of the incest
motif. No doubt this is not a novel reading of them. In the
first of these stories, as in Vis and Ramin, we would again re-
mark on the reversal involved: notably the fact that Mark the
king and surrogate father, like his Persian counterpart
Moubad, has laid claim to a 'daughter', a young woman of
Tristan's generation.

However, both in Tristan and Isolde and Hamlet—stories
rooted in the religious and secular tradition of Christianity in

the feudal world—another of love's complex ingredients receives special accent: the love of the father. Earlier, in our love stories, we have touched on this element in Majnun's tender relationship to his father, or in Moubad's paternal love for both the lovers struggling against the terrible violence which he harbours towards a Vis and Ramin who make a fool of him. Now, though, the tender bond of father and son rises to the fore, the other yearning where the father is the object of desire. Thus Mark adores the youth who fills a special void in his heart while Tristan serves him unstintingly, agonizing when the magic of the woman he has courageously won for his lord washes away his fealty.

In *Hamlet*, a play about the developmentally later fate of the Oedipus complex, persons are replaced by psychic proxies, by the agencies of the mind. Thus Hamlet struggles with incestuous impulses unknown to him and with moral injunctions which, through a series of ingenious and unconscious manoeuvres, divert him from his filial duty.

But now the first of the legends; we have set the stage: enter the inner eye of the analyst.

Tristan and Isolde

Tristan was a child of sadness, born to the sister of King Mark of Cornwall and his devoted ally Rivalen, both dead before the dawn of the hero's consciousness. His identity safeguarded by Rohalt, Tristan as a young man anonymously entered the knightly service of his uncle the king. Embraced by his lord, 'the courageous knight proved his prowess in arms and at the harp.'[2] At last his protector divulged Tristan's genealogy and the intuitive avuncular or indeed paternal love Mark bore his nephew was now secured as 'mutual love grew up in their hearts. By day Tristan followed King Mark at pleas and in saddle; by night he slept in the royal room with the councillors and peers, and if the King was sad he would harp to him to soothe his care.'[3] Echoing the age-old theme in *Layla and Majnun* of the favourite son whose father 'could no longer live in joy without him', Tristan soon became the target of the other lords' fratricidal envy and enmity.

In the service of King Mark Tristan engaged and slew the giant Knight Morholt of Ireland, uncle to Isolde of the Fair Blond Hair. Taking note of a splinter of the youthful victor's sword in the skull of her relative, Princess Isolde declared her hatred of Tristan, as yet a stranger to her, and swore vengeance. Wounded and poisoned, Tristan, playing upon his harp all the while, sailed off in search of cure, eventually drifting to Whitehaven where, again anonymously, he was healed by Isolde, escaping before she could discover who he was.

King Mark is pressed by his barons to take a wife who would give him an heir. Mark, however, wants his dear nephew to inherit the kingdom and would sacrifice his own marital and sexual happiness on Tristan's account. A good son, concerned for his father's welfare, Tristan too joins the importuning of the other lords, threatening that if the king does not take a wife he will himself go overseas and serve some other great king. Hard-pressed on all sides, Mark hits on the ploy of saying that he is ready to marry, but only the mysterious possessor of a long golden hair deposited in his hall by two swallows. Tristan recognizes the hair as that of Isolde and sets sail for Isolde's land to win her as the queen for his revered uncle.

Once more in Whitehaven, Tristan slays a dragon, only to be poisoned by its lethal tongue. Again his health is restored by Isolde the Fair, whose hand he has won by virtue of his heroic feat. She bathes and anoints him, gazing and musing on his body's beauty. But as the knight lies naked and defenseless in his bath, Isolde discovers the heavily notched sword that had broken off in Morholt's skull. Fitting the missing piece to the blade, she realizes that it was he who had conquered her uncle—and, we might add, his niece's heart. She is about to

avenge her uncle when the youth's ardour and nobility overwhelm the princess. She relents, kissing rather than killing the
vulnerable hero.

At the assembly that follows, Tristan's identity is revealed.
Overcoming the Irish lords' natural desire for revenge, he lays
claim to Isolde— not for himself, he further declares, but for
King Mark. The princess's response is more passionate than
dutiful; she is beside herself at being spurned and trembles for
shame and anguish at the betrayal now of her heart. Thus
Tristan, 'having won her, disdained her; the fine story of the
hair of gold was but a lie: it was to another he was delivering
her. So, for the love of King Mark, did Tristan by guile and
force conquer the queen of the hair of gold'.[4] Tristan wins his
lady and cedes her to his lord—fealty in deceit. With this act,
even before imbibing the fateful love potion, the terrible iro-
nies and binds of the love story are set in motion. Truth and
deception, loyalty and betrayal, worth and baseness, can no
longer be pieced out separately. Henceforth they will always
occur together; Tristan's fidelity to Mark would carry with it
infidelity towards Isolde, his constancy towards his lover a
betrayal of filial love and knightly duty he owes and feels for
his uncle and lord. Two loves, filial (perhaps 'homosexual')
and heterosexual passion, vie with each other.

As they embark, Isolde, like Vis in our earlier story and like
women before and after her, bewails the lot in which a marriage necessitates a forcible snapping of a girl's ties with her
home and with those who she has loved, and by whom she
has been loved in turn.

Seated under the tent in which she had secluded herself with Brangien the maid, she wept, remembering her land. Where were these
strangers dragging her? Toward whom? Toward what fate? When
Tristan approached her and sought to soothe her with soft words,
angered, she repulsed him, and hate swelled in her heart. He had
come to Ireland, he the ravisher, he the murderer of Morholt; with
guile he had torn her from her mother and her land; he had not
deigned to keep her for himself, and now he was carrying her away
as his prey, over the waves, to the land of the enemy. 'Accursed be

the sea that bears me, for rather would I be dead on the earth where I was born than live out there beyond . . .'[5]

But does she not also hate Tristan *because* she loves him so? So intensely that she, like him, will renounce all other fealties and the succour they offer?

Isolde's mother has entrusted her maid Brangien with a love potion, the 'philtre', for the lips of Mark and his queen on their wedding night. By chance, Isolde and Tristan drink the brew together, mistaking for mere wine 'Passion and Joy most sharp, and Anguish without end, and Death.' To the more modern eye the fateful externality of the love potion is an excuse and metaphor for an invasion from within, the tide of erotic passion that washes away the dam erected by a vigilant conscience or 'superego'. The drinking of the philtre releases the lovers' sudden realization of the blind impulsion they have already felt for each other and which, in the clarity of their drunkenness, they recognize as irrevocable. The convention is necessary in the Christian and chivalric tradition where duty and goodness, the stuff of conscience, must otherwise win out over passion and desire. Unlike the Islamic value system the Western ethos grants only religious passion a legitimate life of its own. And there is truth in this: most of us relent and yield to our fathers and the values associated with them rather than to the full force of duty-defying desire.

Yet even as Isolde instinctively falls into using the master–servant metaphors so dear to the hearts and tongues of lovers ('you are my lord and my master, and I your slave'), she is aware of the hatred and the torment it will cause her: 'henceforth forever never to know joy without pain again'. While 'a tenderness more sharp than hatred' tears her, Isolde agonizes:

Ah, why did I not sharpen those wounds of my wounded singer, or let die that dragon-slayer in the grasses of the marsh? Why did I not, while he lay helpless in the bath, plant on him the blow of the sword I brandished? But then I did not know what now I know! . . . And what is that you know now, Iseult? What is it that torments you? . . . Ah, all that I know torments me, and all that I see. This sky and this sea torment me, and my body and my life.[6]

Ambivalence, the poles of love and hate, more than in *Romeo and Juliet*, courses through and distorts the passion of the two lovers.

To protect her mistress, Brangien, disguised as Isolde, sacrifices her virginity to King Mark, entranced by the few drams remaining of the potion. But again the potion serves as symbol for inner passion. The noble sensibility of his heart, more than any drugs or sorcery, is what secures the king's tenderness towards his beloved Isolde and Tristan throughout all the trials to follow. His forbearance makes the lovers' guilt–laden plight all the more excruciating.

Subject to a paranoia of sorts, Isolde plans to have her devoted Brangien, privy to the lover's secret, murdered, only to have the would-be slayers take pity on the faithful servant. Once defied, loyalty and morality lose their consistent hold on lovers, imperilling all other ties and the less-than-erotic love that secure them. Notwithstanding her mistress's cruel treachery, Brangien, having escaped, returns to Isolde and is reconciled. What, we may wonder, is so ravishing, so charismatic about their love that they repeatedly win forgiveness from those their blind passion would destroy? The same forces which inexorably draw the two together—their lovability—exert a mesmerizing effect on all the others who also love them: Brangien, Mark, and later Kaherdin.

Deceitful in spite of himself, Tristan continues to betray Mark and to suffer in his betrayal. Unlike the purer loves we have explored earlier, his passion becomes debasing rather than elevating. This is so because of the unwanted cruelties involved and, consequently, the upsurges of self-denigrating guilt. Tristan is doubly moved to surrender—not only to his sensuous mistress but also to a dear overlord. He becomes his own executioner as Mark fails to punish him consistently and thus relieves the remorse which has come to replace his devotion. 'I have come lower by far', Tristan had first lamented after the revelations caused by the love philtre,

for it is not his land I covet. Fair uncle, who loved me orphaned ere even you knew me in the blood of your sister Blanchefleur, you that wept as you bore me to that boat alone, why did you not drive out the boy that was to betray you? Ah! What thought was that! Iseult is yours and I am but your vassal; Iseult is yours and I am your son; Iseult is yours and may not love me.[7]

Now, when 'in the fire of his fever desire without redress bore him like a bolting horse toward the well girdled towers which shut in the Queen', the sexual rivalry between father and son cannot be denied, the thought he shrank away from in the beginning has been long acted upon. Tristan's self-lament bespeaks some of the suffering of the guilt-ridden 'oedipal boy'. Conflict pollutes. 'My body', he groans in secret to a foreking king, 'now exhales the smell of a more repulsive poison, and your love no longer knows how to overcome your honour'. Meanwhile, Isolde's dreams yield her up to ecstatic agonies, of 'running to gates', and 'sharp scythes, traps of felons, that cut her tender knees' of 'weakness and falling', of 'wounds [that] had left her blood upon the grounds'.

Masochistic as well, these are none the less different sentiments from the wounding self-surrender extolled by our pre-oedipal lovers, who would be devoured and absorbed by their beloved. This is 'moral masochism', according to psychoanalytic usage, an acquiescence to the beloved father and the superego which is his psychic imprint.

And what of Mark who finds himself in an unwanted erotic competition with his would-be-son, Tristan? Ignoring all amorous clues that come his way or are called to his attention by Tristan's detractors, he continues to retain his naivete and hence his faith in the pair. Again and again, 'felons' who 'hate beauty and prowess' (but who none the less speak truth) plant seeds of doubt and jealousy in the king, while the adulterous lovers repeatedly win back his confidence. Evidently, goodness requires the fatherly king's willing self-deception, the wink of an eye towards those one cares for.

Mark deserves to be loved—he is the good, gullible, unseeing parent solaced by denials of telltale signs of the child's heart. He simply cannot bring himself to acknowledge the cruelty towards him even when, finally, with the insistent clamour of his barons' voice about the demands of 'honour' ringing in his ears, he must as a ruler act to rid himself of the rebellious lovers.

Eluding falls from cliffs, trials by fire and leprous lechery, all erotic and specifically masochistic metaphors as well, the exiled Tristan and Isolde at last find themselves like animals living off the land, sinking deeper and deeper into mere subsistence and near bestiality. Ogrin, an ascetic hermit, guru-like enjoins Tristan to repent, adding that 'A man that is traitor to his lord is worthy to be torn by horses and burnt upon the faggot, and wherever his ashes fall no grass shall grow and all tillage is waste, and the trees and the green things die'.[8] The threat of eternal immolation and of unrelieved damnation exceeds punishment by death or any so-called 'castration threat'. Tristan remonstrates that the queen is no longer the king's in as much as he gave her up to the lepers. Yet, at some level, Mark's prerogative of royalty and seniority, sanctioned further by the marriage vows, touch Tristan and strike a deep chord. When at last the king rediscovers them lying in the forest, the pair clothed and inexplicably separated by Tristan's naked sword, Mark, in spirit, enfolds them to his bosom, proclaiming the barrier between them a proof of chastity. Reality, it seems, once again, simply cannot impinge on honour and the unthinkable notion that a dear son may successfully covet a woman who belongs to his father. All the baldfaced evidence heretofore of his cuckoldry—trails of blood and flour, nude bodies wrapped round each other—evaporate as if insubstantial in the face of Mark's wish to trust and exonerate. Moreover, the sudden rush of chastity and the reassertion of the marital and generational taboos seem mysteriously to revive the youth and vitality of the lovers, rescuing them from the anomie of an existence without Mark the father's grace and forgiveness. In this epic and its variants the erotic resides essentially in the tension of inaccessibility, and the implicit incest taboo, the alien invasion of the philtre serving to discharge the hero and heroine of any dampening, dulling guilt, while awakening their souls with more poignant and monumental remorse.

The grand oedipal drama reaches a climax when, symbolically, the king replaces Tristan's ring on Isolde's finger, and the sword which lodged in Morholt's skull with his own possessive ornament and implement of power. He enters the young lovers' primal scene, interposing his presence between their bodies such that any love-making—penetration or inception—will perforce involve his claims. At the scene's conclusion Isolde awakens as if in a dream, witness to the claims Mark again makes on her. 'Then in her sleep a vision came to Iseult. She seemed to be in a great wood and two lions near her fought for her, and she gave a cry and woke, and the gloves fell upon her breast; at the cry Tristan woke and made to seize his sword, and saw by the golden hilt that it was the King's'.[9]

The dream in many of its particulars has proved a reality. With this, and the king's demonstration of tender forbearance, Tristan longs to re-enter Mark's retinue to serve him as 'my lord and father' and is given pause only by the notion that in submitting he must relinquish Isolde to him. Sorrow and guilt now overtake him as, along with his lover, he contemplates the king's compassion and longs all the more for his embracing and ennobling love. The lovers' agony in the absence of Mark's patronage is as great as is his in the face of their miscreance; both he and they would restore presence and goodwill. Honour, agape, and perhaps the starker homosexual desire in which they are based exert pressures that would stem the more obvious erotic tide that sweeps the lovers along. Ultimately Tristan is to be banished while Isolde is surrendered to Mark and welcomed back to her husband and lord's chamber. Symbolically, as foretold in Isolde's dream, in exercising his nuptial rights, Mark can now enter and be entered by a Tristan who has been there as well.

Eros, however, the god of heterosexual love, the biology of destiny, reasserts itself. The reunions and ruses continue as

Tristan and Isolde are moved to tryst and connive to prove
their innocence. Tristan reappears in one guise or another,
and in each instance Mark renders himself again and again
gullible. When they are finally parted Tristan, self-exiled in
Wales, sends Isolde as his emissary a little dog with a tinkling
bell reminiscent of the strains of the harp that first carried him
to her breast; a memento in miniature embodying his smaller,
more helpless, abject self, and pointing to his final surrender.
Disengaged, almost a nomad now, he has wandered in and
out of guilt's perimeter—back into a psychologically more
primal realm. Tristan now reminds us of our other lovers—
Romeo and Majnun.

In Brittany, pained and lonely, having again triumphed in
combat, Tristan meets and marries another Isolde, she of the
White Hands. Yet his tie to the first Isolde—the real thing, the
first love—is abiding. The second Isolde, for all her beauty, is
but a poor substitute, and Tristan cannot consummate their
nuptials. He had accused Isolde the Fair of 'treason' in yielding herself to the king, but laments his own betrayal of her
whom he loved. This breach of vows, provoking the jealous
fury of a woman scorned, seals the lovers' doom. Once again
the marriage tie, in this instance Tristan's rather than Mark's,
will intrude on the lover's truer bond, as once more transgressions of the heart vie with those of the social order, rendering
ambiguous any determination as to who and what is being
violated. The major theme of the epic—to whom does Isolde
really belong—receives a minor variation: to which Isolde
does Tristan now owe his constancy? Who possesses him?
Significantly, he has saved his body for Isolde the Fair, owner
of his soul.

He confesses the heartfelt faithfulness belied by momentary lapse in intent and breaks the new Isolde's heart. Accompanied by his brother-in-law, Kaherdin, who in spite of
familial obligation yields to the veracity of illicit and therefore
pure love and to the magnificence of his brother-in-law, Tristan sets out for Cornwall and Isolde. Disguised as a leper, and
then in another abject guise, that of the fool, Tristan and

Isolde meet, part and then meet again. Degraded and mocked, Tristan creeps nightly from his dirty hole to his love's chamber as guilt, agony and now compulsion erode his knightliness. The 'heroic' lover is now truly the 'romantic'. With this the longing for Liebestod overtakes Isolde as well. Like her lover, she pleads to be discharged of any other binding tie, to float in an everlasting and unseeing union— a paradise lost and found anew. 'Oh friend', she says,

> fold your arms round me and strain me so that our hearts may break and our souls go free at last. Take me to that happy place of which you told me long ago. The fields whence none return, but where great singers sing their songs forever. Take me now.[10]

Driven from the land, the death promised in the philtre ready to claim him, Tristan is wounded in an ambush, and feels his life being sapped by the spear's poison. He entreats Kaherdin to effect a reunion with Isolde and, it seems, to tell her half truths:

> Thank you, friend: this is my prayer: take this ring, it is a sign between her and me, and when you come to her land pass yourself at court for a merchant, and show her silk and stuffs, but make so that she sees the ring, for then she will find some ruse by which to speak to you in secret. Then tell her that my heart salutes her; tell her that she alone can bring me comfort; tell her that if she does not come, I shall die. Tell her to remember our past time, and our great sorrows, and all the joy there was in our loyal and tender love. And tell her to remember that draught we drank together. Tell her to remember the oath I swore to serve a single love, for I have kept that oath.[11]

Has he? 'A woman's wrath is a fearful thing.' Nursing her husband, Isolde of the White Hands secretly plots her revenge. Tristan overlooks the sea from the vantage of high cliffs, like Aegeus awaiting the white sail of Theseus' returning vessel. Meanwhile, traversing the perils of storm, Isolde the Fair dreams of a boar's head befouling her skirts—a menstrual symbol perhaps, and, with it, a foretelling of miscarried passion and violent barrenness. The head is

Tristan's as well, the dream an augury of his death, and Isolde realizes she will never see her lover alive again. And indeed, he *is* deceived by his wife, who Medea-like tells him of a black rather than a white sail. Tristan repeats 'Isolde my friend' four times and dies. While one Isolde laments her jealous evil deed, the other kisses the cold eyes of her beloved and gives up her soul.

Parted in life, the lovers now attain their Liebestod despite a grieving Mark's efforts to isolate their graves, testimony again to the inexorability of their compelling passion. Mark cedes his generational mandate at last, conceding the eternal vitality of the lovers united only in death.

When King Mark heard of the death of these lovers, he crossed the sea and came to Brittany; and he had two coffins hewn, for Tristan and Iseult, one of chalcedony for Iseult, and one of beryl for Tristan. And he took their beloved bodies away with him upon his ship to Tintagel, and by a chantry to the left and right of the aspe he had their tombs built round. But in one night there sprang from the tomb of Tristan a green and leafy briar strong in its branches and in the scent of its flowers. It climbed the chantry and fell to root again by Iseult's tomb. Thrice did the peasants cut it down, but thrice it grew again strong. They told the marvel to King Mark, and he forbade them to cut the briar any more.[12]

Hamlet

Hamlet is quite possibly a play more oedipal than *Oedipus Rex* itself, as Freud's disciple Ernest Jones, himself a man by no means immune to the charms of women, so ably pointed out.[13] We are all familiar with the dark brooding play and its black-garbed prince, whose self-torture connotes a sublime metaphysical complexity, which, hand in hand with an obsessional self-indulgence, renders him sick and pale and given to too much thought. He is a man searching for truth but immobilized by conflict. Contemplative and discerning but stupefied, he is quite unlike Tristan—knottier, more complex, slower to act. Yet, we shall argue, the emotional dilemma of the melancholy Dane is heir to that of the child of sadness. Lacking in manifest romance Hamlet's is the most subtle of our tales, one in which lovers exist only in the mind's eye and, for that matter, only in the hero's unconscious. It is a tale of incest desired and of mysterious guilt.

Against the backdrop of a more external drama an inner one is being waged as well, one that is sometimes at odds with real-life imperatives. Hamlet has simply succumbed to a 'neurosis', precipitated by parallelling events but independent of them. It is a neurosis which, like all others, is a psychological story of secret love, intelligible only through interpretation. Such stories ('infantile neurosis'), psychoanalysis informs us, are universal, concluding our oedipal struggles and giving all of us pause before the instinctual rush of adolescence brings us back to our senses.

Shakespeare's story begins, as do so many others, with a feast, at once nuptial and triumphant in nature. Old King Hamlet of Denmark has died, apparently of natural causes, but, we soon discover, at the hands of his brother, Hamlet's uncle, Claudius, who has claimed both his wife Gertrude and his throne. They fete their wedding while Prince Hamlet, son, nephew and stepson, broods apart.

As Claudius' regal ascendancy is celebrated, Hamlet finds himself more preoccupied with the betrayal of devotion on the part of the mother and with her sexuality than with his uncle's ready claim to power, a power that is rightfully Hamlet's own. Perhaps sensing his emotional complicity with Claudius' usurpation, Hamlet is more enraged at his mother, consumed by the images of her lewdness and treachery.

> Ere yet the salt of the most unrighteous tears had
> Left the flushing in her galled eyes,
> She married. O, most wicked speed, to post
> With such dexterity to incestuous sheets!

It is not nor it cannot come to good:
But break, my heart; for I must hold my tongue.[14]

His father's death, the loss of the kingdom, matters of state, these are beyond his clouded purview at the time as he harps on his mother's betrayal of her marital bonds and her failure to mourn.

Why, she would hang on him. As if increase of appetite had
grown
By what it fed on; and yet, within a month
Let me not think on't . . . Frailty, thy name is woman![15]

'Frailty, thy name is woman!' which Freud later echoed when he proclaimed that given a clever seducer a woman's values and sense of self will shift accordingly, is an exclamation charged with irony. Misdirected, Hamlet is easily as 'frail' as any female in the play. His weakness is of a different origin, stemming from excess rather than a want of self-criticism, but it too shakes his masculinity. Sexuality becomes something foul, or, in Hamlet's words, 'rank and gross in nature.' Yet, one senses, his persistent disparagement of his mother's sexuality reveals a profound fascination—with her and with his father. It is against this rather than the usurper that he has fortified himself.

Whatever else he may find himself unconsciously subject to, Hamlet's love for his dead father is as great as is his glorification of him. Indeed its intensity is quite remarkable and Hamlet seems to be in love with the king's image. When the King and Queen, pretenders already in Hamlet's as yet unenlightened eyes, exit, Hamlet compares the interloper to his father as a satyr to Hyperion, the one not only ugly in the face of the other's beauty but also specifically and crudely sensual.

There is a further dimension to Hamlet's idealization of his father's magnificence, one which reveals the workings of his own savage conscience. At the start of the play Hamlet wishes for some sort of self-degradation or dissolution, a release from the tensions he suffers, as he cries out, 'Oh that this too too solid flesh would melt, thaw, and resolve itself into dew, or that the everlasting had not fixed his canon against selt-slaughter!'[16]

As psychoanalysts we have learned that self-surrender of this kind, akin to the sort of self-castration seen in Indian myths of incest, offers itself as a less than sanguine solution to the inner conflicts caused by guilt. In this instance effeminization figures as a compromise wrought of the struggles between the 'agencies' of the mind—dark desire and uncompromising conscience—rather than as a fundamental accession to woman's power. Hamlet imagines assuming a woman's role not out of his admiration of her fleshy virtues but because he seeks to take her place in his father's affections. He would be, perhaps, a more constant wife to Hamlet the Elder than his mother has been.

As if an augury, a fleeting emissary from the collective conscience, a ghost, has appeared periodically to Hamlet's friends, who report his presence to their comrade. The Ghost is not a transparent figure by any means, as an untutored, modern audience might suppose. In Hamlet's Denmark the ethics of the blood feud and vengeance, with which the Greeks would have felt at home, vied with the Christian morality of mercy or, if not mercy, a just punishment for mortal sin. Though he stirs scruples of a more Christian order, this ghost is an emissary and a vision out of the past in which allegiance is owed to the parent or the king rather than to the holier ghost. He would tempt Hamlet to avenge the rupture of his lineage, and with it possibly risk excommunication from the bosom of an ascending Christian deity. His is an invitation, too, to reflexive violence, and this calls into question the reflective bent of the young philosopher prince.

En route to the apparition Hamlet anticipates what he will learn when he contemplates the inevitable sin of all men, an original sin that we suffer despite our actual deeds. Freud will echo his words centuries later when, in *Civilization and its Discontents*, he contemplates the eerie equivalence of deed and desire, and speculates on their common prehistoric origins in remorse over the primal parricide and its ritual expiation. [17] Hamlet senses that like Claudius, the evil-doer, he too is somehow contaminated for some obscure reason, 'some portent within his mind', by the treachery in which he has had no part.

The Ghost's story is a sad one, depicting not only the elder Hamlet's murder and marital betrayal but also his exclusion from grace. Descended from his rootless purgatory, the ghost of his father immediately declares his essential predicament to his son.

> I am thy father's spirit,
> Doom'd for a certain term to walk the night,
> And for the day confin'd to fast in fires,
> Till the foul crimes done in my days of nature
> Are burnt and purg'd away. But that I am forbid
> To tell the secrets of my prison-house,
> I could a tale unfold whose lightest word
> Would harrow up thy soul, freeze thy young blood,
> Make thy two eyes, like stars, start from their spheres,
> Thy knotty and combined locks to part
> And each particular hair to stand on end,
> Like quills upon the fretful porpentine.
> But this eternal blazon must not be
> To ears of flesh and blood. [18]

What the Ghost tells Hamlet, of course, is that he was killed before he had a chance to do penitence and therefore is fated to wander in the limbo of the nether world. This eternal cruelty, as much as the adultery, or the regicide, are the crimes which Hamlet must avenge.

Having told his story of the murder in the orchard, of the drams of poison which Claudius poured into his ears while he slept in seeming safety, Hamlet the Elder enjoins his name-sake to exact vengeance and admonishes him: 'Hamlet, remember me'. But Hamlet is petrified by his father's debasement in death and by his identification with the great man's unknown indiscretions. If a man like him can fall from grace, what, the prince wonders, will be his just reward—especially given the glimmers he has had of his own unsanctioned interests and desires. His 'sinews' threatening to grow instantly old, Hamlet would summon up his courage and have his body 'bear me up stiffly'. He strives to be erect in pursuing the bloodlust. But the same injunction, namely to pursue vengeance, is paradoxically a source of immobility. Erection in the service of aggression and honour goes hand in hand with the tumescence of sexual and incestuous order. Because of the intrusion of the latter and because of the guilt over it, Hamlet becomes impotent.

The Ghost has warned Hamlet, 'Let not the royal bed of Denmark be a couch for luxury and damned incest'. Echoing the living son's sentiments, he is more compassionate and empathic, moved by the affection still felt for his wife:

> But, howsoever thou pursuest this act,
> Taint not thy mind, nor let thy soul contrive
> Against thy mother aught: leave her to heaven,
> And to those thorns that in her bosom lodge
> To prick and sting her.[19]

Bloodlust is the Ghost's aim whereas an unwanted lust remains Hamlet's preoccupation. He will manoeuvre and manipulate to ascertain the truth of the Ghost's pronouncements—he may be after all the evil temptor—and to find out Claudius' guilt. But these ploys and his pondering of his discovery of infidelity lead him to the heart of his own conflicts. By 'indirection', he finds himself out. Like Oedipus, Hamlet recoils from the realization that the evil without abides within. He will try to elude culpability, blaming his mother, indeed all women, for the desire and the rivalry they stir in men's hearts.

Straight from the Ghost, Hamlet heads neither to his own cell to plot the mechanics of his revenge, nor, for that matter, to his mother and Claudius' bedchamber. He goes instead to the room of his beloved fiance Ophelia, daughter of Polonius, the king's minister, and sister of Laertes. In his disarray and mistrust he utterly distresses her and she reports to her father:

> My Lord, as I was sewing in my chamber,
> Lord Hamlet, with his doublet all unbrac'd,
> No hat upon his head, his stockings foul'd,
> Ungart'red, and down-gyved to his ankle,
> Pale as his shirt, his knees knocking each other,
> And with a look so piteous in purport
> As if he had been loosed out of hell
> To speak of horrors,—he comes before me.
>
> He took me by the wrist and held me hard;
> Then goes he to the length of all his arm,
> And with his other hand thus o'er his brow,
> He falls to such perusal of my face
> As he would draw it. Long stay'd he so.
>
> At last, a little shaking of mine arm,
> And thrice his head thus waving up and down,
> He rais'd a sigh so piteous and profound
> That it did seem to shatter all his bulk
> And end his being. That done, he lets me go;[20]

Hamlet is, as we know, feigning madness. But beyond this he is searching for the trail of deceit, not only in his mother, but in all women in whom she finds embodiment. Polonius, reputed fool that he may seem, nevertheless hits the mark in discerning the secret of Hamlet's seeming insanity when he says:

> This is the very ecstasy of love,
> Whose violent property fordoes itself
> And leads the will to desperate undertakings
> As oft as any passion under heaven
> That does afflict our natures.[21]

Ignorant of what has transpired earlier, Polonius does not recognize that this 'passion', apparently for Ophelia, is a displacement of his love for his mother, Gertrude. The love becomes all the more violent because it is suffused and compounded with its own moral condemnation. Yet Hamlet is not mad in the lunatic manner but is, as we have said, overwhelmed by a more circumscribed conflict of a neurotic and erotic kind. He is seized, that is, by the incestuous passion and murderous intent released in him by the Ghost's tale, by the spectre of his fate, and by the harsh pangs of conscience. Partly to escape himself he will decry Ophelia's and all women's sexuality as base, and expect from them inconstancy.

The King and the Queen are all too wary in the wake of their shared crimes. Whether Gertrude was an accomplice in the murder remains moot, though all the evidence points to the contrary. Now, however, she consistently puts her new lord first. She and Claudius despatch Rosencrantz and Guildenstern, initially to find Hamlet out, and later, as events proceed, to terminate his life and his nagging inquiries. The Queen's sentiments, like her deeds, remain ambiguous. What *does* she feel for this son of hers, to whose well being she seems to pay lip-service but whose care, in fact, pales before her passion for her lover, Claudius, and his survival? With the posthumous cuckoldry of Hamlet the Elder comes the emotional as well as political disinheritance of his heir, her son. In betraying a father she has abandoned a son.

Similarly, the strength of Hamlet's love for Ophelia despite his protestations—'But never doubt I love'—is also unclear. Romantic love, like filial or parental, requires trust, hope and an ethos of 'ideality'. With disillusionment in his mother, his faith in his fiancé evaporates as well. She becomes the butt of his irrepressible sadism and spite. In effect, the bonds of family, friendship, and betrothal weaken and begin to snap everywhere as Hamlet loses a father, a mother, a lover and his erstwhile comrades, Rosencrantz and Guildenstern. His 'object world', the images of the people dear to him, becomes, if not barren, contaminated with progressive decay. Exposed to hearts of darkness, disabused of all comfort in human goodness, Hamlet becomes the cynic, his cynicism further giving him to pause about himself. In modern analytic parlance adult sexuality and the readiness for passionate immersion are thrown backwards, dredging up its 'oral and anal sadistic' forerunners, images of 'good kissing carrion'. Not only people but all impulses are to be distrusted. His sense of abandonment further stokes his rage, rendering him cruel and rejecting.

Hamstrung by compunction, adrift like a spurned lost child, wallowing in offal, real and imagined, Hamlet increasingly loses momentum. He is a 'rogue and peasant slave', effectively inert, unable to feel grief and rage. He becomes a prisoner of conscience. Rather then act he is preoccupied with the terrible contrasts that govern him and his purposes.

He wonders of himself: 'Am I a coward?' and recognizes the ease with which he has always addressed the affronts to his honour. Rather, Hamlet implies, he fears himself, cowering before inner accusers. He responds to forces dimly sensed when he continues:

> But I am pigeon-liver'd and lack gall
> To make oppression bitter, or ere this
> I should ha' fatted all the region kites
> With this slave's offal.
>
> Bloody, bawdy villain!
> Remorseless, treacherous, lecherous, kindless villain!
> O! Vengeance![22]

Violence and lechery fall together in his invective against Claudius. By implication, however, for Hamlet to take action and answer destruction with destruction is to acknowledge his own clandestine sexuality, and we submit, his lust for his mother.

Not only foul, but feminine is he in his appraisal of himself. Hamlet likens himself to a cheap prostitute and laments:

> What an ass am I! This is most brave
> That I, the son of a dear father murder'd,
> Prompted to my revenge by heaven and hell,
> Must, like a whore, unpack my heart with words,
> And fall a cursing, like a very drab,
> A scullion![23]

Moreover, as in *Romeo and Juliet*, bestiality joins effeminacy in Hamlet's identification with a wanton mother. To repeat: the feminizing consequences of romantic love in this instance have less to do with any specific desire for union than with the cruelty of the punishing 'superego'. As Freud taught us long ago, our conscience in its critical aspect is heir to the castration threat imagined on the part of the father: therefore when it strikes us it can sever us from our masculinity.

A 'good enough' self-diagnostician, Hamlet in his famous soliloquy contemplates life and suicide. He imagines the torments that might befall him, as they did his dead father, in the nether world. In sleep, he reasons, there is the possibility of dreams, wish fulfilments in the Freudian scheme of mental life, the 'royal roads to the unconscious' and its dreaded contents. Therefore the consummation self-destruction promises, which is 'devoutly to be wished', will be aborted by untoward conflict . . .

> For in that sleep of death what dreams may come,
> When we have shuffl'd off this mortal coil,
> Must give us pause . . . who would fardels bear,
> To grunt and sweat under a weary life,
> But that the dread of something after death,
> The undiscover'd country from whose bourn
> No traveller returns, puzzles the will
> And makes us rather bear those ills we have
> Than fly to others that we know not of?
> Thus conscience does make cowards of us all;
> And thus the native hue of resolution
> Is sicklied o'er with the pale cast of thought,
> And enterprises of great pith and moment
> With this regard their currents turn awry,
> And lose the name of action.[24]

It is in this state, calling up the aftermath of his meeting with the Ghost, that Hamlet again encounters Ophelia. He mistrusts her beauty as inherently dishonest, a sign of women's treacherous nature, recalling his mother's deception of his father and of himself. He envies what seems to him

woman's impulsiveness—continuing to find his mother everywhere. Ophelia's guilelessness, rather like the naivete of his
mother's vulnerability to desire, contrasts with his overween-
ing self-scrutiny, and this drives him more insane.

Hamlet arranges for a play ('something like the murder of
my father') to be performed before Claudius and Gertrude,
setting the stage for his entrapment of the guilty players in his
life: 'The play's the thing wherein I'll catch the conscience of
the king'. As the Player Queen swears to her undying love,
Gertrude exclaims that 'The lady doth protest too much,
methinks'—one owes one's love allegiance only during the
mortal life span. Soon enough, in the play as in her life, the
love of the conjugal couple will end in infidelity and murder.
Claudius cannot bear the torture of confrontation. *His* conscience leads him to cry out 'Give me some light', an allusion
to would-be revelation which would finally discharge him of
his burdensome secret, while bringing down punishment
upon him.

Even at this juncture, rather than pursue Claudius Hamlet
cleaves to his errant mother. Despite the desperate warnings
of the Ghost, he is driven to find *her* conscience out, rushing
to her bedchamber.

> Soft! now to my mother,
> O heart, lose not thy nature! Let not ever
> The soul of Nero enter this firm bosom;
> Let me be cruel, not unnatural.
> I will speak daggers to her, but use none.
> My tongue and soul in this be hypocrites;
> How in my words soever she be shent
> To give them seals never, my soul, consent![25]

Anticipating Hamlet's entrance, Polonius has hidden himself behind the arras to observe his encounter with Gertrude.
Hamlet rushes in. Unaware of the ambiguity and presump-
tion of her words, Gertrude remonstrates that Hamlet has
'thy father much offended'. To this Hamlet replies quite
rightly, 'Mother, *you* have my father much offended.' She ac-

cuses him of an idle tongue and he her of a wicked one. She wonders whether she has been forgotten by him, and oddly Hamlet responds, 'No, by the *rod*, not so.'

Familial relations continue to be at the centre of his attention. 'You are the Queen, your husband's brother's wife, but would it were not so, you are my mother.' Hamlet would have a glass, a mirror to reflect the innermost part of her. Gertrude is terrified and wonders at his purpose; that is, whether he will murder her. She cries out for help. But when Polonius responds, Hamlet draws his sword and kills the unseen spy, only to discover that it is not Claudius the King he has slain but the poor unknowing chancellor.

This is the pivotal and climactic moment of Hamlet's drama. Overwhelmed by unconscious incestuous passion, Hamlet is moved to act blindly and rashly for the first time out of motives of which he is as yet unaware, or only peripherally conscious. The act—the killing of Polonius, the bystander—is, we believe, the displaced enactment both of parricide and vengeance he has so long forsaken. It is an existential moment that frees Hamlet from the chains of his conscience, persuading him of the possibility of action in general. Ironically, it permits him to assume an ethical responsibility for intention and deed.

Now he would wring his mother's heart, having acted on his own. When she wonders at her crime and his accusations, Hamlet holds her accountable for her hypocrisy and proclaims himself thought-sick at the infamy which has doomed her and robbed both parents of their lustre in their son's eyes. Hamlet again shows her the picture of his beautiful father!

> See, what a grace was seated on his brow;
> Hyperion's curls, the front of Jove himself,
> An eye like Mars, to threaten and command,
> A station like the herald Mercury
> New-lighted on a heaven-kissing hill,
> A combination and a form indeed,
> Where every god did seem to set his seal
> To give the world assurance of a man.[26]

His physical adoration of his father is in this context queer, calling up the psychoanalytic notion of a boy's 'negative Oedipus complex', or 'homosexual' love for his father as a defense against his own incestuous wishes towards the mother/woman who intrigues and attracts him. Yet this love, as we have pointed out, is also real. Hamlet compares the two, father and uncle, likening Claudius to a 'mildewed ear', and is baffled by his mother's pure instinctiveness.

> Could you on this fair mountain leave to feed,
> And batten on this moor? Ha! have you eyes?
> You cannot call it love, for at your age
> The hey-day in the blood is tame, it's humble,
> And waits upon judgement; and what judgement
> Would step from this to this?[27]

He accuses her of shamelessness and in the process compares her aging sensuality with his own, touching on the reverberations of her rejection of him.

> Rebellious hell,
> If thou canst mutine in a matron's bones,
> To flaming youth let virtue be as wax
> And melt in her own fire: proclaim no shame
> When the compulsive ardour gives the charge,
> Since frost itself as actively doth burn,
> And reason panders will.[28]

His words have struck a deep chord and Gertrude joins:

> O Hamlet, speak no more!
> Thou turn'st mine eyes into my very soul,
> And there I see such black and grained spots
> As will not leave their tinct.[29]

Hamlet cannot stop himself, for he is overtaken by the imagery of his mother's sexuality:

> *Hamlet*:   Nay, but to live
> In the rank sweat of an enseamed bed,
> Stew'd in corruption, honeying and making love
> Over the nasty sty . . .

> Queen: O, speak to me no more!
> These words like daggers enter in mine ears.
> No more, sweet Hamlet!
>
> Hamlet: A murderer, and a villain!
> A slave that is not twentieth part the tithe
> Of your precedent lord! A vice of kings!
> A cutpurse of the empire and the rule,
> That from a shelf the precious diadem stole,
> And put it in his pocket
>
> Queen: No more![30]

As if to stave off rape or murder, the Ghost enters, the voice of conscience and forbearance, calling a halt to Hamlet's sadomasochistic assault upon his mother's virtue. He reminds Hamlet of his 'blunted purpose' and bids him to step between her and her fighting soul, to spare his mother the terrible torments which are all the more intolerable in her weakness.

The Queen, observing her son's fascination with the unseen apparition, believes him to be simply crazy. Her naivete and crudeness of sensibility seem almost a testimony to Freud's early view of women, the view which won him the animosity of the feminists, in which he suggests that women's consciences and discretion in general are less developed, less 'impersonal' and lofty, than those of men—those 'clever seducers'— to whom they owe their fickle allegiance and who stand in for any morality of their own.[31]

At the same time Gertrude, like Phaedra, the queen to whom we shall turn in the next chapter, is far more earthy than her heady male counterparts. She is far more aware of the realm of instinct, of sensuality, than her son and interprets Hamlet's distress according to its other meaning. She says:

> This is the very coinage of your brain.
> This bodiless creation ecstasy
> Is very cunning in.

The word 'ecstasy', echoing Polonius, releases a new insight not only in her, but now in Hamlet himself about the nature of *his* desires

Ecstasy!
My pulse, as yours, doth temperately keep time.
And makes as healthful music.[32]

They have almost attained union of a bodily order; the Ghost's presence serves as a welcome restraint of the most devastating of passions and psycho-spiritual tensions. Touched in ways his intellectual ken cannot fathom, Hamlet implores his unrepentant mother, lest she be damned:

Mother, for love of grace,
Lay not that flattering unction to your soul,
That not your trespass, but my madness speaks.
It will but skin and film the ulcerous place,
Whilst rank corruption, mining all within,
Infects unseen. Confess yourself to heaven;
Repent what's past, avoid what is to come[33]

As if suddenly aware of some deeper current underlying his hypermoralism, his intended rescue of his mother, the fallen woman, he asks her:

Forgive me this my virtue,
For in the fatness of these pursy times
Virtue itself of vice must pardon beg,
Yea, curb and woo for leave to do him good.[34]

Apprised of her sinfulness, which she might have forgotten, Gertrude concludes that Hamlet has cleft her heart in twain. Hamlet responds that she should throw away the worser part.

He now contemplates Polonius' body, repenting but not regretting his deed. He also understands the fatefulness of it.

but Heaven hath pleas'd it so,
To punish me with this, and this with me,
That I must be their scourge and minister.
I will bestow him, and will answer well
The death I gave him.[35]

He also senses—an intuition beyond deduction—that it is his destiny or at least his circumstance to suffer sins of the world and of heart he would otherwise escape. In this sense, the bearing of culpability is a mark of courage, of heroic resolve. No one can live a guiltless life: to do otherwise, as he has done till now, is to do nothing.

Hamlet drags Polonius away but the impetuous killing has liberated him so that his future actions can be more calculated. He is aware now of his guilt and can tolerate it. Indeed, embracing guilt, Hamlet becomes a man of the world, a worthy successor to a successful king:

> Rightly to be great
> Is not to stir without great argument,
> But greatly to find quarrel in a straw
> When honour's at the stake.[36]

Hamlet now yields in a sort of personal *realpolitik* to fate. He is to be sent to England and, the audience realizes, to be murdered there by Rosencrantz and Guildenstern. Exile offers a relief to him at this point, perhaps, because the dreadful pull towards Gertrude is inexorable. Like Jocasta, mother of Oedipus, who submitted to her husband's jealousy, her self-protectiveness compromising her maternal trust, Gertrude also gives in to Claudius's malevolence towards her only child.

Time passes; Hamlet suffers a further sea-change. No longer driven by impulse and fettered by inhibition, he has become reoriented towards life's more pressing tasks. In a letter to the King, sent him via a messenger, a calmer, more purposeful Hamlet addresses the usurper ironically and enigmatically: 'You should know I am set naked on your kingdom'. Like the usurping ruler we wonder at the word 'naked' and what it means. However, we now know that Hamlet is freed of the black robes of ethical deliberation and has become much more a creature of impulse. Rosencrantz and Guildenstern plot to kill him and Hamlet counterplots. He has Rosencrantz and Guildenstern despatched with the very same order which was to be his own death warrant, an order he has sealed with the royal seal.

In the mean while, the fair Ophelia, quite overwhelmed by her fiancés murder of her own father, has sunk into a true madness of the kind merely simulated by Hamlet. She is, as Claudius puts it, 'divided from herself and her fair judgement/Without which we are pictures or mere beasts'.

In this climate of incest and parricide, real and dreamt upon, true love cannot flower. Attempting to reassert her and its innocence, Ophelia drowns, having garlanded herself in flowers, among them 'dead men's fingers'. These are tentacles of the claims of the grave—Polonius's and the Elder Hamlet's. She sinks into the water and dies. Indeed, watery imagery has begun to become quite prominent.

It is on the seas, as we have said, that Hamlet has suffered his existential transformation. On the sea, employing his father's signet, he is at last able to identify with him and to accept his and the older man's sexuality, as he has learned to do his mother's, and with it the onus of original sin. Woman's corruptibility and immorality no longer astonish and repel him. Nor does his own, for Hamlet has discovered his own instinctuality. He tells Horatio:

> Methought I lay
> Worse than the mutines in the bilboes. Rashly,—
> And prais'd be rashness for it; let us know
> Our indiscretion sometimes serves us well
> When our deep plots do pall; and that should teach us
> There's a divinity that shapes our ends,
> Rough-hew them how we will.[37]

and proceeds to describe his betrayal of Rosencrantz and Guildenstern. They are, he says, not near his conscience and their defeat was a by-product of their own insinuation. Hamlet has discharged himself of paralysing excruciation for the misdeeds of others. In the process he is free to fulfil his filial duty. Having assumed an identification with his kingly, perforce worldly and therefore tainted father, an aggressive and sexual man, Hamlet replaces a faint-hearted moralism with the ethic of choice, action and personal responsibility.

> is't not perfect conscience,
> To quit him with this arm? And is't not to be damn'd,
> To let this canker of our nature come
> In further evil?[38]

Hamlet asks these questions rhetorically, however, for he has already answered them. He accepts the price exacted of him and will not let Laertes' moral indignation outweigh his own. A fateful duel with Laertes follows and with it the deaths of the guilty Queen, King, of Laertes and Hamlet himself—his death being the only possible conclusion to his tortuous conflict. In the end Fortinbras can say that Hamlet is a free man, the incestuous ties snapped along with the strictures of a primitive conscience.

As a primal danger of love, guilt has occupied a uniquely privileged position in the development of psychoanalysis. It was guilt, his patients' and his own, the latter manifest in a series of hysterical and hypochondriacal concerns in the wake of his father's death, which moved Freud to plumb the secret of dreams and to discover the unconscious in himself. And as he listened to the musings of his patients supine upon the couch, guilt—whether manifest as remorse for deeds actually done or suffered privately as a consequence of intentions known and unknown—sins of the heart, seemed to be the hallmark of their associative ramblings.

The guilt which beset his patients, Freud discovered, was traceable to some otherwise obscure or forgotten incestuous impulse. Daughters loved their fathers, were stimulated by their rumoured indiscretions and suffered the covert and sometimes not so disguised advances offered by them or their surrogates (witness Freud's Dora, her syphilitic father, and the infamous Herr K., in Freud's first full-fledged psychoanalytic case-history). Sons, in their turn, however virtuous or prideful they might be—and in the self-declared decent man, pride and moral purity are very much of a piece. Such sons, we have seen, are willy nilly the victims of their unwanted wishes.

'Repugnant to morality yet forced upon them by nature!' Freud lamented in *The Interpretation of Dreams*, as he contemplated Oedipus' and Everyman's fate. A man's and boy's yearnings for a less than hallowed 'mother love', he asserted, gave rise to the paradigmatic conflict at the very heart of civilization. Guilt itself was fated, a function of instinct and possibly the dark deeds of prehistory. In individual development, we have argued, it is a precipitate of both fear and love of the father.[39]

In this conception of the child, notwithstanding the fact that Freud chronicled at length the indiscretions and violations of innocence perpetrated by reputedly upright parents, it is as if the caretaker was the victim of the dependent child's unwanted wishes. Matters, however, are never that simple, as we have shown with fathers and will next do with mothers in our last stories of love.

The omission of Islamic and Indian stories from this chapter is due to the fact that guilt as a primal danger of love seems to be generally absent from the tales of these cultures. One reason for this absence may be that the Judeo-Christian presuppositions—the dualistic division of man's nature between natural and moral realms, with guilt as an essential symptom of this bifurcation, guilt as *the* curse of man's lower, sexual nature—which is a part of Western cultural and literary heritage—is not shared by the other two cultures. Guilt in Islam and Hinduism is related less to the sinfulness of sexual love than simply to man's sense of imperfection and anxiety. The core psychoreligious issue in the Hindu view, for example, is man's *ignorance* of his essential nature rather than guilt. Most Indian religious endeavours are directed towards removing this ignorance—the veil of *maya*—and not to the expiation of guilt.

Classical psychoanalysis, then, is also a child of the Western heritage when it places a central emphasis on guilt in its theory of human development. In searching for the roots of guilt in the oedipal situation or in the 'original sin' of a prehistoric murder of the father, psychoanalysis does not overturn the Judeo-Christian mythology but amplifies and deepens its semantics and symbols. Lacking a historical preoccupation with guilt, it is quite understandable that Indian and Islamic literary imaginations did not elaborate· upon themes other than those contained in their own cultural lexicons.

CHAPTER SEVEN

MOTHER-LOVE: WHEN DESIRE BECOMES REALITY

Mai Zetterling's girlish nude body had once tempted and enchanted audiences of an early Ingmar Bergman film, her lithe back and inviting buttocks receding from the camera's lens as from her lover's eye to the reeds and to the river below, a silver streak across the screen. Years later she tried her own hand at film directing. In one of the films, *Night Games*, her actors portrayed perversions infusing a decadent mansion. Of the parade of disquieting erotica, more graphic than the nudist romps two decades earlier, one scene stood out as perhaps the most poignant. A naked little boy lies across his mother's ample canopy bed as she holds court. Absently, vaguely, she half caresses him, as he jiggles his penis. Suddenly she notices the masturbation, admonishes her son harshly and summarily dismisses him from their intimacy.

A psychoanalytic patient in his late thirties haltingly

approaches a memory of adolescence which he has successfully forgotten for many years. One summer, when he was
fifteen years old, he used to doze off in the heat of the
afternoon while lying on a mattress on the floor. There his
mother would usually join him after finishing her household
chores. Often, he now remembers, he felt himself grow hard.
Half awake and perhaps half responsible, he would rub his
erect penis against his mother's buttocks, quickly turning
away after ejaculating, now detumescent and somnolent. The
mother, he believed, was fast asleep and noticed neither his
erection nor its thrusts.

One day, however, as the patient is once again erotically
but, he thinks, privately, engaged with his object, both real
and illusory, pressing himself against his mother's back,
suddenly she comes to life. She turns over to face him and in a
voice husky with excitement complains, 'You always satisfy
yourself but never think of me'. The patient faints. Recollect-
ing the scene twenty years later on the couch, his adult
waking consciousness is confronted with the full impact of
what proved to be the mutual exchange of the illicit. The
session is, in fact, followed by a transient psychotic episode.
At its close he succeeds in banishing from awareness once
again the terrible knowledge of his desire and the confession
of her own.

Freud, as we know, struggled with his 'seduction theory' for a
long time. Having impugned parents in the etiology of his
children's neuroses, in the end he exculpated them, granting
to fantasy or 'psychic reality' a peremptory power equal to
historical actuality. But what of Freud's own early or 'screen'
memories? His infamous nurse seduced and mocked him,
now inviting him to gaze upon the naked female body, now
carrying young Sigmund off to the Christian church with its
arch morality and promises of hell-fire and damnation should
the transgressors succumb to any interdicted libidinal inclina-
tion. His mother nearly exposed herself to her son. He

remembers that once on a railroad journey, he caught a glimpse of her 'ad nudam', as Freud put it with latinate decorousness.[1] Later he recalled that in the fashion of more primitive mammals, a wolf cub of sorts, he laid territorial claim to the parental bedroom by urinating upon its floor, only to be shamed in the process, told by his father in one of the more famous vignettes of Freud's reminiscences, that 'this boy will amount to nothing!'[2] Freud had been, it seems, like most little sons, seduced into a heightened, sensual sensibility, linked in its turn to overwhelming ambition and the wish to rid himself of rivals blocking his way, only to have his initiative curtailed.

It is striking that sons bear the culpability for being aroused. Men punish themselves, or else retribution is exacted of them from those who govern their existence. Mothers, as we shall see, also excruciate in the face of what amounts to a potential violation of the security they owe their infants, even on into adulthood. But their transgressions and psychic turmoil, perhaps because of the obviousness of a man's erection in contrast to a woman's secretions, is harder to see.

In this chapter we will scrutinize the motif of incestuous love between mothers and sons in its more oblique manifestations: the mythology of Phaedra and her stepson Hippolytus (dramatized in two ages—by the classical Greek Euripides and two thousand years later by the Jansenist Racine), and an Indian tale of incest generally told by women to their daughters. If the pre-genital seductions of parent and child, transpiring long before consummation is possible, are disquieting enough, the genital tensions of adolescence are even more perilous.

Phaedra

In fairy tales the less acceptable qualities of the mother are often attributed to the stepmother who abandons or attempts to kill her predecessor's progeny. In the story of Queen Phaedra's passion for the beautiful but priggish Hippolytus it is not hate but love which is at issue, a love that is no less dangerous to its luckless recipient.

The tale of Phaedra's plight is but one in the series of great adventures which befell the legendary Athenian, King Theseus—an episode, that is, which largely took place in his absence. Rescuer of the youth thrown to the Minotaur, founder of the great Athenian democracy, Theseus none the less, like most heroic leaders from Jason to John Kennedy, also proved to be something of a philanderer. Theseus eventually married Phaedra, the daughter of Minos, king of Crete, who bore him two sons. Two other wives may have intervened, but their fate is uncertain. The marriage to Phaedra was a political one, uniting the two great states. Phaedra's sons were to succeed in the rule of Athens, which Theseus had wrested from the rival family of Pallas.

Meanwhile, there is the parallel story of Theseus's conquest of the Amazons. In one version it is said that Queen Antiope or Hippolyte fell in love with the handsome Athenian and betrayed her city to him. As he sailed home with her they conceived a child, Hippolytus, Theseus's bastard but beloved son. The Amazons, those paradigmatic 'phallic women' whose female spears-penises men would wrest from them, followed Theseus, encamped near Athens, and were about to attack the city when the greater part of their force was killed by the Athenian army. In the aftermath of the killing Theseus retired to Troezen, where he had already sent Hippolytus. Theseus felt secure in these living arrangements, for he believed that his wife Phaedra would not protest the presence of the concubine's son so long as he did not bar the way to her own children's political succession. But he made a fateful error. In stressing Phaedra's *maternal* jealousy, he overlooked her womanly sentiments as well as the limits of his own charisma.

The queen had seen Hippolytus upon visiting Attica, when she was initiated into the cult of Eleusis, and had fallen madly

and secretly in love with him at first sight. She was a south-
erner, a sensualist, and Aphrodite was already her goddess.
On the corner of the Acropolis she built a shrine to love over-
looking the Saronic Gulf all the way to Troezen, pointing the
way to her unlikely would-be-lover. It is in this amorous and
political setting that the action of her drama begins.

Euripides's Phaedra appears in *Hippolytus*, which was
first presented in 428 BC. This is in fact the second version of
the play. The first version, which has been lost, was deemed
scandalous because of its debunking of tradition, and badly
received, while the second version won the first prize (Sophocles' time-honoured *Oedipus Rex* garnered only the second).
The traditional view of the play is that Phaedra is a sympathetic character overcome by her passions or, in the Greek
scheme of things, by the love goddess, Aphrodite. Mortals
must, unfortunately, suffer the clash between the goddesses
Artemis and Aphrodite, deities of virtue and sex, of the dictates of the 'superego' and the 'id'. The Hellenic dialectic has a
more unabashedly anthropomorphic cast to it than Freudian
notions of 'structural conflict' but shares with the latter a de-
terministic deference to the forcefulness and fatefulness of
love.

The play begins with an invocation on the part of Aphrodite reminiscent of Dionysus's apology and declaration of
vengeance which begins Euripides's famous *Bacchae*. The
gods will have their due and are not to be ignored, however
much man's scruples and vanity would deny them.
Aphrodite informs us that she is mighty among men and
much honoured. She demands that her power be worshipped
in all humility.

> But those whose pride is stiffened against me,
> I lay by the heels.[3]

The implication is that she will have no patience for moralistic machismo, a 'phallic narcissistic pride' of the kind
triumphed by Hippolytus, son of Theseus by the Amazon.
An implacable foe of his own emotions and his instincts. Hip-

polytus abhors the company of those who are consumed by emotion and instinct. Instead, according to Aphrodite, he honours Artemis, Zeus's daughter, with whom 'he hunts with hounds and clears the land of wild things. Mortal with immortal in companionship.'

Artemis is reminiscent of his mother's asexual warrior spirit. This is hubris, perhaps, but it is not what galls Aphrodite. It is the affronts to her station and homage which rankle the goddess, and for these she wants redress.

Much of her work has already been done, she tells us, for Phaedra, after seeing Hippolytus and moved by him, dedicated her temple to Aphrodite. She remarks that Theseus, having condemned himself to a year's exile after the murder of Pallas's son, had sailed with his wife to this land, only to leave there in order to pursue other adventures. Love's power has already infected Phaedra, who 'groans in bitterness of heart and the goads of love prick her cruelly, and she is like to die'. The servants do not know the nature of the sickness afflicting her. It is the secrecy, too, of her passion, which quite ravages the prostrate queen, who must suffer the stabs of illicit longing in complete isolation.

So Aphrodite does not have to work her celestial magic, as did Dionysus on the women of *Bacchae*, in order to invade men's hearts. What she will do, however, is to make her worshipper's secret known. With the revelation of the would-be incest she sets in motion a power struggle between a once loving father and beloved son. While Phaedra will be renowned rather than reviled in death and Hippolytus will have a cult erected around him, die they both will. In a clear reference to women's sexual power over man's pretensions to the contrary, Aphrodite concludes:

> He does not know
> That the doors of death are open for him
> That he is looking on his last sun.[4]

In Euripides's rendering of the story we are introduced to Hippolytus before we meet Phaedra. Hippolytus repeatedly invokes Artemis and her virginal purity—Artemis, maiden daughter of Zeus and Leto, maid of the mighty father, maid of the golden gristling goose, maiden goddess most beautiful of all the heavenly hosts that live in Olympus, and so on. He emphasizes her chastity in contrast to the easier eroticism embodied by Aphrodite,

> Not those who by instruction have profited to learn,
> But in whose very soul the seed of Chastity toward all
> Things alike nature has deeply rooted, they alone
> Gather flowers there! the wicked may not.[5]

Hippolytus seems almost prototypical of a Christian ascetic, haughty and violent in his scrupulous condemnation of the flesh and of lasciviousness. In his self-righteousness he is playing God, and his servant, recognizing the young man's temerity, asserts that he will call him king rather than master, for 'Master' is an appellation belonging to the gods. He offers the chaste young man some chastening advice, 'Will you not worship the goddess Cypris [Aphrodite]?'

To this Hippolytus responds that yes, he will, but from afar. In the spirit that the Christian world cannot understand, the servant responds that she is a holy goddess revered throughout the world. Erotic or romantic love is not to be dismissed so easily as a lesser sentiment. Therefore, Fortune should guard Hippolytus from his prudery. Hippolytus counters once more: 'The God of nocturnal prowess is not my God'.

Once Hippolytus has departed to recover form his Dianian hunt (Diana being the Roman name for Artemis), Euripides intercedes in the voice of an old man, begging forgiveness of the goddess Aphrodite. Being a god she is entreated to simply turn a deaf ear to Hippolytus' foolish words and ignore his tempestuous heart.

We know better. The gods are easily as imperious as any man. All the Greeks, from Homer on, were well aware of their deities' foibles. But conceit can overrule common sense. Hippolytus's conscience is irksome and at times downright crude in its steadfastness. He wavers neither in deed nor in thought—not for a moment; he is dull to reason's voice.

The chorus then introduces the second act. It tells of Phaedra's mysterious illness, her lovesickness, rather like the fever seizing the sanatorium's inhabitants and visitors alike in Thomas Mann's *The Magic Mountain*. The verse begins with many references to water.

> There is a rock streaming with water,
> Whose source, men say, is Ocean,
> And it pours from the heart of its stone a spring
> Where pitchers may dip and can be filled.
> My friend was there, and in the river water,
> She dipped and washed the royal purple robes,
> And spread them on the rock's warm back
> Where the sunbeams played.[6]

There are more references to waters of the lake in contrast to the dry land and the 'eddying salt sea'.

Evidently the Greeks, like Freud, seemed to conceive sexuality or sensuality as some mysterious vital fluid—libido—emanating from a source, which was somehow inherent in the animal nature of women. This men could dabble in or else eschew altogether, but it was essentially beyond their compass. A female chorus debates the relative weights of sexuality and chastity, the last speaker concluding that she bows to Artemis, Queen of the Bow—an airy, hard goddess, a rather boyish figure in fact, ensconced well above the water's reach.

At this point Phaedra appears with her nurse. This nurse, in both Euripides' and Racine's versions, figures as the spokesperson for the rule of passion, suggesting that if we yield to our impulses we will be emancipated and they will turn to good rather than devour us. Discerning the erotic or incestuous impulses lying at the heart of emotional agony, she continues:

> But something other dearer still than life
> The darkness hides, the mist encompasses;
> We are proved luckless loves of this thing

> That glitters in the underworld: No man
> Can tell us of the stuff of it, expounding
> What it is, and what it is not; we know nothing of it
> Idly we drift, on idle stories carried.[7]

What a telling statement about the unconscious scenarios that govern our lives and about the narratives that we concoct in order to give them rational substance!

Phaedra moans and groans, lamenting her state, enjoining the world and begging the nurse to lift her from her agony. Hers is a depression partly brought upon her by guilt. She cannot 'draw from the dewy spring, a draught of fresh spring water'. Nor can she 'lie beneath the poplars and the tufted meadow and find her rest there'; suicide is not open to her. She is also loath to go to the mountains and to seek out the hunt, and we know of the hunter, Hippolytus, who has seized her heart. She can yield neither to self-punishment nor desire, for as yet they carry equal weight. The nurse comments,

> Here at one moment you're afire with longing to
> Hunt wild beasts and you go to the hills, and then
> Again all you desire is horses,
> Horses on the sands beyond the reach of breakers.
> Indeed, it would need to be a mighty prophet
> To tell which of the gods (mischievously)
> Jerks you from your true course and thwarts your wits.[8]

Phaedra disclaims responsibility for her torment:

> O, I am miserable!
> What is't I have done?
> Where have I strayed from the highway of good sense?
> I was mad. It was madness sent from some God
> That caused my fall.[9]

She wants to cover her face because she is so ashamed. Her tears are flowing and the blush of her cheek has turned to shame. Yet, like Potiphar's wife, consumed with a similar passion for Joseph in Thomas Mann's novel, Phaedra becomes acutely conscious of her body, the vessel of love, and the changes being wrought in it by frustrated desire. With mingled pride and misgiving she exults in her beauty:

> Here, you take my hands.
> They're beautiful, my hands and arms!
> Take away this hat! It is too heavy to wear.
> Take it away! Let my hair fall free on my shoulders.[10]

She cannot allow herself the love of Hippolytus since it defies the marriage tie and, although Euripides does not say this (Racine does), the incest taboo. Nor can she do so, for conscience is also a protector, and should she stray, acquiescing to her unsanctioned wishes, all havoc will be set in motion. Even so defiance of desire is a most painful and tense undertaking, an effort most often doomed to fail.

Asserting her worldly, seasoned wisdom, the nurse suggests that she has learned much from a long life:

> The mixing bowl of friendship,
> The love of one for the other must be tempered.
> Love must not touch the marrow of the soul.
> Our affections must be breakable chains that we
> Can cast them off or tighten them
> That one soul so for two should be in travail
> As I for her, that is a heavy burden.
> The ways of life are most fanatical
> Trips us up more, they say, than brings us joy.
> They're enemies to health, so I pray, less
> The extreme than temperance in everything.
> The wise will bear me out.[11]

The nurse is an exponent of 'free love'. For her proprieties, ties and their concomitant obligations are but hypocritical sources of distress. Such views, however, do not take cognizance of the jealousies and the malevolence unleashed once the erotic impulse towards another is acknowledged. This is the fallacy of free love, of sex that is without romance.

Phaedra's great secret is still not revealed. In the 'mythology' of psychoanalysis the nurse represents the 'pleasure ego', whereas in a previous chapter we have suggested that Friar Laurence serves as the embodiment of that agency's rationality. Both are dangerous to their possessors for, unlike the conscience in all of its unwanted primitiveness, they underestimate the destructiveness of the instinctual forces. Our executive faculties fail to heed the violence both of our instincts and of our innermost injunctions. These are, in William Blake's words, the priests in 'black gowns walking their rounds and binding with briars my joys and desires'.[12]

The nurse pursues her inquiry, and savvy as she is hits on a part of the truth. She tells Phaedra:

> No, by the Amazon queen the mighty rider
> Who bore a master for your children, one
> Bastard in birth but true–born son in mind,
> You know him well—Hippolytus . . .
> So that has touched you?[13]

Phaedra responds prophetically:

> You have killed me, nurse, For god's sake!
> I entreat you, never again speak that man's
> Name to me.[14]

How many times does the analyst encounter similar remonstrations on the part of his patients when he confronts their incestuous longings! In the safety of the psychoanalytic situation, where these are played out in the 'as if' world of the transference, such wishes, surprisingly, prove therapeutically benign. But in reality, where the politics of family prevail, they are lethal.

Phaedra has committed no deed; as she puts it, 'My hands are clean; the stain is in my heart'. But at a certain point wishes brought to the day, known by others as by the self, must perforce initiate action. Desire has its own inexorable course. Phaedra pleads: 'Leave me to my sins, my sins are not against you',—to the psychoanalyst a familiar disclaimer of old, yet extant love. 'Sorrow, nurse, sorrow, nurse, sorrow you will find my secret'. The nurse counters, pleading that

Phaedra's death is worse than the revelation to follow. Phaedra says: 'You will kill me, My honour lies in silence.' Phaedra thinks of her family, her unhappy mother and sister, Ariadne, the bride of Dionysus, either wrested from or abandoned by her husband Theseus, and concludes that hers is an inherited curse. It is not new—her defiance of the social order and of the reigning father monarch.

This is an old theme in the Greek scheme of things, as in the psychoanalytic world view. Our incestuous wishes and parricidal inclinations are forced upon us by our heritage. Either we are hounded by the forgotten memory of some dim deed of prehistory, as in Freud's fanciful notion of the primal horde, and the killing of the father in pursuit of the women he possessed, and the cannibalizing of the patriarch. Or else, simply, we are creatures of our animal nature as well as of our childish mind and of the brutal discipline to which dependent creatures are subject. Freud finally invoked these to explain the inevitability of desires that threatened the family order and that move us to build the defensive edifices that make our psychosocial topography.

Finally the revelation is rendered explicit:

> PHAEDRA: There is a man . . . His mother was an Amazon.
> NURSE: You mean, Hippolytus?
> PHAEDRA: You have spoken it, not I.[15]

At this point the nurse herself is appalled. She cries out to Aphrodite that she is not a true god. As the principle that governs the world and makes of order chaos, Aphrodite is indeed something stronger than a god. She has 'ruined her and me and all this house.'

Phaedra tells how naively she believed 'that I could conquer love, conquer it with discretion and good sense.' She continues, as if giving credence to Hamlet's sense of woman and her all-devouring sexuality, as engulfing for her as for her would-be lover:

> I know what I have done; I know the scandal:
> And all too well, I know that I am a woman,

> Object of hate to all. Destruction lights
> Upon the wife who herself plays the tempter
> And strains her loyalty to her husband's bed
> By dalliance with strangers.[16]

She might say, 'sons.'

Here the multiple infidelities of the incest, while never made explicit by Euripides, though later by Racine, are unmistakable. 'I cannot bear that I should be discovered a traitor to my husband and my children.' Guilt wracks her, and she reiterates the proverb which runs—'There is one thing alone that stands the brunt of life throughout its course—a quiet conscience, a just and quiet conscience, whoever can attain it'. She speaks of innocence and the wisdom that should come with age, and of overripe desires no longer enhanced by the blush of youth. Shame compounds remorse:

> Time holds a mirror, as for a young girl
> And sometimes as occasion falls, he shows us
> The ugly rogues of the world. I would not wish
> That I should be seen among them.[17]

In the manner of the seasoned clinician the nurse avers that Phaedra's case is 'not so extraordinary'. It is not beyond thought or reason. She is simply the victim of passion; the goddess in her anger has smitten her. She is in love. 'What wonder is this? There are so many who suffer with you.' How many times would the therapist indirectly tell his patient something so similar! 'So you will die for love and all the others who love and will love, must they die too? How will it profit them?'

> The tide of love,
> At its full surge is not withstandable.
> Upon the yielding spirit she comes gently,
> But to the proud and fanatic heart
> She is a torturer with the brand of shame.
> She wings her way through the air; she is in the sea
> In its foaming billows; from her everything,
> That is, is born. For she engenders us

> And sows the seed of desire whereof we're born,
> All we her children, living on earth.[18]

She recalls Semele, mother of Dionysus, the lover of Zeus, whose cruel treatment by her city stirred Dionysus' revenge and set the whole tragedy of the House of Thebes in motion. Smitten with a savage hedonism, Agave too forsook her motherly duties, decapitating her son—a fate not unlike that awaiting Hippolytus. She enjoins Phaedra to blind herself to what is ugly in lust. She summons up the imagery of water once again, equating passion and the sea. Such is the 'great lot of women', dangerous to her and man alike:

> You've fallen into the great sea of love
> And with your puny swimming would escape!
> If in the sun you have more good luck than ill,
> Count yourself fortunate—for you are mortal.[19]

What the nurse suggests and what the psychoanalysts have learned is that genital love has its wellsprings in our very origination, that is, in the womb of our mothers, whence we came. We must return to it, and this compulsion for re-entry rules our lives, however much we try to tame or navigate the waters. To do otherwise is, according to the nurse, only insolent pride, representing a wish to be superior to the gods that govern our mortal bodies. Our loves must be endured. In the spirit of analysis she suggests to Phaedra that she challenge her defenses: 'Endure your love. The gods have willed it so. You are sick. Then try to find some subtle means to turn your sickness into health again'. The modern clinician would say, *soto voce*—to himself if not to his patient—sublimate, or find another 'object' for your passion. Be easy with yourself, look elsewhere. Phaedra, who suffers what the nurse no longer does, counters: 'This is the deadly thing which devastates well-ordered cities and the homes of men'. The nurse retorts that hers is but high moralizing:

> What you want
> Is not fine words, but the man!

> Come, let's be done.
> And tell your story frankly and directly.[20]

She tells Phaedra to forego any foolish narcissism. Her words may be shameful, but they are better in being truer than Phaedra's noble-sounding moral sentiments. The deed is better if it saves your life and your good name in which you die exulting.

So much again for moralistic pride. It is a theme that will be echoed through the millennia, evident, for example, in Hawthorne's *Scarlet Letter*, in which Hester defies the insensitive puritanism of her time. From the psychoanalytic perspective on development it is the upsurge of adolescence along with a lascivious older generation which undoes the teenager's composure. In coming of age and into his handsome manhood, Hippolytus has rekindled his stepmother's youth.

Phaedra fears being seduced by the nurse's words. 'I am afraid of you', she says, 'I am afraid that you will be too clever for my good'. The nurse rejoins: 'You're afraid of everything. What is it?' Phaedra has a presentiment. Bent on her course, the nurse trusts instinct, and Phaedra frets: 'You surely will not tell this to Hippolytus?' The nurse reassures her with a sage smugness equal to the arrogance of Hippolytus himself, 'Come, let that be: I will arrange all well.'

The argument is brought to a halt by the entrance of the young man at issue. Overhearing Hippolytus cursing a bawdy servant maid, Phaedra is aware of his scorn for human frailty. She tells him that it is natural we should sin, being human. Echoing Hamlet, Hippolytus declares:

> Women! This cant coin which men find counterfeit!
> Why, why, Lord Zeus, did you put them in the world,
> In the light of the sun? [21]

For the moralist and the misogynist women are whores:

> We have proof how great a curse is woman,
> For the father who begets her, rears her up,
> Must add dowry gift to pack her off

To another's house and must be rid of the load.
And he again that takes the cursed creature
Rejoices and enriches his heart's jewel
With dear ornament, beauty heaped on vileness.[22]

Hippolytus is a chauvinist of the first order. Is it that his mother was a proud androgynous queen laid low by the greater force of arms and, more than this, by the virile charms of his own father, Theseus? Is he, the psychoanalyst wonders, secretly identified with the once phallic woman who bore and reared him?

At any event he shuns the allure of all women, however much he may cleave to Artemis, his mother's immortal reflection. Despite his pretensions to virtue Hippolytus is a phallic sadist. He may not seduce or conquer them sexually, but is so overwhelmed and appalled by the sexuality of mothers that he can adhere only to bravado, asceticism or some overt or concealed homosexual refuge in the company of men. He uses women as foils aggrandizing his superiority.

In Euripides's play, charged with irony as well as passion, the incestuous motif is not explicit. Manifestly, Euripides represents a clash of forces beyond mortal comprehension and control, a clash which modern man interprets as the great inner or psychic conflict. Racine's *Phaedra* retains some of the paganism of Euripides's original view, while at the same time bringing the issue of incestuous passion and family honour into the forefront of dramatic action and lending it greater clarity. He reinterprets the tale in the context of the Jansenism which ruled his age, a religiosity to which the once licentious and later tamed dramaturge reverted, seeking refuge after the creation of his greatest tragedy.

In the process of probing Phaedra's secret Racine came closer to the incestuous impulses which, we have learned from analysis, suffuse all secret passions, perhaps especially adultery. In Racine's version of the encounter between Phaedra and Hippolytus the queen is an older and more matronly wife of Theseus, who is rumoured to be dead. Encour-

aged by the nurse, Phaedra at last approaches Hippolytus. She
says that she has come to join her tears to his and to tell him
of a mother's fears:

> My son is fatherless, and soon, too soon,
> He must behold my death as well. Even now,
> Numberless enemies beset his youth.
> You, only you, can see to his defence
> But I am harried by remorse within.
> I fear lest you refuse to hear his cries.
> I trembled lest you visit on a son
> Your righteous anger at a mother's crimes.[23]

Phaedra describes how she has sought to separate herself from
Hippolytus and lead herself out of temptation, going so far as
to have none in her presence speak Hippolytus's name. Failing to pick up her innuendos Hippolytus interprets her words
in terms of filial obligation. He believes Phaedra hates him because of his favoured position in Theseus' affections and tells
her: 'A mother jealous of her children's rights rarely forgives
another woman's son'.

He thinks he sees in her the wonder of her love for
Theseus. But Phaedra tells him the truth.

> Yes, Prince, I pine, I am on fire for him.
> I love King Theseus, not as once he was,
> The fickle worshipper at countless shrines,
> Dishonouring the couch of Hades' god;
> But constant, proud, and even a little shy;
> Enchanting, young, the darling of all hearts,
> Fair as the gods; or fair as you are now.[24]

She cannot stop: 'He had your eyes, your bearing, and
your speech. His face flushed with your noble modesty'. A
mother, and an adult woman, she loves the youth in man before it becomes corrupted by his inconstancies, peccadiloes
and the conquests that have come his way. She yearns for
freshness and revitalization. Hers is a paradoxical striving,
one where fulfilment destroys the goal. There is a longing
then, for renewal, for the innocence and revival also inherent

in the incestuous impulse. She loves Hippolytus's purity and yet would claim him with the great ocean of her own desires and give him rebirth. She tells Hippolytus: 'You would have slain the monstrous Cretan bull despite the windings of his endless lair.'

The labyrinth where the Cretan bull lurks is almost a metaphor for the mystery of a woman's genital cavern and the illusion of the protective phallic policeman guarding her inner sanctuary from youthful interlopers. Danger energizes the quest, adding the thrill in flirting with death to the undulations of sensual discovery.

Phaedra continues in her impassioned wooing of Hippolytus, becoming urgent and, finally, unmistakable in confessing her intentions.

> For my love would instantly have fired me with the thought
> I, only I, would have revealed to you
> The subtle windings of the labyrinth.
> What care I would have lavished on your head!
> A thread would not have reassured my fears.
> Affronting danger side by side with you,
> I would myself have wished to lead the way,
> And Phaedra, with you in the labyrinth,
> Would have returned with you or met her doom.[25]

She is talking, of course, about inducting this proud young man into the dangerous mysteries of intercourse and, with this, have him take his father's place. Hippolytus can no longer deny what he has heard and wonders whether Phaedra has forgotten that she is Theseus's wife and he his son. 'No, I am mindful of my name', Phaedra answers. Hippolytus seizes on this cue and asks forgiveness as if her words were innocent. He cannot bear her gaze. At last, Phaedra confesses fully. She tells him that he has understood only too well and that she has revealed enough. She says:

> Know Phaedra then, and all her wild desires.
> I burn with love. Yet, even as I speak,
> Do not imagine I feel innocent,

> Nor think that my complacency has fed
> The poison of the love that clouds my mind.
> The hapless victim of heaven's vengeances,
> I loathe myself more then you ever will.[26]

She describes her suffering and asks Hippolytus to relieve and release her through punishment. Her imagery calls up Bernini's famed and once notorious St Theresa in ecstasy, hardly beatific in her receipt of the stigmata.

> Punish me for loving you.
> Come, prove yourself your father's worthy son,
> And of a vicious monster rid the world.
> I, Theseus's widow, dare to love his son!
> This frightful monster must now escape.
> Here is my heart. Here must your blow strike home.[27]

Punishment would be an immolation which serves not only as an expiation but as the fulfilment of this woman's raging and evermore masochistic cravings.

Returning to Euripides' version, we find Phaedra resolved on suicide. Her suicide is a sacrifice to love, an offering to the might of the goddess. 'When I shake off the burden of this life, I shall delight the Goddess who destroys me, the Goddess Cypris. Bitter will have been the love that conquers me, but in my death. I shall at least bring sorrow upon another too.' Thoughts of revenge predominate as she contemplates her destruction of the haughty Hippolytus,

> Whose high heart
> May know no arrogant joy at my life's
> Shipwreck; He will have his share in
> This, my mortal sickness and learn of
> Chastity in moderation.[28]

As the Chorus puts it:

> The presage of the omen was true;
> Aphrodite has broken her spirit with the terrible
> Sickness of impious love.

> The waves of destruction are over her head,
> From the roof of her room with its marriage bed.
> She is tying the twisted noose.
> And now it is around her fair white neck!
> The shame of her cruel fate has conquered.
> She has chosen good name, rather than life:
> She is easing her heart of its bitter load of love.[29]

The seas of her own sexuality, wearing the robes of despair, have engulfed her very person—as they will the contentious son who is its object. She will speak of Hippolytus in her suicide note, impugning him for crimes which will incur Theseus's rage.

The suicide note comes into Theseus's hands, and he immediately responds to the putative offender. As in *Hamlet*, the ties of marriage linking members of one generation with their own kind prevail over the bonds between the generations. Theseus is quick to believe his wife, despite Hippolytus's chaste reputation, and cries out

> I shall no longer hold this secret prisoner
> In the gates of my mouth. It is horrible,
> Yet I will speak,
> Hippolytus has dared to rape my wife.
> He has dishonoured god's holy sunlight.[30]

How different is this Theseus from timorous Mark and Moubad, as he readily curses his once beloved illegitimate son, invoking Poseidon and asking him to kill his boy with the horrific bull from the sea. Hippolytus, it appears to him, has challenged his generational claim to a woman already belonging to the king rather than taking a daughter of the land. With the horror of this threat to his authority he sweeps aside logic and probability in a reflexive rage. He banishes Hippolytus, unaware that it is his son's chastity and not his accession to incestuous impulses which has destroyed Phaedra and the family. He curses his son and questions all of his pretenses to asceticism and purity. Hippolytus's remonstrations and recollections of virtuousness are in vain. Theseus expels him from the fatherland to beg his way. Like Oedipus, Hippolytus must bear the brunt of the guilt of the parental generation. Theseus hits the mark when he accuses Hippolytus of self-worship, but misses the truth as far as the actual transgression is concerned. Pride, he says, has felled him. He is more at home in self-worship than in the other virtues—justice, for instance, and duty towards a father.

Invoking Artemis, the dearest of the gods to him, Hippolytus accepts his exile. We learn later how the bull from the sea, the phallic figure from within the great womb, frightens Hippolytus's horses so that they drag, maim and kill him. The bull is also the symbol of the power of Crete and of Phaedra's origins. He bespeaks her revenge, however much Theseus may believe that it is his god, a male god, Poseidon, who is responsible for Hippolytus's demise.

Artemis proclaims that she and Theseus are the chief sufferers of the tragedy of Hippolytus and Phaedra. She eulogizes the nobility of Hippolytus's soul when he reappears, a battered wreck of a body—a nobility which has proved his ruin. After his death Hippolytus will be worshipped in a cult established by Artemis in his name. But, dying, he can see the great gates of death which beckon him—the eternal womb—the vulva of the desirous mother luring the son back into her dark inner regions, sensual or destructive according to his desserts. Our own proverbs have it that hell hath no fury like a woman scorned.

To expound on mother/son incest is to speak immediately of a shared and promiscuous guilt, perhaps unlike other passionate loves that stand outside the family or social order. Once the secret is leaked and the conflicts and inhibitions give way, mothers and their sons are swept up in a veritable tidal wave of incestuous urgings. Such compulsions are lethal and further sound the collapse of the existing family and social edifices that depend on their containment. At least this is true in Western mythology and its fictional and dramatic renderings.

An Indian Interlude

As with incest between fathers and daughters, 'mother love' in India is not to be found in the culture's drama and poetry but in its oral legends and folk tales. In the Indian literary tradition love and lovers remain determinedly exogamous— confined to the same generation and constrained from conjoining within the family. An exception is found in the legends of Kunala, the son of the great king Ashoka. Kunala was desired by his stepmother but, like Hippolytus, rejected her proffered love. Phaedra-like, the queen accused him of making improper advances and Kunala was blinded by his father as punishment.

Strangely enough, the Kunala story never found an Indian Euripides or Racine. One reason for this striking literary omission may well be that the spirit of Eros in the mother– son relationship in India is much too powerful to be summoned lightly through poetry and drama. We know (and there is no reason to believe it was otherwise in the past), that from the moment of birth the Indian son is greeted and surrounded by direct, sensual body contact, by relentless physical ministrations.[31] Constantly cuddled in the mother's arms, the son's experience of the mother's body is a heady one. When the infant is a few months old and able to rest on his stomach, he may be carried astride the mother's hip, his legs on each side of her body, as she goes about on visits to neighbours, to the market, to the fields and on other errands. At other times (and in other places) the infant may also be transported in a similar way, lying along the stomach or the back of the mother or her substitute.

For many years the child will sleep at night with the mother in the same bed, shifting to that of some other family member only when the maternal bed has become too crowded, for instance, after the birth of a third child. Patients who have slept with their mothers until the onset of puberty are not uncommon in Indian analytic practice. The mother's smell and bodily warmth and the texture of her skin, in a climate which ensures that a minimum or no clothing at all is worn by the young child, pervade the early sensory and sensuous experience of most Indian men. It is an experience different from the more disengaged, less enveloping and stimulating lot of the Western boy.

The sexual arousal by the mother, however well integrated it may become during the course of development in most men, nevertheless continues to lurk under the surface as a seductive restlessness. Along with its transformation into extremes of filial love, there remains the threat of an unbidden and uncontrollable surge of sexual emotion in relation to the mother which can evoke acute anxiety. For its transfiguration into literature this erotic arousal hits too close to the heart for the poet and the writer to recollect it in aesthetic tranquillity.

Myths and folktales, on the other hand, are collective rather than individual productions, and do not suffer from the limitations imposed by the artist's life-historical defenses. One example of a direct depiction of 'mother love' is the myth about the goddess Durga whose intercourse with her son was observed and noisily interrupted by peacocks. In her anger Durga cursed the peacocks with impotence and an ugly, raucous voice. Later she relented and permitted the poor fowl to procreate by means of their tears. (Incidentally both the Kunala legend and the Durga myth support the psychoanalytic postulation of the existence of an unconscious, symbolic equation between blindness and castration, eyes and penis, tears and semen.)

Indian tales of mother–son incest centre on the mother and the fatefulness of her wishes. Collected in its many variations by the folklorist A.K. Ramanujan, the paradigmatic story runs as follows:

A girl is born with a curse on her head that she would marry her own son and beget a son by him. As soon as she hears of the curse, she wilfully vows she'd try and escape it: she secludes herself in a dense forest, eating only fruit, forswearing all male company. But when she attains puberty, as fate would have it, she eats a mango from a tree under which a passing king has urinated. The mango impregnates her; bewildered, she gives birth to a male child; she wraps him in a piece of her sari and throws him in a nearby stream. The child is picked up by the king of the next kingdom, and he grows up to be a handsome young adventurous prince. He comes hunting in the self-same jungle, and the cursed woman falls in love with the stranger, telling herself she is not in danger any more as she has no son alive. She marries him and bears him a child. According to custom, the father's swaddling clothes are preserved and brought out for the newborn son. The woman recognizes at once the piece of sari with which she had swaddled her first son, now her husband, and understands that her fate had really caught up with her. She waits till everyone is asleep, and sings a lullaby to her newborn baby:

> Sleep
> O son
> O grandson
> O brother to my husband
> Sleep O Sleep Sleep Well

and hangs herself by the rafter with her sari twisted to a rope.[32]

What is striking in this Indian story, and its variants, is the absence of the father of the Oedipal triangulation so characteristic of ancient Greek or European drama. It is indeed solely a woman's story which, in the culture, is invariably narrated to and by women.

The mother's disavowal of her incestuous wishes by transferring the responsibility for the act to the workings of fate—a curse, the gods—is present in all versions of the tale. Common in all, too, is the attempt to elevate the object of the incest, and hence the impulse itself, to a domain where natural laws, the rule of the body and the social order are inoperative. A son is conceived without intercourse, thus leaving both the mother and son initially untainted by her sexuality. Moreover, it is a *king's* liquids—sweat, tears, blood, semen, in different variations—which make for the birth of the son, always a prince of sorts, rendering the incestuous possibility more acceptable, a 'royal incest'. Yet, in spite of the denial of the wish, the effort to strip it of original sin and all the other stratagems employed by fantasy, the revelation of the great secret still results in the woman's suicide in most versions of the tale. As in the story of Phaedra, the self-sacrifice serves as a testimony to the power of guilt in the mother's desire for the son as a lover. It is a desire driving to the very heart of passion while endangering at the same time the very soul of the family and the society surrounding it.

There are, however, other versions of the tale in which the mother, after learning the incestuous secret, sensibly keeps it to herself while she continues to live as a lover and wife to her son-husband. (This, according to some commentators, was the intention of Oedipus' mother-wife Jocasta, who may have known of the incest all along but whose hopes were dashed on the shoals of a man's uncompromising moral curiosity.) We can only speculate that this less-than-tragic conclusion to the tale reflects its deeper feminine perspective in ways quite different from the blood and thunder climaxes spun out by Euripides and Racine—both men. Perhaps women, in their own imaginative fictions, are more matter-of-fact and accepting of the paradoxes of sensual immersion and the dangers that lurk in the sexual realm. As mothers they seem better able to accept the guilt of incestuous urgings than their sons who, in their literary creations, would destroy them for all too natural transgressions.

As a developmental phenomenon the Oedipus complex is constructed of illusion and unidirectional desire. A little boy is beleaguered by his erotic yearnings for his mother and does not truly conceive of hers for him, which are known only to sage adults privy to the murmurs of a chaste mother's heart. Indeed when these are too much in evidence in a boy's life, confronting him in his bitterness and vulnerability, his passionate development may be thrown awry. A downright seductive mother and the cruelly precocious triumph offered in her intimations of incest move her admirer to retreat. Often he will damn and dam up the tides of heterosexuality, neuter himself or seek out sensual solace in other males.

When, at last, the developing lover encounters woman in adolescence, not merely as a creation of his 'heat-oppressed brain' but as a hot, desirous person in her own right, he sees deeper into his past and his destiny. The cardbord construction, making mother both desired and safe, crumbles to reveal an aching personhood. Only the glue of shared morality protected them, he learns, from that 'tragic bliss' that is a cataclysm as far as the social and familial orders are concerned.

The moment of hitherto forbidden pleasure—one of Freud's patients tasting desire's fruit exclaimed that he would murder his father for the sensation—is also a rite of passage and an omen. It signals the end of a protected childhood, the assumption of generational authority, the demise of those dearly loved and direly needed, the utter reality of desire in the flesh. In literature at its best, the paradoxical onslaught is embraced and given form. In real life the young lover may recoil, resurrecting his childish Oedipus complex as a defence against adult actuality.

Whether mothers or not, then, all women present challenges of this sort to a sexual initiate. Long awaited, embodiment in the flesh of a fantasy hitherto entertained in the mind's eye alone, the conjunction of action and physical arousal—all these may move some men to flee the moment of climax. But, for most, in the fitful embraces of warm womanhood, reality falls wonderfully into place as the teenager strives to accept the gift proffered him, aspiring to the courage required by love and of lovers.

PART III

LOVE THEORY AND LOVE STORY

Othello tells of Desdemona and himself wooing each other, deeming it an 'unvarnished tale'. Simply enough she 'loved him for the dangers [he] did pass', and 'he loved her that she did pity them'. He is describing a pure moment, and pure feeling, of course, and suggesting that reflections and ideational embellishments do little to capture love's essence as it exists in 'the love story'.

It is only in the loving encounter of two people, the meeting of their bodies and their perusal of each other's souls, that love finds form, or else perhaps, in the invocations and evocations of music, poetry and the like. The analytic enterprise, which tries to break down all of psychic life into its component parts, rather than distilling or synthesizing them in one single moment of expression, may seem by its very nature antithetical to its subject's veracity. Why, then, even attempt a 'conclusion' on the general theme of love—a 'love theory'? Our aim, like the technical and developmental percepts which govern the clinical analyst, is to allow ourselves and our readers to deepen these erotic and aesthetic moments when they occur by adding to them, a sort of anticipatory knowledge, a self-knowledge in fact. Having opened further chambers for reverberation, generalization and explanations can then disappear, at the point of expression and attention, into the background lest they clutter or deform. Forget us, in other words, as the patient so often forgets her or his analyst's interpretations, but attend somehow differently in the future.

CHAPTER EIGHT

THE PHENOMENOLOGY OF PASSIONATE LOVE

In the intermediary space between body and mind, bounded by biological instinct on one side and imaginative impulse on the other, lies the country of passionate love. In both Western and Eastern cultures this has been considered a new territory, a recent phenomenon in historical time, a province no more than two thousand years old in India and classical Greece, and younger in Europe. It was 'discovered' only after sexual love between man and woman had begun to emancipate itself from its biological function of reproduction alone. Progressively conquering nature, the survival of old and young alike assured in diminishing infant mortality rates, men and women could begin to choose each other according to spiritual and sensual lights rather than biological and social dictates. No longer merely instinctive or crudely purposeful, eroticism *per se* began to free itself from moralities and kinship laws subserving the preservation of the family and, ultimately, the larger social order. With this there followed its romatic elaboration.

Indeed, there is but one activity in love's country. As its philosophers have defined it, its religion and commerce consist of the single-minded and relentless search of individuals desiring to constitute themselves into two-person universes. In the words of Teilhard de Chardin, this activity is 'the play of countless subtle antennae seeking one another in the light and darkness of the soul; the pull towards mutual sensibility and completion, in which preoccupation with preserving the species gradually dissolves in the greater intoxication of two people consummating the world'.[1] In the many 'dividual' or contained universes within this country the delirium of love's passion is both 'normal' and avidly sought. The dread, in fact, lies in a loss of such feverishness and a consequent return to a world of ordinary consciousness becomes in its distantiated realism arid and alien.

These deliria and the delusions and illusions they foster have been condemned by men of so-called good sense— Christian theologians, Muslim divines, Hindu pundits, even perhaps a few psychoanalysts. As spokesmen of their societies they have for many centuries tried to bring the rule of the law to the erotic spontaneity which in their eyes runs wild in this profane terrain. Rarely have they recognized that the attractions of passionate love lie not only, or even primarily, in the promise of an orgiastic license but in the fascination exercised by its paradoxes. On the one hand there do exist those burning torments of unrequited or unconsummated love, the sharp stabs of jealous possession and the high pitch of love's 'supreme joy'—the *hoechste Lust* of Wagner's Isolde. On the other, however, are found the devotion and the meditation, 'the religious intimacy' and the 'gravity' of the lovers' world. The land of love is not only overgrown with steamy jungles and criss-crossed by untamed torrents but, at the same time, dotted with many a 'tolerant and enchanted slope' on which, as Auden tells us, while the lovers die in their ordinary swoon, 'Grave the vision Venus sends / Of supernatural sympathy / Universal love and hope.'[2]

Passionate Love: Desire and Longing

Freud, as the first psychoanalyst, was in fact a natural philosopher. His views of love have their clear sources in the spirit of the nineteenth century. In his first book on Eros and the wellsprings of love, Freud posited an initial union of the two currents of *Sinnlichkeit* and *Zaertlichkeit*—the sensual and the affectionate. For Freud both flowed out of the single subterranean reservoir of the libido, that ratio-mystical pool of the sexual instinctual drives, its rivers coursing along the frontiers of the body and mind.[3] The tender, protective stream, Freud felt, was one of desire, diverted by inhibitory dams and delaying its gratification to preserve the well-being and abiding availability of the other person. The second had an openly lustful intent, imperiously and precipitously seeking satisfaction for its own sake, a tidal rush of gut instinct. According to Freud these currents diverge during the course of life, crisscrossing now and then to converge again in what he called 'adult object love'. It is in the plumbing of subcurrents and their interrelation with one another that we have sought to fathom the core of passionate love.

Freud's stress on the physical or sensual underpinnings of love has troubled many, not all of them simplistic moralists. Some have proposed a different category of love altogether—more platonic 'true love' or 'loving', where the role of sexual impulsion *per se* is lacking, or at least muted.

The contemporary challenge to the primacy of physical desire does not derive from an anachronistic resurgence of some Rousseauan romantic puritanism. Rather, this deep uneasiness with the instinctual element of love, we would surmise, stems from an inchoate understanding of dimly perceived and unexpected fantasies which are largely unconscious. These hidden products of our unknown minds show themselves in the form of unexpected and often frightening shades of stabbings of the heart. These suggest that sexual desire as we typically know it may also have aims other than the keen pleasure of genital intercourse and orgasm. One elemental urge tends to dredge up other instinctual elements—witness, for instance, Romeo's devouring, insatiable hunger.

Psychoanalysis became belatedly a 'dual instinct theory', granting libido and aggression equal footing. Criticizing his erstwhile disciple Alfred Adler, Freud commented that his psychology of power omitted to consider 'love', the very heart of the psychoanalytic enterprise. It was a long time before Freud could countenance violence as an essential element of psychic life. Reluctantly, in the wake of the First World War, twenty years into psychoanalysis, Freud came to speak of an elemental death instinct directed towards the self and its obliteration, subsequently turned outwards against others. His followers were eventually to speak of the aggression drives, thereby emphasizing man's cruelty and murderousness towards his fellows. In any event, the cauldron of the instinctual drives was now seen to contain two sets of drives; lift the lid for one and the other might pour forth without rhyme or reason. Violence and loving might even be bound together in some terrifying unity.

In unconscious erotic fantasies the darker purposes of destructive aggression come into play. According to Sartre, possession is paramount in sexual intercourse—the chaining of the partner's will to one's own and therefore the reduction of his or her consciousness to a reactivity of the flesh alone.[4] The urge to subjugate, he continues, prevails over the wish for pleasure as the individual seeks to assault and degrade the partner. Thus, for instance, a man's arousal and attention concentrate on the least personal, most inert parts of the woman's body—breasts, thighs, stomach.

There is resonance in Sartre's view, however incomplete as it is in its didacticism. A variant of the 'possession fantasy', for example, finds its way into classical Sanskrit love poetry, with its rhapsodic descriptions of female breasts and hips, thighs and navels, and its predilection for love scenes where woman trembles in a state of diffuse but nongenital bodily excitement as if timorously anticipating a sadistic attack, her terror a source of excitement for both herself and her would-be assailant. In Kalidas's *Kumara Sambhava*, a fourth-century masterpiece of erotic poetry, for instance, Siva becomes impassioned at the sight of nail marks at the root of Parvati's thighs, deep tooth marks on her injured lower lip and her dishevelled hair. His excitement reaches a crescendo when Parvati 'in the beginning felt both fear and love'. And in our own tales the violence of the 'possession fantasy' is most graphic in the description of the sexual intercourse between Vis and Ramin.

While not equivalent with it, the hostility of sexual conquest is reminiscent of the 'normal' displays of aggression and apparent violence observable in the mating of many mammals. Briffault eloquently depicts the spectacle:

With both the male and female, 'love' or sexual attraction is originally and pre-eminently 'sadi'; it is positively gratified by the infliction of pain; it is as cruel as hunger. That is the direct, fundamental, and longest established sentiment connected with the sexual impulse. The male animal captures, mauls and bites the female, who in turn uses her teeth and claws freely, and the lovers issue from the sexual combat bleeding and mangled. Crustaceans usually lose a limb or two in the encounter. All mammals without exception use their teeth on these occasions. . . The congress of the sexes is assimilated by the impulse to hurt, to shed blood, to kill, to the encounter between a beast of prey and its victim and all distinction between the two is not infrequently lost. It would be more accurate to speak of the sexual impulse as pervading nature with a yell of cruelty than with a hymn of love.[5]

Aggression in the service of self-gratification is no doubt an essential ingredient of the paradoxes of which passion is composed. Sexual violence bespeaks instinctual desire in its rawer form. Phylogenetically it harkens back to the procreative and territorial prerogatives which the male animal asserts when it lays claim to a female—baser motives from sociobiology still very much with us. It finds its ontogenetic origins in each child's fanciful misconception of the sheer physicality of the so-called 'primal scene'. As he overhears their groaning, senses the sweating and abandon to feeling, the child is quite overwhelmed by the bestiality and power of his caretakers as sexual beings. To a child's unschooled imagination the parents in sexual congress seem to be engaged in a sort of mutual violence. That they survive a fight to death seems miraculous to many for whom the terror of it all halts or erodes erotic development.

Many cultures have sought to civilize and transform this aggression into exquisite refinements of the pleasure it ultimately serves. In the *Kamasutra*, for instance, the 'bestiality' of intercourse or, better, foreplay elaborated and extolled, is evident in its chapters on the eight forms of 'the love scratch' and 'the love bite'. A scratch made on the foreparts of a woman's breast is compared to the marks of 'a tiger's claw'; tooth marks on the base of the breast are compared to the 'chewing of a boar'.

This rather benign or playful violence, civilized into foreplay, is delectable for all involved in it. Hostility proper—the wish to *harm* and *degrade* the object—frequently does not express itself in convulsive overt violence at all. It is more detached, manifest in cold rage rather than hot lust. The possessive and hostile 'lover' does not give up his self-possession, seeking instead a reversal of trauma and a revenge for the early slights and the hidden injuries of the parent–child relationship. And indeed the French sensibility does touch on a dynamic truth known to the psychoanalyst from his studies. Sadism subserves self, the clinician knows all too well. The degradation of the other, through sexual instruments of power, is exploited as testimony to one's own would-be grandeur, fostering all manner of ritualized cruelty—most notably, of course, misogyny.

In women the counterpart of the phallocentric possession—encompassing the woman's urge to attract, 'entrap' and control the male—is rarely expressed in the same way as in men, namely in conscious or unconscious fantasies of conquest, ravishment and mastery. Rather it takes a more circuitous route, wherein, as Erich Fromm once put it, mirroring their typical coital posture, women—in subtle and not so subtle ways—would undermine the man who thinks he dominates her.[6]

Given woman's social dependence and vulnerability to masculine whims through centuries, and their inevitable impact on her psyche and specific sense of femininity, it follows that her vindictiveness should be expressed in images of herself as a self-abasing and self-humiliating slave—a slave, that is, who mocks the pretentious master that is man. As the sociologist Evelyne Sullerot observes of French feminine writings over the centuries

There is no weightier set of chains, no more paralysing trap, than a woman 'who has totally surrendered' to a man ... They escape their would-be masters by the very excess of the dependence forced upon them, paralysing them, devouring them.[7]

Treated as chattel, woman, in other words, seeks to debase and control man through a caricature of masochistic slavery which veils her more fundamental control of his appetites and emotions. She toys with his sexual urges and needs while perpetuating for him an illusion of his supremacy. In the process she charges him with utter responsibility for her lot, shackling him with the ball and chain of a guilty conscience. She then becomes the possessor of good will and absolution in the granting of her sexual favours.

Freud's sensual current, then, the *Sinnlichkeit*, falls under the rubric of an even more complex and encompassing instinctual *desire*. In this the body's wanting and its violence, the mind's yearning for sexual pleasure but also the need to rid itself of ancient pain and noxious hate, the excitement of orgasm and the fierce exultation of possession, all flow together. Where desire alone holds sway and the body overtakes the soul the boundaries of the self are not expanded to include another, but rather the self and its impulses are propelled outwards, effectively effacing what lies in their path.

The kinds of wishes we have just described, wherein aggression comes into play, are inevitable but insufficient components of love.

The urge towards conquest is an incentive on the way to a passionate embrace. Yet love does, as the psychoanalyst puts it, transform or 'neutralize' hostility, even sublimates it, such that its aims and form are no longer recognizable. Dominance and intrusiveness make entry into a woman possible for a man, and with it the loss of his self-composure when he yields something of his self, his seed to her. The act of union is, as we shall soon argue, also therefore one of parting with something of one's self, of willing surrender. Aggression therefore is not *the* central theme, we contend, but an inevitable corollary of love. Heightened, hostility may in fact sever the bonds that unite two individuals in love. Here we part company from the studied cynic who cavils only at what is for him or her, mawkish, outworn or dishonest romanticism.

A stress on desire alone leaves out the human need to preserve what is possessed. As far as intercourse is concerned, penetration and domination constitute penultimate acts en route to a higher goal—that of union. Entering the body of the lover, or taking it into oneself, the individual cannot fully embrace the psyche of another. The quest for oneness finds its object elusive and illusory. It may be that it is a foreknowledge of this ultimate privation which moves the individual to hate in advance what or who cannot be had, confounding love with lust as the onlookers do in *Romeo and Juliet*.

In passionate love there is, then, another stream—Freud's tender current—in which the adoration and cherishing of the person for whom one lusts override the forces of ambivalence, selfishness and destruction which, we must concede, accompany the quest for pleasure. This tender stream we would signify with the idea of *longing*, which in conjunction with desire gives birth to the dialectic of romantic eroticism. In Roland Barthes' words,

I want to possess, fiercely, but I also know how to give, actively . . . I see the other with a double vision; sometimes as object, sometimes as subject; I hesitate between my tyranny and oblation. I am condemned to be a saint or a monster; unable to be one, unwilling to be the other.[8]

The prototypes of the 'longing' in passionate love can be found in three well-known myths from Greece, India and Persia which are among the earliest attempts of the human imagination to formulate in poetic images and symbols an explanation of heterosexual love. They offer metaphors for the hermaphroditic quest for self-completion and fulfilment which underlies it.

According to Plato's myth in his *Symposium*, with Aristophanes as his spokesman, humans began life as spherical creatures with eight limbs, two faces and two genital organs facing in the opposite direction. These beings were so mighty and strong that they posed a threat to the gods. Zeus retaliated against their *hubris* when they attacked the gods, not by destroying them but by cutting them in two. From then on, the two parts of human beings, each desiring his (or her) other half 'came together, and throwing their arms about one another, entwined in mutual embraces, longing to grow into one: they were on the point of dying from hunger and self-neglect, because they did not like to do anything apart.'[9] They were in the process of thus destroying themselves when Zeus at last took pity on them, relented, and turned their genitals around to the front so that they could at least embrace in intercourse. Thus they 'might be satisfied, and rest, and go their ways to the business of life: so ancient is the desire of one another which is implanted in us, reuniting our original nature, making one of two, and healing the state of man.'[10]

In the Indian myth of creation from the Upanishads, Purusha was alone at the beginning of the universe. Looking around, he saw nothing other than himself. 'He found no pleasure at all. So, [even now] a man who is all alone finds no pleasure. He longed for a second. Now he was the size of a man and woman in close embrace. He split this Self in two: and from this arose husband and wife . . . He copulated with her and there were human beings born'.[11] Besides the myth of an original androgynous being, formally expressed in literature and art in the figure of Siva as half man and half woman, Indians conceived of another explanation for human origins. In this story the first man, Manu or Yama, and his sister, Yami, were twins. After the latter had overcome the former's scruples, they produced the human race.

This myth is very similar to the ancient Persian story of Mashya and Mashyoi, who grew up intertwined in the form of a tree. The twins were united in such a manner that their arms rested behind on their shoulders while their waists were brought close and so connected below that it was impossible to distinguish what belonged to one and what to the other. Later they were changed from the plant into human shape, received a soul, and copulated to sire the human race.

In all these narratives, as well as in the terse Koranic statement, based on the creation myth of Genesis, 'It is He that created you of one soul, and fashioned thereof its spouse, that he might find repose in her' (Koran, 189), there is a striking lack of stress on sensual exuberance. Correspondingly, they underplay the roles of sexual desire and heterosexual intercourse in the conjunction of man and woman. Rather, these myths contend, lovers strive for a sort of swaddling in the contours of another, a person whose gender fits the mould but whose flesh is almost incidental to the primeval quest for wholeness. Commenting on his own myth Plato remarks, 'for the intense yearning which each of them has towards the other does not appear to be the desire of lover's intercourse, but of something else which the soul of either evidently desires and cannot tell and of which he has only a dark and doubtful presentiment.'[12] The myths make it clear that 'this something else', which we have called longing, lies anterior to desire.

The longing for union is not for a *fusion*, with which it is often confused, which would recreate the original androgynous entity. Union makes the boundary of the self permeable; it does not altogether erase it. It heightens the sense of both the self and the other; it does not create a new, merged state which screens a secret solipsism by obliterating, finally, our awareness of another. The narcissistic self-sufficiency of an undifferentiated being who does not require another is implicitly condemned by all the myths; Plato's globular monsters are, after all, not only unattractive but in danger of annihilation; Purusha, alone, 'does not enjoy happiness', while the tree of Mashya and Mashyoi, joined at the trunk, lacks soul.

The myths also suggest that the solution to the anxiety of separation does not lie in a regressive 'dedifferentiation' of self and another, which blurs the difference between I and you, and subsequently male and female. The answer resides in a specifically heterosexual commingling which temporarily assuages the ache of this longing for release, rest and immersion. Even if it cannot erase felt solitude altogether, intercourse provides a respite which is both immediate and evanescent. Granted no amount of physical and emotional mingling of lovers can undo their sense of distinctness from one another—to obliterate the fateful sexual distinction that one is the 'he' and one the 'she'. Yet moments of deep sexual intimacy and the ambisexual illusion they tender permit men and women to transcend the reality of their corporeal boundaries, to join longing to desire, as in the embrace of Radha and Krishna, and fulfil both in the cataclysmic tenderness of the orgasm.

Longing presupposes, first, a special kind of identification that makes the person of the beloved attain for the lover a centrality at least the equal of his own. Infusing sexual sensibility and action, such identification heightens a man's masculinity (and its acceptance) by satisfying his feminine aspirations in the embrace and vicarious enjoyment of his lover's womanhood—and *vice versa*. These identifications are complex phenomena, as elusive as they are compelling, and to which many mental processes contribute. We have tried to plumb their nature in some of our tales—in *Romeo and Juliet*, and perhaps, most starkly, in the secret passion of Radha and Krishna.

Longing requires, also, an idealization, that great construct of imagination which is capable of conceiving with the conviction of known fact a more perfect and valuable reality while ensuring that what is idealized is inevitably adored, admired and held in awe. Idealization makes 'me' experience the loved one as an infinitely superior being to whom 'I' willingly subordinate my desire. I need the other outside of myself as a *telos* to which or whom I can surrender and obey and thus reverse the accents of the master–servant metaphor of possessive desire. Somehow I sense that without this *telos* of another I shall share the futility of Narcissus who, in Auden's interpretation, 'falls in love with his reflection; he wishes to become its servant, but instead his reflection insists upon being his slave.'[13] The idealizing fervour of passionate love, which recognizes only the spontaneity of religious passion and grateful devotion as its equal, reveals the beloved as a being of almost sacred stature—the Layla of Majnun's vision. It is that part of the lover's 'discourse' (i.e. passion) which, to quote Barthes,

is usually a smooth envelope which encases the image, a very gentle glove around the sacred being. It is a devout, orthodox discourse. When the image alters, the envelope of devotion rips apart, a shock capsizes my own language (the horror of spoiling [the idealization]) is stronger than the anxiety of losing.[14]

The great imaginative creations of identification and idealization are only preliminary achievements in the work of longing. They are, so to say, psychic looseners, jarring the soul out of the narcissistic sheath of normal, everyday, self-limiting routines. They serve as a prelude, establishing in the lover a special receptivity, a readiness to risk transcending individual boundaries so that he can become as one with the beloved. As Ortega y Gasset remarks, whereas in every other situation in life nothing upsets us so much as to see the frontiers of our individual existence trespassed upon by another person, the rapture of love consists in feeling ourselves so metaphysically porous to another person that only in the fusion of both can it find fulfilment.[15] In it we hunger for that which otherwise threatens our individual survival.

The striving for ineffable union, *the* longing par excellence, has been traditionally considered love's greatest gift, Yeats' 'marvellous moon' that love tears from the clouds. Suffusing our relationships, such yearning becomes the fount of what is most exalted in human beings and their aspirations. It constitutes much of the subject matter of poetry (as also the more poetic aspects of theology and metaphysics), and it provides the starting point for various aesthetic and mystical ventures.

Love's longing to transcend personal boundaries in a union with the other suggests many parallels to mysticism, especially to its devotional variety. The relationship between the two has been pondered by theologians over many centuries, leading in the Christian tradition to a distinction between sacred and profane love. No wonder so many secular and profane lovers have hitherto taken divine vows in search of oneness and tranquillity while others, then and now, have fled their ecclesiastical communities, spurred on by erotic passion. The poets, though, the ecstatics of love, scorned such distinctions in favour of giving expression to the underlying identity between the two. In much of Sufi and Hindu erotic/religious poetry, as also in John Donne's songs and sonnets, for instance, it is impossible to know whether the beloved is human or divine, and whether the poet himself makes this distinction or even considers it important!

In both East and West, religious traditions would interpret the longings of passionate love as essentially a vain quest for a *unio mystica*, fated to founder since it has found only an inferior object. They would contend that the lover needs to take one further step from the person of the beloved creature to the Person of their common Creator, for the love of the individual to the love of All. Profane love falls short of the sacred, dooming the lover to mortality's frustrations.

Where the mystic envisions a yearning for oneness with that which is everlasting, the psychoanalyst will often see a forlorn attempt to recapture long-lost unity from the infant's earliest experience. In the emotional and sensual riches granted in the fleeting moments of oneness with the mother and the maternal universe, there, too, was a similar quality of (in Ibn Hazm's words)

that pure happiness which is without alloy, and gladness unsullied by sorrow, the perfect realization of hopes and the complete fulfilment of one's dreams . . . a miracle of wonder surpassing the tongues of the eloquent, and far beyond the reach of the most cunning speech to describe: the mind reels before it, and the intellect stands abashed.[16]

This is not to say that longing is reducible only to its infantile origins, for novelty is fundamental to this sort of over-reaching. All *recherches du temps perdus* are transfigured by the changing consciousness of psychic growth, each evolving mode of knowing obliterating the contents of previous experience, so different in its qualities of perceiving and encoding, seeing and remembering. Attempts like this, entailing what analysis calls the twin processes of regression and restitution, induce the tensions of colliding, irreconcilable realities. Sometimes the dissonances are so unbearable as to produce anxieties of psychotic proportions. Yet in art, love and mysticism, with their consensual and sometimes ritualized rules of illusion, the longing for union erotic or mystical, need not imply a psychotic dissolution of the demarcators between self and object, fantasy and consensual reality. Conjoining with the *newly* idealized other, and identifying with this *novel* perspective, the lover's sense of himself, more secure initially than the madman's, and of the world around him, becomes heightened, as if discovered anew. The lover is filled to the brim, not depleted, and there is no need for that restitution in delusion and hallucination that is the prime work of insanity. Quite the contrary, a lover's ache is anything but a void.

The lover is akin to the mystic who, when in a state of grace, rekindles the world with a fresh vision, discovering or rather endowing it with new-found beauty and harmony. In the moving verses of St John of the Cross:

> Overflowing with God's grace
> He passed through the groves in haste
> And, though he saw them
> In their natural state
> He left them garbed in
> Beauty to his taste.[17]

Erotic grace illuminates what have been hitherto perceived as shadows, background figures, animates a lover's relationship with nature and art, and deepens his sensate and metaphysical responsiveness. The garbing of the world with 'beauty to his taste' is, of course, most striking in first love. In a quieter vein, however, this basic creation of meaning and a subjective ordering of the outside world is equally true of any mature lover who falls in love passionately. In the full circle of love, what is familiar is also surprising.

The ecstasy—from *ek stasis*, to be outside one's self and the world—which comes with the fulfilment of longing, reaches beyond the cold triumph of aggressive conquest and the transience of orgasmic explosion in the satisfying of genital desire. It is, put simply, a feeling of complete peace in an ineffable intimacy. Thus, the eighth-century Sanskrit poet Bhavabhuti lets Rama, with Sita asleep across his arm, reflect on it as 'this state where there is no twoness in responses of joy or sorrow / where the heart finds rest; where feeling does not dry with age / where concealments fall away in time and essential love is ripened.'[18] The hidden promise of all passionate love, the eye of the instinctual storm—this peace is not as much quiescence, a complacence of the heart, as voluptuous absorption and repose. Yeats evokes this in verses from the poem, 'The Indian to his love':

> The island dreams under the dawn
> And great boughs drop tranquillity;
> The peahens dance on a smooth lawn,

A parrot sways upon a tree,
Raging at his own image in the enamelled sea.

Here we will moor our lonely ship
And wander ever with woven hands
Murmuring softly lip to lip,
Along the grass, along the sands,
Murmuring how far away are the unquiet lands.

How we alone of mortals are,
Hid under quiet boughs apart
While our love grows an Indian star,
A meteor of the burning heart
One with the tide that gleans,
The wings that gleam and dart.[19]

Just as some philosophers have equated the whole of erotic desire with one of its parts—possessive violence, for example—so have others discerned at the core of longing nothing more than a masochistic offering, suffrance, and ultimately a nirvana of self-destruction and death. With all the anguish in lyric poetry and the glorification of woe and wretchedness in novels of forlorn love, it is indeed a seductive idea, namely to believe that torment is love's aim.

In one such view, derived from a less than careful application of psychoanalysis to literature, one which does credit to neither, love is seen to be motivated by unconscious guilt and its tortured expiation—by a 'moral masochism', in short. 'In the love story', William Evans observes,

it is as if both author and the reader enter into an unconscious pact and the writer says, 'You want a pretext to enjoy a masochistic fantasy and to enjoy it without the reproaches of conscience. I will provide you with a most skilfully devised rationalization—all the more so as it is the name of love.'[20]

It is, however, often forgotten that one major reason for the preponderance of pain and anguish in the literature of love has to do with the nature of the literary enterprise itself. 'Happy love has no history', de Rougemont ruefully remarks—an observation familiar to everyone since novels were written.[21] Auden, with his usual lucidity, argues in the same fashion for poetry:

Of the many (far too many) love poems written in the first person which I have read, the most convincing were either fal-la-la's of a good natured sensuality which made no pretense at serious love, or howls of grief because the beloved had died and was no longer capable of love, or roars of disapproval because she loved another or nobody but herself; the least convincing were those in which the poet claimed to be earnest, yet had no complaints to make.[22]

Passionate love is not solely the stuff of raw nerves, bleeding wounds and sheer pain. It is not a pathological variant of 'algolagnia', to borrow from the sexologists of the nineteenth century. To reduce its periods of inevitable self-doubt and despair to masochism, in itself a notoriously ambiguous and over-inclusive notion, is to close one's eyes to the limitations of human existence and seriously to overestimate, in a way the novelist and the poet do not, the range of human freedom and available choices.

A second argument advanced in favour of love as moral masochism takes as its evidence its power to subjugate the lover—a truth which has distressed scores of poets, among them Shakespeare: 'Being your slave, what should I do but tend / Upon the hours and times of your desire?'[23] This fear of a dangerous vulnerability to the power and whims of the beloved again seems to be of greater concern to men, with their fears of emasculation and inability to become habituated to receptivity. Their timorousness contrasts with the sanguine optimism of women, who are more accustomed to taking in and being invaded and even used by others (their babies even more than their men). Once more it is the man's terror most in evidence, especially so in the West. The lament is relatively absent in Indian love poetry where a large number of poets— especially those influenced by *bhakti* and Sufi ideas—positively welcomed their 'enslavement'. In this culture greater sanction is granted to the sacrifice of a delimited selfhood to something—be it a godly abstraction or a joint family—

transcendent or at least overarching. In medieval Islam, too, with Majnun as a prototype, there were cultivated men of letters who applauded love's slavery as a state of being that enhanced a man rather than diminished him.

One of the wonderful things that occurs in Love is the way the lover submits to the beloved, and adjusts his own character by main force to that of his loved one. Often and often you will see a man stubborn by disposition, intractable, jibbing at all control, determined, arrogant, always ready to take umbrage, yet no sooner let him sniff the soft air of love, plunge into its waves, and swim in its sea, than his stubbornness will have suddenly changed to docility, his intractability to gentleness, his determination to easy-going, his arrogance to submission.[24]

Man's dismay at his surrender to woman centres less on the possibility of a breakthrough of his masochistic urges than on the twin dreads of 'feminization' and 'annihilation' in adoring and, inevitably, identifying with her. These fears are, once again, rooted in infancy, the era when the child is helplessly dependent upon the mother and has yet to differentiate his male psyche from her feminine aura. Both anxieties belong to the shadow side of the longing for union, fears which have expressed themselves so variously in our tales of love.

In passion, longing is revealed to desire as if to lend to the latter permanency and stability. Yet, and this is love's greatest paradox, the urgency of sexual excitement and possessive violence, in which desire finds shape, cannot, after all, be reconciled with the still tempo of mutual repose. Desire and longing do not combine to build a solution in some chemical sense; but at least, and only at certain moments, they may temporarily be in a state of amicable suspension. As Barthes observes: 'The tender gesture says: ask me anything that can put your body to sleep, but also do not forget that I desire you—a little, lightly, without trying to seize anything right away.'[25] The firm contours of the self presupposed by one aspect of passionate love—desire—stands in opposition to the willingness to yield and accede to the union demanded by the other—longing. Sensual and possessive desire aspires to be fulfilled by the overpowering of its object while longing would have her or him indestructible, immortal, and ascendant.

This disclosure of desire and longing to each other is, to paraphrase Octavio Paz's observation, almost always painful because the existence of the other person presents itself as a body that is penetrated and a consciousness which is impenetrable.[26] In the erotic pursuit the soul is also 'a vision that is not insensible to touch'. These and other similar dilemmas pervade passionate love with irreducible ambiguity and potential tragedy. At one end of the long tunnel there is no rejoicing, no song and verse extolling its glory, but often enough lovers' cries cursing it as a plague and a poisonous affliction. Here, in Bedier's ringing words in *Tristan and Isolde*, the onlooker is called upon to witness 'Passion and Joy most sharp, and Anguish without end, and Death.'[27]

An awareness of love's simultaneous joy and anguish conforms with what has become the 'modern' view. Traditional Sanskrit poetry, in contrast, with its myriad rules for creating a particular mood, deemed inappropriate the intermingling in the same love poem of love's happiness with its sorrow.[28] Whereas the erotic may combine on equal terms with the comic and on unequal terms with the compassionate, the combination which Sanskrit so studiously avoids characterizes much of what is best in modern Western literature, with its Marxist and Freudian emphasis on the dialectics of human nature. It is the exception, the rare Sanskrit love poem, that breaks this rule, which has the greatest resonance for the modern reader.

The torment and obsessive quality of passionate love derives not only from the inherent conflict—a collision, a squashing together—of desire and longing, but also from the unyielding reality each encounters. Hence the wish for Liebestod, for the fateful conclusion to it all and the release promised in it, as the ironic outcome of erotic vitality. In longing, the 'purest' state is one when the soul nearly contains the body. Lovers like Tristan and Isolde or Layla and Majnun, who yearn for their souls to merge and become one, find consummation impossible as long as they do have bodies. Their ultimate goal becomes no longer to live but rather die in each other's arms, escaping the flesh that once excited their aspiration but has become a prison. In *The Merchant of Venice* Lorenzo tells his Jessica, 'Such harmony is in immortal souls; But whilst this muddy vesture of decay / Doth grossly close it in, we cannot hear it.'[29] Corporeal reality forces lovers to doubt what they most believe by insisting on the existence of a final mystery that separates one from the other. It dictates that the challenge to death and to the transitory nature of the individual, contained in love's transcendence of self, is doomed to fail. This reality enjoins us to accept the sadness of our 'savage solitude' and, if we are lucky, to learn in the beloved's eyes, 'that existence is enough'.

The fate of instinctual desire, all-wanting and all-consuming, is no better, for it must perforce grapple with finitude and freedom of the other. As Auden states it,

Tristan and Isolde (the symbol of longing) are tormented because they are compelled to count up to two when they long to be able only to count up to one; Don Juan (the symbol of desire) is in torment because, however great the number of his seductions, it still remains a finite number and he cannot rest until he has counted up to infinity.[30]

Freud's first version of the pleasure principle proves inadequate. Desire does not subside with seeming satiation. Each orgasmic encounter merely whets the appetite in self-perpetuity. Memory as well as deliciousness of pleasure's ache gnaw at us, making it impossible to rest.

The suffering of passionate love is felt by individuals differently, in consonance with the variety of the lives they have led. As psychoanalysts Martin Bergmann and Otto Kernberg, among others, have pointed out, all crossings of borders amount to a defiant sally into forbidden territory, challenging time-honoured prohibitions against breaching sexual and family barriers and taboos which are so basic a component of human society.[31] In crossing individual, sexual and, as we saw in the stories of Hamlet, Phaedra and the Indian tales, generational boundaries, passionate love collides with the culture and its inner emissary, the 'superego', Freud's term for conscience and the ideas and critical faculties of which it is composed. The rigidity and unyielding cruelty of this conscience, the extent to which it is punitive or benign, will influence the intensity of the guilt and the suffering which are, alas, in some measure inevitable corollaries of love. Christendom, antipathetic as it is to fleshy appetites, seems to have engendered some of the guiltiest of lovers. But other factors too, as we saw in our tales from Islamic and Hindu cultures, conspire to suffuse erotic elation with its sombre or tearful opposites.

All lovers weep. The sadness of each is related to his or her particular capacity to mourn. Whether the individual has inwardly succeeded in detaching himself from the allure of his parents; whether he has grieved their loss at the same time that he has reconfirmed their past and continuing goodness in his inner life; whether he brings to love a ceaseless effort to undo his earlier expulsion from the maternal Eden; whether he has more or less resigned himself to his later exclusion from the sexual life of father and mother as man and woman—all enter into his present anguish. Inevitably, however, all passionate love is built on a trembling foundation of loss and depression. This, too, is what is meant by longing.

Even now, as we must remember, we are culturally and historically bound. The notion that desire and longing—the two prime movers of passion—are products of individual needs and wishes is a modern one. It is far removed in spirit from the older conception of passion as an overwhelming alien invasion. In the Greek scheme, as we saw in our chapter on 'mother love', the goddess Aphrodite made her presence felt unequivocally. She claimed individuals and toppled the pride of ascetics, stoics and warriors who tried to discredit her in favour of her more chaste sibling. The modern notion has also led to a weakening of the emphasis on 'love at first sight'. In the past it was not infrequent that a man fell violently in love with a woman after catching the merest glimpse of her, as she went about on everyday business. Indeed there are many tales, in both East and West, of love flowering to its fullest splendour (and anguish) at the sight of a woman's portrait, at the hearing of her voice raised in song, or a description of her charms. A modern psychologically informed society, attuned to the mind's boundless capacity for projecting inner events onto the outer world, now takes issue with the reality of any external agent that can simply overpower one completely without his wanting it, expecting it, or participating actively in its seizure of himself. Yet in spite of contemporary cavilling, the older view has not disappeared from our sensibilities. Its continued presence is not a merely picturesque ruin of an abandoned theory but, in its emphasis on novelty and uniqueness, challenges any easy disposition we might have towards psychoanalytic determinism. Lovers are more than shadows projected on the screen of their individual unconscious infantile pasts. There is a 'chemistry' of sorts in their encounter, an alchemy beyond analysis.

Nor are the historians or anthropologists in possession of the revelation of love's truth. The artist plays on love's transcendence of cultural context, as we have said, turning over the social expectations that govern audiences he knows all too well. That one poem can reach from one culture and era to another is further testimony to the transcendence of time and place inherent in art and love. As the psychiatrist Harry Stack Sullivan put it: 'We are all more human than otherwise' . . . forever human, we might add.

Perhaps our somatic selves yield the metaphorical secrets of love better than any purely psychic exegesis. The body's expression of passionate intercourse contains and condenses its varied psychological themes. Indeed, the progression may amount to a sort of amorous archaeology, containing clues as to love's history, allowing us to reach back into bygone eras of desire and longing beyond articulation, representation and recollection.

Wooing and craving call up the theme of (as yet) unrequited love, the poise and the vibrancy of expectant pleasure and the edge of union. In this stage idealization and novelty are paramount, as from a distance the beloved is contemplated as a total and separate person. Forepleasure is a savouring of one's own and the other's body, heightening desire and awakening, enlivening senses dormant in everyday life. Witness to the joy he induces and receives, he finds himself (or herself) identifying with the responses of the lover—in their shared pleasure and anticipation. Soon enough, it matters not whose response is whose—'the love you get (being) equal to the love you make', in the lyrics of the Beatles. The lover can then enter a different realm, an interpenetration of psyche and soma. Penetration by the man and inception by the woman indeed constitute acts of aggression in which tender lovers are conquered, seized—and joined. Penultimately, with 'ejaculatory inevitability', in the apt if crude language of Masters and Johnson, comes our last gasp, the final line of resistance to orgasm, to the lost selfconsciousness of the little death. Climax, when achieved, carries with it myriad illusions of union and a flooding in of all past and future pleasure. A whole lifetime collapses into an instant, in a process of which we are dimly aware, reviving sensations submerged in everyday adult life. In ecstasy, the self is freed from its sensory and temporal confines and finds a second birth as if immersed in another.

This is passion, the concatenation of longing and desire, seemingly dangerous and even grief-laden, but profoundly vitalizing. Its aftermath, when the two bodies must again divide, is a cherishing, the aftertaste whetting an appetite for the beloved and her or his inner regions which can never be satisfied. We never have enough, for even while possessing the body of another, his or her soul eludes our grasp—the butterfly eternally pursued by an indefatigable Cupid.

CHAPTER NINE

THE ONTOGENY OF LOVE

The act of erotic love exposes its history by reversing it, retracing the embrace of two individual adult lovers back to passion's origins in the essential union of infant and mother. In this concluding chapter we shall follow love's evolution. We shall meander through sensuous detours to discover the beloved's unfolding and often unexpected forms, the diversity betraying some basic unity or at least a continuity in multiplicity.

Psychoanalysts underscore a commonality in the infinite variety of vital pleasures with terms like the 'libido', 'the primary object', the 'interdependence of representations of self and other'. We live with these unifying drives, objects and images all our lives yet uncover or discover their power again and again; they continually take us by surprise.

The Greeks captured the quest in Cupid's mythical pursuit of Psyche, the butterfly. The search for the beloved is then a quest for one's soul—the soul transcendent, the immortal psyche, mother of pleasure. For the Russian-American writer Vladimir Nabokov too, lepidoptera—from caterpillar to bucolic silken butterfly to the captured, frozen but unaging specimen for contemplation—became a metaphor for soulful love and its transformations.

Literally and figuratively, these creatures enticed this erotic, ironic chronicler of our times from the gardens of St Petersburg through exile in Europe to the academic institutions of America's New England and its expansive West. Shortly before he wrote *Lolita*, considered by critics to be the last of the love stories,[1] at a point when his literary life was then but occasional, Nabokov had, in fact, busied himself with the morphological distinctions to be made among lepidopterous genitalia. The climax of the novel that catapulted its author to notoriety, Lolita's *nuit extraordinaire*, when the crude young heroine seduced the stealthy hunter, takes place in Leppingville! For Nabokov, as for the psychoanalyst, life is love, haunting our sensibilities from cradle to grave.

In point of fact, Nabokov suffered a lifelong antipathy to the 'crankish medievalism of Dr. Freud' and his followers. He was resentful no doubt of the language of universals and of the arrogant sorties of self-styled conquistadors into literature, where form is everything, perhaps the only thing. He might have found 'ego psychology' more congenial, and his own memoirs cannot help revealing a convergence with its view of emerging consciousness (just as *Lolita*, almost self-consciously, perhaps in pardoy, is a study of the very sexual symbolism Nabokov disparaged). At all events, Nabokov has given us a narrative and a body of words which make the ontogeny of love come to brilliant life. With reverence, delight and a sense of irony akin to his, we shall allude to his work now and then as we chart our course through passion's changing terrain.

Thus, in *Speak Memory*, the very readable autobiographical tale of his life and loves, Nabokov's hunt for the butterfly, ranging over the various settings and guises of his life cycle—the 'pretty boy in knickerbockers and sailor cap', the lanky (and appropriately libertinous) expatriate in 'flannel togs and beret', and the 'fat hatless old man in shorts'—provides for a special continuity. It is Everyman's search, capturing in metaphor man's evolving quest for woman, fragile and yet enduring in her various and elusive incarnations.

Loss begins it all. For Nabokov the eve of life is captured in an acquaintance's encounter with family home movies taken before he was born, therefore unmissed and unmourned. An empty carriage awaiting him figures as a grotesque coffin at one end of personal time. Like a cooler Margaret Mahler and Réné Spitz, but with a shudder, the Russian envisions a life without a self, without awareness, without others, a stark purity of solitude, a black hole of the soul. His symbol, the prenatal world, serves as a metaphor for postnatal existence without psychology—a period deemed by these psychoanalytic students of infancy as 'autistic' or 'objectless'. It is solitude without self. Too strange and terrible to contemplate, if such were feasible, life's beginnings, like death, make us 'chronophobic', fearful of the life cycle, of mortality, of life without another. In loving, as in art, we would freeze time and hold on forever to the beloved for the sake of ourselves, the terrifying irony being that in so doing we risk destroying him/her.

'Love' during the earliest era can be equated with gratification alone—the felt meeting of mouth and breast, in fact, or as what Freud referred to as 'hallucination'. It is the simple fulfilment of desire, in a form beyond the adult's ken, since the primitive 'sensori-motor' schemata (to borrow from Swiss psychologist Jean Piaget) know neither an 'I' nor an 'other' but only some interpenetration of action and sensation. From the start, then, the self and the love object are found in each other and, above all, in the body. Moreover, in suckling, sucking an absent breast, the infant can be said to defy time, creating what is no longer and not yet there. Still, what is loved is not a person but a gut feeling, what abjured 'unpleasure'. No one can be certain, of course, since (unlike poets) babies do not talk, and we have only their observable reactions and behaviours as intimations of the inner rudiments of sentiment.

In fact, using films and videotapes, more recent infant observers have challenged established notions of an unpeopled world at the inception of life. Even as mindless little creatures—feeding, burrowing, thrashing aimlessly—we are by nature social and therefore loving beings.[2] Witness the neonate turning towards, the high pitch of a woman's voice, of 'rooting' to the smell of the mother's breast pad; the baby gazing fixedly into an animated face or collapsing in despair when confronted with a still one. Are these not signs of sentience, of life, of love, of 'people' in the purview of the babe, or even of mother in some crude guise? The traditionalist argues, to the contrary, that the indices are merely of crude 'gestalts' and of reflexive instincts. The world is one of 'part objects', not whole persons. And this cannot be the bond of love, no matter how intense the desire.

Be that as it may, whatever the eventual verdict on the neonate's sociability, it does seem now that early on the baby is capable of brilliant instants of awareness, brought to life by the very person, mother, who becomes their focus. At first these evanescent glimpses of her and her universe are discrete and discontinuous. 'Islands of memory', Jung called them in retrospect; 'a series of spaced flashes' according to Nabokov.[3] As the intervals between them diminish, perception and then memory—consciousness—begin to take a tenuous hold.

This writer's is an apt rendition of the very 'object relations theory' he himself would have found anathema—a boorish imposition on aesthetic liberty and elegance. All of ego development, mind, devolves upon, is motivated by, the unfolding forces of love and the need to know its object. Another of Nabokov's aphorisms captures the essence of psychoanalytic formulations of life's first task and of the love story that is development: 'the inner knowledge that I was I and that my parents were my parents'. Nabokov echoes our view of a dynamic epistemology, one fraught with emotional turbulence and constantly created anew by the dialectics of persons and impulses in conflict. It evolves through sequences of processes labelled first 'separation-individuation' (from four to five months to roughly two and a half years), and then 'oedipal triangulation' (beginning at perhaps three years).

Sentient life begins its gestation six to eight weeks after parturition, with a 'symbiosis' or 'dual unity' of mother and child when the latter 'falls in love', or more precisely 'imprints' a 'pre-object'. It is a time when the baby becomes orally enamoured of maternal envelopment. He feels enfolded by the mystery of life's fount; self-fulfilment, self-preservation and love are as one; there is a rhythmicity, a conjunction of two souls. This meeting of body-minds is the first form assumed by 'true love', object love.

The artist puts it more eloquently and equivocally. Nabokov cautions his readers that the 'primordial cave' at the dawn of his consciousness is *not* what Freudians might suppose, presumably the womb. However, his images and memories have much to do with 'Mother' as an enveloping presence and the various maternal proxies which a child, magically, animistically endows with her vital maternal spirit—'part' or 'transitional objects' in psychoanalytic language. Nabokov's narrative illustrates the manifest acts of imagination through which what Réné Spitz called the cradle of perception is lovingly reconstructed in the play and whimsy of later childhood. We cannot really recollect the primal longings, for we and our mothers have become so different, i.e. in the modalities with which we perceive and remember. The cave in fact can be many things: a narrow passage between a divan and a wall, arranged by understanding adults, caretakers attuned to the eerie delights of pitch-dark and to the lonesome vibrations of imaginary melodies. It is the hollow of the tent made of the bedclothes by the little author-to-be, filled with the workings of his imagination upon the bedsheet, the 'fair light penetrating the penumbral coverlet.' It is Nabokov the child's own mouth when he wrapped a garnet-dark Easter egg in a thoroughly sucked and salivated corner of a bedsheet and then both visually and orally savoured the synesthetic warmth of colour and texture. He adds, in anticipation of his sexual and literary destiny, that this was not yet the closest he got to feasting on beauty.

Yet clearly close indeed; Nabokov succeeds in guiding us through a paradise of visual and tactile sensuousness, the scrumptuous world of the child we have all been. The light beckoning through the window of a moving train becomes 'diamonds stepping into pockets of black velvet' when the nostalgic adult uses language to unburden himself of secret riches by giving it to his characters. Nothing is more delightful and mysterious than to contemplate those first thrills. He asserts that all Russian children—all children, we would assert—pass through a period of 'genius', the sort of brilliance that disappears when everything is secreted, saved and stored away—yielding, we would say, to the vague, inevitable, universal depression of the adult severed from his childhood sensuality and, with it, more or less dead to the vibrancy of unremitting discovery. But we are all geniuses at rediscovering in eroticism and art our *originality*.

Encased in wool, woolly-eyed, the adult goes about his daily affairs, his body and the sensorium numbed, anaesthetized by habit and necessity. He becomes quite unlike the 'carefree' child who once responded to sensation and form for the first time with psychic freedom and fulsome fantasy. Children do not require the studied sybaritics of the adult, who must caress the gaze or the palate with aesthetic sensual elegance. Because he feels so fully, however, the infant 'lover' also suffers greatly: a trickle of gas in the gut is an agony wrenching apart a tenuous sense of the body, the absence of the caretaker goddess a horror of the highest order. No wonder we later fear love, so much like the painful awakening of a frost-bitten limb.

For a while, in infancy, anyone or anything will do, even a grotesquely elemental mask. As long as the basic configuration or gestalt is there, the mere geometry will 'release' the baby's social smile—a promiscuous precursor of true love. This is the kingdom of primary narcissism, well beyond the reach of later ethical evaluation or, for that matter, rational understanding. 'His majesty, the baby', Freud once said.

However, by four to six months or perhaps even earlier, the baby begins to 'hatch' from its solipsistic cocoon. Now the 'lap baby' pushes and pummells at his mother, arching as he strains away from her in order to see her all the better. Pulling and poking, experimenting with what of her belongs to her and to him, with what endures and what comes off, the transfixed infant more and more devours mother with his eyes. It is as if he senses that, like himself, she too has mass and place and that he should take her all in, possess her before she disappears.

Strange and dark forces enter; light and generous quick moods and sinister and grasping frustrations invade the sinuous world of advancing selfhood, knowledge and emotion. The dummies developmentalists devise to toy with terror for the sake of science will no longer do. Present a clown face and the baby 'averts', as they say in the language of infant study, reaching out and then turning away in panic, despair and, finally, apathy.[4] Nor will other friendly adults, humans, find a congenial welcome. The baby senses a mismatch of maternal images when superimposed upon the mind's registration of the live stranger. It is not that he dislikes you, you see, but you are not she. He knows now who she is and you do not fit the scheme. The baby's fear is a sign of a defter mind and, with it, a more loving heart.

To wax 'adultomorphic', it just might be that our baby's feat is a glimpse of the fact, as well, that all who coo and woo him are not mother, 'good mother'. The beings who come and go—at whose will the child knows not—are not to be trusted unreservedly. 'Badness' begins to exist in absence or simply in abrupt contours. Suffering and rage erupt from teething and aching gums. It is 'eight month's anxiety', and it is filled with a gnawing hunger. This, too, is love—this self-consuming cannibalism which would crush what is cherished.

The child's 'separation-individuation'—the demarcation of persons and of consciousness—proceeds inexorably as the once supine and then sedentary infant learns to crawl and then to toddle, surveying the world laid out before him. His first steps applauded by admirers not yet with a complete life of their own, he now becomes elated by *self*-love. The investment of the self is greatly enhanced by illusions of omnipotence borrowed from the mother, who is believed to be an omnipresent support for his upright sallies. With the maturation of locomotor skills and a variety of psychological corollaries, the toddler gives free rein to a 'secondary narcissism', one an adult cannot remember but which is certainly recognizable as a human attribute. People, even mothers, fade into the background, as in Margaret Mahler's Viennese accenting of American argot: 'the world is the child's oyster'; or, the child's is a 'love affair with the world' and with the powers of the self. For a while mothers pale by comparison except in those moments of 'mini-anaclitic depression' when, sinkingly, he senses that she is not there and returns to her for a tug or touch, for a little 'emotional refuelling'.

The 'rapprochement crisis' which ensues—with its determinants in symbolic, semantic and representational growth and emotional vagaries—opens wide the oyster and sets our developing lover loose from a self-congratulatory shell. He is thrust by the forces of maturation into full contact and prototypic conflict with the people whom once more he adores. Suddenly, the adventurous explorer, at a year and a half, turns timorous. He rushes from his sorties back to his mother, sensing that he is helpless and afraid. For the moment he hopes to wed the two as one, to surrender autonomy and self to her person, only to push her violently away the next instant, protesting the limits to his self and declaring his boundaries. His struggle is one with a lost paradise no longer wished for so devoutly. Even the devoted Krishna or entranced Tristan will wrench themselves from their beloveds to protest and admire their heroic selves. But for only a time: Radha's or Isode's pull is too great and draws them back again.

The one and a half year old's love of mother, the desired and feared death of a newborn psyche in perpetual entanglement with the beloved, prefigures all those love-deaths which are the unsettling consummation of many of our elegiac or tragic narratives. Recoiling from the morbidity, none the less we sense in these denouements something familiar, ineffable. The allure and horror of the *Liebestod* in its prototypic state are great indeed, and a little lover clings and darts away, shadowing, approaching and fleeing the very person he most desires.

Salvation lies in sifting out love and aversion from the totalities of self and other, in somehow refining this gravitation towards merger into forms of true affective expression. The crude love of this era becomes increasingly differentiated and profound, as the child grows more cognizant of himself and of the complexities of the person he cleaves to, capable of beholding the beloved. Maturation, having precipitated the process, comes to the rescue. With it there is the recognition that she who is loved also tenders, or withholds, her affections. Her emotions can now be played upon.

Foreshadowing the lover's passionate offering of his seed, or the conqueror's cruel usage of it, the 'senior toddler', as he has been called, also becomes fixed on the by-products of his body and tosses these substances into the arena of desire and longing. Faeces and urine, the soft and warm solids and liquids from his inner body regions, ripe and ugly in the heat of the day, become alternatively gifts to a cherished caretaker and vindictive symbols of self-assertion, sullying her efforts at control, cleanliness, continence and composure. Thus, the most devoted admirer is capable of sadism and inconstancy.

The openings from which the stuff issues become vibrant to the touch, especially to the ministrations of the mother. That all of this should sometimes be greeted impatiently or derisively as dirty or wasteful becomes perplexing. They are the confounding omens of the inevitable doubts and self-loathing of the later lover, abased and abject before the acceptance or rejection of a cruel mistress.

Nor can the anus or urethra provide as yet the orgasmic explosion and release reserved for the mature and the fully reproductive adult. Even when for some, through developmental deviations, they become prime erogenous zones, it is always the penis and testicles that will accomplish the actual ejaculating. The unslaked desires of these areas in this era are by their very nature—their libidinal seat within the body—unrequitable. For all his shows of independence, pride and containment, then, the child finds himself subject to an essential and sacrificial masochism as he concedes his body and its byproducts to his beloved ruler. The earlier, near objectless cannibalism has now acquired subject and object, evolving into ambivalence.

Fortunately for our passionate boy, the father enters as a purveyor of his own male destiny, an erect counterpoint to his prone or squat surrender or defiance. He becomes an amorously tinged object of awe in his own right, and a model for masculinity. His hairy, virile presence is a solid anchor. The knowledge of him is a tie-line, permitting the son to meander through the liquid mazes of femininity and yet return to a secure masculine mooring.

The world of fathers—Mark, Moubad, Theseus, the Ghost and more—repeatedly draws the lover from a dyadic entrapment, reassuring the lover that he is and has been a man. This is 'early triangulation', preparing the way for real romance.

The entry into the age of Oedipus is not so abrupt, so phallic as was once thought. With the father and mother now presenting themselves as male and female prototypes, the young lover discovers and explores these essences in the interpersonal surroundings and in himself. Sex differences reside in anatomy, the two and a half year old learns.

His penis calls itself to his attention. He prides himself on it and fears its loss even as mother beckons to him like some luxurious dark continent about to swallow him up in a vaginal tropicality. In his mind's eye she smothers him with her mountainous breasts, biting and even beating him with an imaginary phallus of her own. Now and then, perhaps for a time, in the era of phallic narcissism, of ithyphallic display and power playing, the boy wrenches himself loose from her hold, imagining himself to be her conqueror and colonizer. Yet the mystery of this larger being again proves more compelling than self-spectacle. Thus it is that in later life the heroic warrior yields armour and weaponry to the so-called weaker sex. The god Krishna gleefully prostrates himself before a mere cowherdess. Mother, in fact, hovers everywhere, breathing into every circumstance of childhood, making of sons poised to begin their oedipal passage half hermaphrodites at heart, encompassed by and infused with her womanliness.

The full flowering of the love affair with the mother corresponds, as Nabokov notes, with the dawning of consciousness and identity. These processes—the progressions of romance and of humanity itself—unfold in synchronous evolution. As in our more private screen memories, the autobiographer's recollection and artifice telescope and fix the flow in a dramatic instant, a 'well-realized' moment. At four, on his family's country estate, Nabokov tells us, flanked by a 'thirty-three year old being in white and gold', and one 'twenty-seven in soft white and pink', on her, his mother's birthday, he celebrated the 'birth of sentient life'.

Mother gives us birth, and then she gives us the world. *Speak Memory*, for example, offers an elegiac rhapsody on her bequeathal to her adored boy of 'unreal estate'—a series of verbal tableaux calling up the images and special pleasures of childhood, the minutiae of utterly precise sensations, especially piquant and intense because they are as yet uncategorized, without the conceptual order that levels novelty into predictability. In Nabokov's book, as in all genealogies, other adults—tutors or political figures, for instance—provide a punctuation, an historical and social context for the earthy and ephemeral. In the journalist's memory, as in the perceptions of the adoring child, the human characters in his life assume a vitality of particulars akin to that which he endows the sundry inanimate treasures of his earliest years. Mother lives in them, too.

Yet, for all her importance, Nabokov's mother, like most

of her kind, paradoxically retains throughout the character of one of the 'mild hallucinations' or 'hypnagogic mirages' to which Nabokov was subject his whole life. Hers is a diffuse yet abiding and beckoning presence. She is a being luminous but lacking definition, invigorating yet given life by her little boy's responses to her. In his childhood retrospective, she is said to have a rather 'soothing flo quality', informed with that total sensory and at times synesthetic potential which coloured her son's alphabet. Towards the end of the memoir, when in his young adulthood she becomes a distinct person in her own right, Nabokov's mother simply drifts into obscurity—to be, like all mothers, reincarnated in later lovers. The narrative truth corresponds with the paradoxical findings of researchers on the younger child's ability to label persons in the social environment. At certain points the mother, to whom the child is vitally attached, is none the less harder to identify or categorize than far less significant others. Oedipal immersion in her revives this earlier envelopment, once again both enlarging and softening the image.

All boys identify with the womanliness that enchants them. As we have demonstrated in earlier chapters, the eve of Oedipus is characterized by a fluidity of the boundaries and roles dividing the genders. A mother and a loving son are as one in a unified 'anima', their shared feminine soul.

Nabokov and his mother, in fact, shared the 'synesthete's sensibility'—that peculiar blending of perceptions which is the artist's gift. She, too, heard her letters in hues and 'did everything to encourage the general sensitiveness (he) had to visual stimulation'. Painting for him, enlivening his consciousness of nature's coloured landscapes, at night she would offer masses of jewelry for her son to relish at bedtime, jewels which mirrored the light and forms of the darkening cityscape outside his window. No wonder that, throughout his life, Nabokov, an intractable insomniac, was loath to relinquish consciousness to the comforting but dull blackness of sleep. His mother had aspirated life into his waking world and was herself infused with its miraculous variety. Why give her or it up?

In this communion there is the risk of passivity in intensity, of an undoing of the masculinity which will bring man to woman in later heterosexual life. The phallic narcissist in him will move the Oedipal boy to seek in and from the mother the gift, the renewal, of the masculinity ceded to her—an affirmation, not a loss, of self and of sex. Mother continues to make a man of him. Indeed she promises to make him and his phallus grow beyond the realm of the senses, drawing him forth into virility at the height of his absorption in her with imaginary portents of a stupendous future.

Childhood illness brought the pair still closer together. 'Beneath [the] delirium [which undid an early mathematical aptitude] she recognized sensations she had known herself.' Ill, Nabokov imagined the daily gift she would bring to ease the pangs of fever or perhaps transform them into pleasures, making of convalescence a delight. He envisions her riding on a horse-drawn sleigh, perched comfortably behind the coachman's huge rump and the smacking of the courser's scrotum. He sees with her eyes. Snow thuds against the front of the sleigh, as his mother raises her fur muff to her face and exhales vapour through the 'reticulated tenderness' of the tightly drawn veil, one through which she has so often kissed him. She enters a store and retrieves for him a pencil. It seems ordinary at first, yet when she offers it to his sickbed it proves to be a Faber pencil, four feet long and of proportionate circumference. Nor is it merely *ersatz*, as the boy first fears; the point is genuine graphite. Nabokov's mother has intuited what all good oedipal mothers know in their bones—an understanding of what cannot be coveted but which her son does covet—and gives it to him in symbolic form.

The 'objets sexuelles' of the imagery are unmistakable, but even so they stand out by virtue of the conjured sights and sounds in which they take form. The more pathographically minded analyst would discern in this and other sense memories of mother the son's incestuous yearnings. Such a mother, he might argue, has overstimulated her son and foolishly, falsely proffered him an oedipal triumph in a more than man-sized penis—'the coachman's', the father's. This is fabricated delicacy, he would argue, an extension of her own illusory phallus. He might find in her 'seductiveness' and 'overstimulation' the seeds of a defensive, fearful feminine identification and infantile regression. She is a siren and has but seduced and abandoned him.

Alas, such cavilling efforts would meet with their subject's derision and ingenious rebuttal. This is all true, he might admonish us, but there is so much more. And, indeed, more poignant than any unstated precocious liaison is Nabokov's mother's having heeded the simple rule, 'love with all one's soul, and leave the rest to fate'. Feeling and image are at issue—more so than the singular desires that give rise to them. The more sophisticated analyst—the student of healthy development—would concur, of course. The oedipal mother offers her son the beauty of the imagination, fantasy and the potential 'family romance'.

To return to the oedipal boy: sinister psychic forces again conspire to dim his romance with his mother. Fifty pages into his narrative, before the fact, Nabokov anticipates a moment of horror in his adult life—the evening in exile when his father will be felled by an assassin's bullet. With the tragic event he then leaves his widowed mother in Prague, playing solitaire, her husband's wedding ring affixed by a thread to her own. Their visits have become increasingly rare. The gay child-woman is portrayed abruptly as having become old, bereft, clearly less capable of frivolity and illusion—a free spirit felled by history and grief. Without lustre, spectral at best, she is no longer the mother of childhood. Nabokov's sad fate, in its particulars, once again serves as metaphor for the universal grief of childhood.

The threat, albeit in the mind's eye, of the beloved and protective father's death at his murderous hands conjures up the spectre of loss and of the lord's vengeance according to the law of the talion—eye for eye, tooth for tooth, phallus for phallus. Triangulation makes for a confrontation with parental reality and with searing guilt. All these Swiftean imperfections are perceived close up on a dismal landscape by our Lilliputian.

With their advent, the sensuality, or rather the incestuous ties of the oedipal era, are forgotten, not so much because they are structurally foreign to adult awareness but rather because these pulsings and ambitions challenge other loves and the security and sanctity of the family. The 'superego', fully formed now, demands of 'ego' their repression. For a while, the child's love life is relegated to 'id'.

Like an ice age, what Freud called 'latency' passes over the steamy seas of passionate life. More self-contained, a boy now busies himself with the mere derivatives of his first and truest love. Erotically, he touches other boys and girls in the time-honoured scramblings we euphemistically call 'playing doctor'. But he ignores, for the most part, his parents' bodies and is moved by things around him—the birds and the bees. Their origins and habits become the origins and facts of life. Butterflies and literature seized Nabokov's imagination. Yet the dormancy of middle childhood is spotty and short-lived enough, and the researches of the period lead both back to and away from the obsessions of Oedipus.

Conceded to father, a man of appropriate generational status, mother sinks back into herself. Instead, the hue of passion for her begins to colour other female, and even male proxies. Coming of age, a boy must contend with a relentless itch and unpredictable stirrings which take him by surprise. His erections, over which he has little control, precede ejaculations, and a pulsing genital—yet to explode in orgasm—points him on his way. At first arousal is promiscuous. A chafe, a wrestling match with another of like sex, even fear, can prompt tumescence.

The teenaged boy retreats from the world of women into the safety of his camaraderie with other males, occasionally expressing more frankly the homoeroticism beneath the banter and ceaseless activity. His experiments with love, and now and then with sex, are in the guise of testing or demonstrating a new-found genital prowess. Thus Nabokov and a cousin play at cavaliers (the latter will later be killed in the real Revolution), make up romances replete with heroines, and espy girls of their own age from afar. Thomas Mann told us of this in *Tonio Kruger*, and there is the triumvirate of Romeo, Mercutio and Benvolio—the gay blades.

In the process of bonding boys silently divide the feminine population, catching their eye from afar, into 'good' and 'bad'. All boys do so, individually and especially collectively—categorize, that is, their would-be conquests into those who 'do' and the ones, more chaste, who 'don't'. Freud first identified what came to be called the 'mother–whore syndrome', implying that the attempt of many young men to sever romance from sex represented a flight from incestuous feeling and, with it, a horror of 'de-idealizing' a mother on whose image, in its purity, the boy still relies for nurturance and undying support. The idea that 'they', and by extension 'she', desires him—the transformation of the protective mother into the Phaedra-like seductress—is still too hard, too human to bear, portending loss on the eve of the second great separation.

Butterflies, mere insects, led Nabokov to real women. At eleven, moved to explore a vast marshland, skirting a river in search of Parnassian 'nymphs', the pre-adolescent Nabokov finds a rickety footbridge—all imagery of precariousness suggestive of the prepubescent boy's uneasy inklings of desire for union with woman. Bright patches are made on the turf by the scattered clothes of peasant girls who romp stark naked in the shallow water. One of these is a certain Polenka. Radiant in the distance, the barefoot girl's pretty round face is sobered with her young master's approach.

Theirs was an 'ocular relationship'. Her bosom softening, she was the first to have a poignant power over him, searing his sleep, thrusting him into 'clammy consciousness'. He dreamt of her even while he feared being revolted in reality by her dirt-caked feet. Her description is the first wholeheartedly erotic presence in the autobiography.

From the disintegrating dormancies of late boyhood, the

flow of life moves on to the fiery emissions of youth. The adolescent achieves his orgasms now, if not mutually, alone. Wet dreams yield to voluntary manipulation, sometimes tutored by a more experienced hedonist. Through masturbation he seeks to reassure himself of his phallic durability even in the throes of a 'little death', not yet ready to concede his manly power to a real woman. He has come to the brink of what psychoanalysts dub 'genitality' and is, to put it crudely, capable of discharge. The problem is that, drug-like, each sweet salving whets the appetite for another once his fleeting regrets and fears settle. He wants more and more, wants to lay hands on and hold a woman; the push towards her is inexorable.

In *Ada*, as in his autobiography, but with the license of a novelist, Nabokov describes the sensual gravitation of the moth to the flame, the coming together of the adolescent boy and girl through the wisps of fabric cloaking their bodies and their soulful search for each other.[5]

The fleshy gropings of adolescence depicted by him intimate bona fide passionate love, one in which impediments in the way of fulfilment have as much to do with separateness as with any social or interior taboo. The youthful lover would consume and be consumed by the beloved. As this is not possible and not quite desirable, he drinks her in through foretastes of sex. He privately savours every morsel which his senses offer him.

In the boy's adolescence, however, the sensory routes lead more and more to his penis. Gradually, visual, olfactory and other indulgences give way to the pulsations of the young hero's as yet forlorn genitals. No longer are 'oral' or incorporative pleasures, the 'kissing phase', the centre of the childman's quest, but rather penultimate satisfactions arrived at before the exquisite genital moment can be achieved.

Finally, Nabokov provides us with the wonderful anticlimax and harbinger of all things to come. The two 'children' are left alone when a barn catches fire. Clad only in the tartan toga of a lap robe, Van enters the library, a significant setting. The drama now unfolds in which the distant becomes proximate, reality a reflection, stranger and greater and scarier than fantasy. Desire has become reality. Mistaking the girl's reflection in the window for a distant image, the youth is drawn to her person close at hand. They begin to caress and explore each other's body, and now *he* seems to *himself* a distant reflection, an echo of himself. In this delectable encounter it almost matters not whose body is whose as the two discover and possess one another.

His hands become like labia, 'fleshy folds', as they search out her body, her hot pale vulva. The bodies intertwine; positions become confused, their parts interchangeable. The girl strips her lover and investigates his phallus. On the brink of entering her, driving towards her, the boy, like so many others, merely dissolves in a 'puddle of pleasure'.[6] Trying once more, he again ejaculates prematurely.

The realities and sensual moments of imminent adulthood are thus both less and more than what has preceded them. It will be some time before the adolescent is inherently capable of feeding upon a woman's inner treasures, of intermingling the excitement and terror, of transgressing the boundaries of the generational prerogative, of sexual selfhood and of self and others.

When Tamara, Nabokov's own first love, finally comes into his life, she seems to a young Nabokov 'a girl out of a novel'. He continues, 'I took my adorable girl to all those secret spots in the woods where I had daydreamed so ardently of meeting her, of *creating* her'. He adds, with a decorum foreign to the novelist but befitting a respectful lover: 'In one particular grove, everything fell into place, I parted the fabric of fancy, I tasted reality.' We need no more, for we see in their discreet intercourse the coming together of aspiration, illusion and imagination, of longing and sexual desire. The past funnels into youth and leads in unseen rivulets into the ambiguity of 'the future'.

Such metaphors are obvious to clinical decoders, clear in their allusion to the contact of his and her genitals. Yet they also hark back to a mother's fancifulness, her theatricality and her oblique relation in the mind of the child to real people—again and again, to her 'unreal estate'. The lap of loveliness has opened itself to the lover with a familiar (ironically so) whoof of theatricality, yet also with a surprisingly real and penetrable access. Again erotic love halts time, further informing us that the future anticipated in past fantasy was real, that illusions of union at all developmental junctures were destined to find a genital embodiment.

In continuing to look for love the late adolescent searches for his soul, his sexual identity, his self-continuity. He is a 'hundred different young men at once, all pursuing one changeful girl'.[7] A single encounter, crossing over the boundaries, does not suffice for a young man—though sometimes for a young woman. He needs to enter and return from many new inner places before he can discover in variety his sameness and wholeness.

Having discovered what psychoanalysts abstract as their 'genitality', most adolescent boys test it to the hilt. To the extent that they retreat from the erotic, they are more phallic than romantic. They conquer girls and body parts. They notch their gun belts with each quick copulation, refurbishing their masculinity retroactively, even as women, one after another, hold for a time and implicitly threaten to seize forever the erect penis, bathing and penetrating it with their soft labia and the labyrinth within, leading right back to the womb itself. When he does not return the love to the woman with whom he has sex, however, the adolescent boy finds his erection withering to reveal an aftertaste of regret and remorse. He may hide these feelings from himself. Still, he learns, only romance and surrender, ironically, will make a man of him. That is, a truly sexual man.

A youthful lover cannot elude the ambisexuality and dissolution of self at the heart of the quest for woman and still revel in the voluptuousness of sex. In concert with all the taboos and triangles conspiring to keep lovers apart this intrinsic instinctual paradox has to be somehow integrated and the hesitancy it creates is swept away in a rush of impulse. Having found desire's reality at last, the youthful lover must halt his own flight from it, wedding wish to fear in ecstasy, in being outside and beside oneself.

The sublimity and sensuality of youthful first love are virtually impossible to revive later in their genuine form. To do so in mid life risks a foolish perversity of the sort but half parodied in the memoirs of Humbert Humbert, the abject, hapless hero of *Lolita*,[8] his nostalgia gone awry. And thus it is that our fully fictitious tales of love succeed where pornography and perversion, the erotic love of the incomplete and the two dimensional, fail, fail to reanoint the past and its bygone pleasures. We expect that all 'true' lovers be young, treading the border between childhood and maturity, in sexual ripeness and in a physical and emotional convulsiveness which undoes the distance between the erotic subject and his object.

All adolescent boys, like Van or the young Humbert with his Annabel, at one time or another, come too soon, or have been exposed to other shameful frustrations. Hobbled by past disappointments, some have then shrunk into a sexual solipsism—a self referential world of eroticized 'part objects' and peculiarity—of a universe such as is rarely seen in the literature of love because it is, in its potential, more pathetic or ridiculous than tragic or romantic. 'The idiotic mutual masturbation, the slums of sex of American novels', Nabokov called it, stressing how much they missed the point, falling short of the sublime and of temporal transcendence.

Yet Nabokov's self-avowed 'obsessive nostalgia' is what a Humbert Humbert's 'insanity' and 'passion' are all about: the oblique yearning for an altogether terrifying mother love in the redundant ritualized revivals of rites of wrong passage. For all his seeming idiocy the erotic pervert, the dirty old man, too desperately attempts to stop time's passage, or better, as Nabokov suggests, make the successive moments simply accumulate—so that nothing is lost, ever, ever. Deviants, about whom we have said little, are lovers too, though, like 'macho men', they flee from and obfuscate the romanticism of their endeavour.

In retracing this evolution of love we have also glossed over much in the way of passion that does not pertain to women, herein our own obsessive and nostalgic subject. In so doing we have not told a whole love story; obviously, one cannot have the one without the other. For example, one psychoanalyst, Peter Blos, has gone so far as to suggest that with the closing of the oedipal age in middle childhood, mother love tumbles into repression and quiescence, to be replaced for boys and girls alike with the unrequited passion for their father.[9] Such a love of man exists in tandem with, hovers about, the individual's adulation of woman, now standing in conflict with it, now informing our 'negative oedipal' or 'quasi-homosexual' wishes to be like her for him. Further, as we have suggested earlier, it is an inner paternal presence that allows a male to love and play with a woman's femininity.

Most important, idealizing the father, a boy and later a young man will strive to *be* him, to plant his seed deep in woman–mother and 'give' her a child. He would recreate himself as a child and, however ambivalently, give back his mother/wife to a son who is also an *alter ego*. Whatever the meanderings of passion, within the marriage and family it is the conception of the child which constitutes the lover's shared and most enduring and romantic creation. A child is the embodiment of their souls' conjunction, realizing in its flesh the generation of two as one. This, too, defies time and loss. To return to our love historian, to *Speak Memory*.

Having alluded to his amorous adventures as a young man and then having described in some detail the unlikely lot of his family in exile, Nabokov speaks of love and brings us full circle back to his mother in Russia. He guides us to the heart of his despair and aspiration, even as he reflects on the 'vast, enduring infinity of sensation' inherent in the love of a son, one of 'nature's marvels'. The fruit of sexual passion, it is the child who at last brings us back to our childhood and our mothers, he seems to say, unifying as one a potentially dangerous opposition of eros and agape, embodying the conjunction of all manner of love, bringing immortality down to earth:

Whenever I start thinking of my love for a person, I am in the habit of immediately drawing radii from my love—from my heart, from the tender nucleus of a personal matter—to monstrously remote points of the universe. Something impels me to measure the consciousness of my love against such unimaginable and incalculable things as the behaviour of nebulae (whose very remoteness seems a form of insanity), the dreadful pitfalls of eternity, the unknowledgeable beyond the unknown, the helplessness, the cold, the sickening involutions and the interpenetrations of space and time.[10]

So much remains to be told. There are also in life the Cleopatras and Blue Angels who lay low emperors (like Moubad) at the close of mid life or on the brink of dotage. In all humility, however, having not yet tasted the ashes of age or the sting of revitalization in rekindled sexuality, we shall stop here. The story of love is never complete, anyway; recounted many times, it has never been told to the end.

We will hear it again and again, the sometimes soothing and at others ominous sounds (to borrow from Melville) of the 'endless flowing river in the cave of man'.

NOTES

REFERENCES TO CHAPTER ONE
INTRODUCTION

1. Denis de Rougemont, *The Myths of Love* (London: Faber and Faber, 1963), p. 74
2. Ibid.
3. Milan Kundera, *The Unbearable Lightness of Being* (New York: Harper & Row, 1984), p. 199.

REFERENCES TO CHAPTER TWO
THE AMOROUS DEATH OF ROMEO AND JULIET

1. William Shakespeare, *Twelfth Night*, I.i.1–4, in *The Complete Plays and Poems of William Shakespeare*, ed. W.A. Neilson and C.J. Hill (Cambridge: Mass: Houghton Mifflin, 1942), p. 281.
2. *Romeo and Juliet*, Prologue, 5–6.
3. Denis de Rougemont, *Love in the Western World* (New York: Anchor Books, 1956), p. 193.

4. 'Fancy', Coleridge dubbed this self-indulgence, transfigured into bonafide "imagination" according to some modern critics like Chambers. See E.K. Chambers, *Shakespeare: A Survey*, (New York: Hill and Wang, 1925).

5. *Romeo and Juliet*, I.iii.40–4.

6. Ibid., I.v.140–3.

7. Ibid. Prologue in II.

8. Ibid., II.ii.133–5.

9. Ibid., II.vi.9–12.

10. Ibid., III.iii.110–13.

11. Ibid., IV.v.77–8.

12. John Keats, 'La Belle Dame Sans Merci' in *Complete Poems and Selected Letters of John Keats* ed. C.D. Thorpe (New York: Odyssey Press, 1935), p. 343.

13. Norman Holland, 'Romeo's dream and the paradox of literary realism,' *Literature and Psychology*, 13, 1963, pp. 97–103.

14. See M.D. Faber, 'The adolescent suicides of Romeo and Juliet,' *Psychoanalytic Review*, 59(2), 1972, pp. 169–81; M. Cox, 'Adolescent processes in *Romeo and Juliet*,' *Psychoanalytic Review*, 63(3), 1976, pp. 379–92.

15. Sigmund Freud, 'Three Essays on Sexuality' (1905), *Standard Edition*, vol. 7, p. 173.

16. Sandor Ferenczi, *Thalassa: A Theory of Genitality* (1924) (New York: Norton, 1968); Karl Abraham, *Selected Papers* (London: Hogarth Press, 1942).

REFERENCES TO CHAPTER THREE

LOVE IN THE MIDDLE EASTERN WORLD: LAYLA AND MAJNUN

1. Nizami, *The Story of Layla and Majnun*, trans. and ed. R. Gelpke (Boulder, Colorado: Shambhala, 1978).

2. Ibid., pp. 13–14.

3. Ibid., p. 25.

4. Ibid., p. 38.

5. Ibid., p. 52.

6. Ibid., p. 116.

7. Ibid., p. 118.

8. Ibid., pp. 177–9.

9. Annemarie Schimmel, *The Triumphant Soul* (London: East-West Press, 1978), p. 336. See also H. Ritter, *Die Bildersprache Nizamis* (Hamburg, 1925). For a good survey of Sufism see A.J. Arberry, *Sufism: An Account of the Mystics of Islam* (London: Allen and Unwin, 1950).

10. For a brief account of Muslim attitudes towards sexual love see Ch. Pellat, 'Djins' in B. Lewis, Ch. Pellat and J. Schacht (eds), *Encyclopedia of Islam*, vol. II (Leiden: E. J. Brill, 1965), pp. 550–3. See also A. Bouhdiba, *La Sexualité en Islam* (Paris: Presses Universitaires de France, 1975).

11. *Alf Laila*, p. 4, cited in Jerome W. Clinton, 'Madness and Cure in the 1001 Nights', *Studia Islamic* (forthcoming).

12. Nizami, pp. 107–8.

13. See, for instance, the collection of Middle Eastern and Turkish tales in E. Power Mathys (ed.), *Eastern Love*, 10 volumes (London: John Rodker, 1929).

14. Nizami, pp. 145–6.

15. These versions of the Pakistani tales are taken from Zainab G. Abbas, *Folk Tales of Pakistan* (Karachi: Pakistan Publications, 1957).

16. Nizami, pp. 186–7.

17. Joel Kovel, 'On Reading *Madame Bovary* Psychoanalytically', *Seminars in Psychiatry*, 5(3), 1973, p. 335.

18. Nizami, p. 32.

19. Ibid., p. 34.

20. Ibid., pp. 34–5.

21. Norman Holland, 'Romeo's dream and the paradox of literary realism', *Literature and Psychology*, 13, 1963, pp. 97–103.

22. See A. Bouhdiba 'The Son and the Mother in Arab-Muslim Society', in L. Carl Brown and N. Itzkowitz (eds), *Psychological Dimensions of Near Eastern Studies* (Princeton, NJ: Darwin Press, 1977), pp. 126–41; see also, Hisham Sharabi and Mukhtar Ani, 'Impact of Class and Culture on Social Behaviour: The Feudal-Bourgeois Family in Arab Society', in *Psychological Dimensions of Near Eastern Studies*, pp. 240–56.

23. Sharabi, p. 245.

24. Bouhdiba, p. 130.

25. Nizami, p. 26.

26. Ibid., p. 184.
27. Ibid., p. 130.
28. Ibid., p. 139.
29. Ibid., p. 139.
30. S. Freud, 'Delusion and Dream in Wilhelm Jensen's *Gradiva*', (1909), *Standard Edition*, vol. 9, pp. 7–93.

REFERENCES TO CHAPTER FOUR
THE CLOISTERED PASSION OF RADHA AND KRISHNA

1. The verses from the *Gitagovinda* quoted here are taken from the scholarly yet intensely lyrical translation by Barbara Stoler Miller. See her *Love Song of the Dark Lord: Jayadeva's Gitagovinda* (New York: Columbia University Press, 1977).
2. Maurice Valency, *In Praise of Love* (New York: Macmillan, 1958), p. 18.
3. Lee Siegel, *Sacred and Profane Dimensions of Love in Indian Tradition* (Delhi: Oxford University Press, 1978), pp. 26–7.
4. For a discussion of erotic love in ancient India see, Sushil K. De, *Ancient Indian Erotics and Erotic Literature* (Calcutta: Firma K.L. Mukhopadhyaya, 1959); J. J. Meyer, *Sexual Life in Ancient India* (New York: E.P. Dutton, 1930).
5. Miller, p. 15.
6. W.H. Auden, *Forewords and Afterwords* (London: Faber, 1973), p. 67
7. W. Shakespeare, Sonnet 130.
8. On this see A.K. Ramanujan, *Hymns for the Drowning* (Princeton: Princeton University Press, 1981), pp. 127–33.
9. For a further discussion see Siegel, pp. 178–84, and Ramanujan, *Hymns for the Drowning*, pp. 152–7.
10. Translated by Edward C. Dimock and D. Levertov, *In Praise of Krishna: Songs from Bengali* (New York: Anchor Books, 1967), p. 18.
11. Frederique Marglin, 'Types of Sexual Union and Their Implicit Meanings', in J.S. Hawley and D.M. Wulff (eds), *The Divine Consort* (Berkeley: Religious Studies Series, 1982), pp. 305–7.

12. Ibid., pp. 306–7.
13. Auden, *Collected Poems*, p. 536.
14. Miller, p. 89. See also the poems in Dimock, p. 7 and p. 11.
15. D. Bhattacharya, *Love Songs of Vidyapati* (London: George Allen and Unwin, 1963), p. 41.
16. Denis de Rougemont, *The Myths of Love* (London: Faber and Faber, 1963), p. 21.
17. Robert Stoller, *Sexual Excitement* (New York: Pantheon, 1979), p. 21.
18. The third-century Tamil epic of *Shilappadikaram* (The Ankle Bracelet) is perhaps the earliest illustration of the 'separate but equal' attraction of the adulterous and the conjugal for the Indian man. See Ilango Adigal, *Shilapaddikaram* (The Ankle Bracelet), trans. A Danielou (New York: New Directions, 1965).
19. *Mahabharata*, XIII, 104.20ff. Cited in Meyer, pp. 246–7. See also *The Laws of Manu*, XII, 165.63ff.
20. Daniel H.H. Ingalls, *An Anthology of Sanskrit Court Poetry* (Cambridge, Mass: Harvard University Press, 1965), p. 256.
21. W.S. Merwin and J. Moussaief Masson, *Sanskrit Love Poetry* (New York: Columbia University Press, 1977), p. 169.
22. Dimock, p. 28.
23. Andreas Capellanus, *The Art of Courtly Love*, trans. John J. Parry (New York: Columbia University Press, 1941), book I, ch. VI, Seventh Dialogue.
24. Walter M. Spink, *Krishnamandala* (Ann Arbor, Michigan: Center for South and South East Asian Studies, 1971), p. 88.
25. Dimock, *In Praise of Krishna*, p. 56.
26. Miller, p. 113.
27. Quoted by Barbara Miller, 'The Divine Duality of Radha and Krishna', in *The Divine Consort*, p. 25.
28. A.J. Alston, *The Devotional Poems of Mirabai* (Delhi: Motilal Banarasidass, 1980), pp. 24–5.
29. Ramanujan, *Hymns for the Drowning*, p. 154.
30. Ibid.
31. Sigmund Freud, 'Psychoanalytic Notes Upon an Autobiographical Account of a Case of Paranoia' (1911), *Standard Edition*, vol. 12, pp. 3–82.
32. Miller, *Love Song of the Dark Lord*, p. 92.
33. M.S. Randhawa and S.D. Bambri, 'Basholi Paintings of

Bhanudatta's Rasamanjari', *Roop Lekha* 36 (n. d.), p. 99.

34. Miller, *Love Song of the Dark Lord*, p. 122.
35. Quoted by D.M. Wulff, 'A Sanskrit Portrait: Radha in the Plays of Rupa Gosvami', in *The Divine Consort*, p. 39.
36. Dimock, *In Praise of Krishna*, p. 21.

REFERENCES TO CHAPTER FIVE

KINGS AND CUCKOLDS: PASSION AS POWER

1. S. Freud, 'Dostoevsky and Parricide' (1928), *Standard Edition*, vol. 21, p. 188.
2. Fakhr-ud-din Gurgani, *Vis and Ramin*, trans. G. Morrison (New York: Columbia University Press, 1972), p. 24.
3. Quoted in Julius Evola, *The Metaphysics of Sex* (New York: Inner Tradition, 1983), p. 160.
4. *Vis and Ramin*, p. 30.
5. Ibid., p. 30.
6. Ibid., p. 36.
7. Ibid., pp. 47–8.
8. Ibid., p. 48.
9. Ibid., p. 52.
10. Ibid., p. 52.
11. Ibid., p. 60.
12. Ibid., p. 64.
13. Ibid., p. 67.
14. Ibid., p. 84.
15. Ibid., p. 111.
16. Ibid., p. 113.
17. Ibid., p. 114.
18. Ibid., p. 123.
19. Ibid., pp. 139–40.
20. Mayura, *Mayurastaka*, trans. E. Power Mathys, in *Eastern Love*, vol. II (London: John Rodker, 1929), pp. 108–11.
21. *Vis and Ramin*, p. 117.
22. Ibid., pp. 207–8.
23. Quoted from Jagajivana's *Mansamangal* by Ralph Nicholas,

'On the (Non-existent) Incest Taboo in India, with Particular Reference to Bengal', typescript (Department of Anthropology, University of Chicago, 1978), p. 13.

24. A.K. Ramanujan, 'The Indian Oedipus', in L. Edwards and A. Dundes, (eds), *Oedipus: A Folklore Casebook* (New York: Garland Publishing, 1983), p. 249.

25. Nicholas, p. 11.

26. Ramanujan, p. 248.

27. Ibid., p. 249.

28. Matsya Purana III, 30–4, cited in Ramanujan, p. 248.

29. *Brahma Vaivarta Purana*, cited in *The Koka Shastra*, trans. A. Comfort (London: George Allen and Unwin, 1964), p. 231.

30. Judith L. Herman, *Father-Daughter Incest* (Cambridge, Mass: Harvard University Press, 1981).

31. Ibid., p. 62.

32. *Naradasmrti*, cited by Nicholas, p. 16.

33. *Sathapatha Brahma* 1.7.41–4, in Ramanujan, p. 248.

34. On this issue see Ramanujan, but also R.P. Goldman, 'Fathers, Sons and Gurus: Oedipal Conflict in the Sanskrit Epics', *Journal of Indian Philosophy* 6(1978), pp. 325–92.

35. *The Mahabharata*, trans. and ed. J.A.B. Van Buitenen, vol. I, (Chicago: University of Chicago Press, 1974), p. 227.

36. Ibid., p. 193.

REFERENCES TO CHAPTER SIX

THE CONSCIENCE OF THE KING

1. Michael Foucault, 'Introduction' to *Hercule Barbin*, trans. R. McDougall (New York: Pantheon Books, 1980).

2. Joseph Bedier, *The Romance of Tristan and Iseult*, trans. H. Belloc (New York: Pantheon Books, 1945), p. 18.

3. Ibid., p. 54.

4. Ibid., p. 60.

5. Ibid., p. 62.

6. Ibid., p. 61.

7. Ibid., p. 118.

8. Ibid., p. 129.

9. Ibid., p. 236.

10. Ibid., p. 241.

11. Ibid., pp. 245–9.

12. Ibid.

13. Ernest Jones, *Hamlet and Oedipus* (New York: W.W. Norton, 1949).

14. William Shakespeare *Hamlet*, from *The Complete Plays and Poems of William Shakespeare* ed. W.A. Neilson and C.J. Hill (New York: Houghton Mifflin, 1942), I.ii.153.

15. Ibid., I.ii.143.

16. Ibid., I.ii.29.

17. Freud, 'Civilization and its Discontents' (1930), *Standard Edition*, vol. 21, pp. 59–145.

18. *Hamlet*, I.v.9.

19. Ibid., I.v.84.

20. Ibid., II.i.77.

21. Ibid., II.i.102.

22. Ibid., II.ii.605.

23. Ibid., II.ii.611.

24. Ibid., III.i.66.

25. Ibid., III.ii.410.

26. Ibid., III.iv.55.

27. Ibid., III.iv.66.

28. Ibid., III.iv.82.

29. Ibid., III.iv.88.

30. Ibid., III.iv.92.

31. Freud, 'Some psychical consequences of the anatomical distinction between the sexes' (1925), *Standard Edition*, vol. 19, pp. 243–58.

32. *Hamlet*, III.iv.137

33. Ibid., III.iv.144.

34. Ibid., III.iv.152.

35. Ibid., III.iv.173.

36. Ibid., IV.iv.53.

37. Ibid., V.ii.5.

38. Ibid., V.ii.67.

39. Freud. 'The Interpretation of Dreams' (1900), *Standard Edition*, vol. 4.

REFERENCES TO CHAPTER SEVEN

MOTHER LOVE:
WHEN DESIRE BECOMES REALITY

1. Freud, 'Letter to Fliess, 3 Oct. 1897', *The Complete Letters of Sigmund Freud to Wilhelm Fliess (1897–1904)*, ed. J. Moussaief (Cambridge, Mass: Harvard Univ. Press, 1985), p. 258.
2. Freud, 'The Interpretation of Dreams' (1900), *Standard Edition*, vol. 4, p. 216.
3. Euripides, 'Hippolytus', in *Greek Tragedies*, ed. David Grene and R. Lattimore, vol. I (Chicago: University of Chicago Press, 1960), pp. 8–9.
4. Ibid., pp. 55–7.
5. Ibid., pp. 79–84.
6. Ibid., pp. 121–8.
7. Ibid., pp. 191–7.
8. Ibid., pp. 234–8.
9. Ibid., pp. 239–42.
10. Ibid., pp. 199–202.
11. Ibid., pp. 252–66.
12. William Blake, 'The Garden of Love', from *Songs of Experience: Selected Poetry and Prose of William Blake* ed. Northrop Frye (New York: Modern Library, 1953).
13. 'Hippolytus,' pp. 307–11.
14. Ibid., pp. 312–13.
15. Ibid., pp. 350–3.
16. Ibid., p. 405.
17. Ibid., pp. 427–30 and 443–51.
18. Ibid., pp. 469–72.
19. Ibid., pp. 490–2.
20. Ibid., pp. 616–18.
21. Ibid., pp. 627–32.
22. Ibid.
23. Racine. *Phaedra*, trans. John Caincross (New York: Penguin Books, 1983), II.v.587.
24. Ibid., II.v.634.
25. Ibid., II.v.653.
26. Ibid., II.v.672.
27. Ibid., II.v.699.

28. 'Hippolytus', pp. 727–31.

29. Ibid., pp. 765–75.

30. Ibid., pp. 882–6.

31. For a detailed description see S. Kakar, *The Inner World: A Psychoanalytic Study of Childhood and Society in India* (New York and Delhi: Oxford University Press, 1978), chapter III.

32. A.K. Ramanujan, 'The Indian Oedipus' in L. Edmunds and A. Dundes (eds), *Oedipus: A Folklore Casebook* (New York: Garland Publishing, 1983), p. 237.

REFERENCES TO CHAPTER EIGHT
THE PHENOMENOLOGY OF PASSIONATE LOVE

1. Pierre Teilhard de Chardin, *On Love* (New York: Harper & Row, 1972), p. 11.

2. W.H. Auden, 'Lullaby', *Collected Poems* (New York: Random House, 1976), p. 131.

3. Freud, 'On the Universal Tendency to Debasement in the Sphere of Love' (1912), *Standard Edition*, vol. 11, p. 180.

4. See Jean Paul Sartre, *Being and Nothingness* (New York: Philosophical Library, 1956), part III. For Freud's views on the importance of sado-masochism in erotic life, with its component of humiliation, see 'On the Universal Tendency . . .', and 'A Child is Being Beaten' (1919), *Standard Edition*, vol. 17.

5. R. Briffault, *The Mothers*, vol. 1 (London: 1927), p. 119.

6. Erich Fromm, *The Forgotten Language* (New York: Holt, Rinehart & Winston, 1957).

7. Evelyne Sullerot, *Women on Love: Eight Centuries of Feminine Writing* (New York: Doubleday, 1979), pp. 30–1.

8. Roland Barthes, *A Lover's Discourse* (New York: Hill and Wang, 1978), p. 42.

9. Plato, 'Symposium' in B. Jowett (tr.), *The Portable Plato* (New York: Viking Press, 1950), p. 145.

10. Ibid.

11. *Brahadranayka Upanishad*, I–IV, 1–3.

12. Plato, p. 146. For a psychoanalytic discussion see William

Binstock, 'On the Two Forms of Intimacy', *Journal of American Psychoanalytic Association*, 21 (1), 1973, pp. 93–107.

13. W.H. Auden, *The Dyer's Hand* (New York: Vintage Books), p. 115.

14. Barthes, p. 28.

15. Ortega y Gasset, *On Love* (New York: Greenwich Editions, 1957).

16. Ibn Hazm, *The Ring of the Dove*, trans. A.J. Arberry (London: Luzac & Co., 1953), p. 118.

17. St. John of the Cross, *Poems*, trans. R. Campbell (Baltimore: Penguin Books, 1960).

18. Bhavabhuti, *Uttara Rama Carita* (The Later Story of Rama) in *Six Sanskrit Plays* (Bombay: Asia, 1964), p. 368.

19. W.B. Yeats, 'The Indian to His Love', *Collected Poems* (New York: Macmillan, 1956), p. 14.

20. William N. Evans, 'Two kinds of Romantic Love', in *Psychoanalytic Quarterly*, 22, 1953, p. 76.

21. de Rougemont, *The Myths of Love*, p. 65.

22. Auden, *Collected Poems*, p. 498.

23. Shakespeare, Sonnet 57.

24. Ibn Hazm, p. 87.

25. Barthes, p. 224.

26. Cited in Otto F. Kernberg, 'Boundaries and Structure in Love Relations', *Journal of the American Psychoanalytic Association*, 25 (1), 1977, p. 96.

27. Bedier, *Tristan and Iseult*.

28. See Daniel H.H. Ingalls, *An Anthology of Sanskrit Court Poetry* (Cambridge, Mass: Harvard University Press, 1965), p. 15.

29. William Shakespeare, *The Merchant of Venice*, V.i.63–5.

30. W.H. Auden, *Forewords and Afterwords* (London: Faber and Faber, 1973), p. 24.

31. Martin Bergmann, 'Platonic love, transference love and love in real life', *Journal of the American Psychoanalytic Association*, 30 (1982), pp. 87–111; Kernberg, p. 95. See also Leon L. Altman, 'Some Vicissitudes of Love', *Journal of the American Psychoanalytic Association*, 25(1), 1977, p. 42.

REFERENCES TO CHAPTER NINE
THE ONTOGENY OF LOVE

1. Lionel Trilling, Frontispiece of *Lolita* (New York: Berkeley Books, 1982).
2. See T. B. Brazelton, M. W. Yogman, H. Als & E. Tronick, 'The Infant as a focus in family reciprocity', in *The Social Network of the Developing Infant* ed. M. Lewis & L. Rosenblum (New York: Plenum Press, 1978), pp. 29–43; see L.W. Sander, 'Issues in early mother-child interaction', *Journal of the American Academy of Child Psychiatry* (1962), 1:141–66 and D. Stern, 'The goal and structure of mother-infant play', *Journal of the American Academy of Child Psychiatry* (1964), 3, 321–64.
3. Vladimir Nabokov, *Speak Memory* (New York: G. Putnam & Sons, 1966), p. 21.
4. See Brazelton *et al.*
5. Vladimir Nabokov, *Ada* (New York: McGraw Hill, 1969).
6. Ibid., p. 118.
7. *Speak Memory*, p. 240.
8. Vladimir Nabokov, *Lolita* (New York: Berkeley Books, 1982).
9. Peter Blos, 'Son and Father', *Journal of the American Psychoanalytic Association*, 32:301–24.
10. *Speak Memory*, p. 296.